BRENT POPE

If You Really Knew Me

Brent Pope

with Kevin MacDermot

Published by Irish Sports Publishing (ISP)

Unit 11, Tandy's Lane

Lucan, Co Dublin

Ireland

www.irishsportspublishing.com

kevin@irishsportspublishing.com

First published, 2012

A CIP record for this book is available from the British Library

ISBN 978-0-9573954-5-9

Printed in Ireland with Print Procedure Ltd

Cover Design and Typesetting: Anú Design www.anu-design.ie

Cover Photograph: © Karina Finegan Alves

Inside Photographs: Inpho Sports Agency, Karina Finegan Alves

and Brent Pope's personal collection.

This book is dedicated to my loving family,
Mum, Dad and Mark, who always encouraged me to be different,
empathetic and honest. Who allowed me to pursue my dreams,
no matter where and how far they took me from home. I miss you.

Acknowledgments

When I was first approached and asked if I would be interested in writing an account of my life, my reaction was to say 'no', who'd want to read it? But Liam and Kevin from Irish Sports Publishing persisted and I finally caved in. It's been a long journey ever since, trying to remember back to my wonderful schooldays as an insecure, chubby-faced, bare-footed rugby player in Ashburton, New Zealand.

It's been impossible to remember all the wonderful faces and friends that I have known. In writing this book, I often feel I've missed someone out and I'm sure that I have. If I've missed anyone, I'm very sorry: trying to recall all the great teammates, flatmates and heartaches has been difficult. It hasn't all been plain sailing – I questioned the chapters on my 'down days' as they were extremely raw and painful for me. They were days that I never thought would pass.

But I am proud to say I've tried to live a varied life. I've travelled the world through rugby, explored far-flung cultures and had the luxury of being able to work on TV in a sport I love. I've written children's books, opened art galleries, sung, and played clarinet with the RTÉ orchestra. As the song says, "I have loved and lost" but I am still here, still trucking and eager to see what the next fifty years hold in store. I regret not being able to spend more time with a family I love, and I miss them every day, more so at Christmas time, but they know I am in good hands with the Irish people.

I want to thank my agent, John Baker, and of course the team at ISP who believed that this book may appeal to someone and worked to make it a reality. A big thank you to Karina Finegan Alves for her amazing photographs and to the Finegan family for their support over the years. Thanks, also, to all the contributors to this book, not necessarily for the written word but for what it meant to just know you. Thanks to Kevin for all his hard work, patience and, most of all, his friendship. He's a man who pushed me to open up about things I had only shared with my closest confidants.

Most of all, I value the friendships I have made, the people who have come into my life and made it a better, safer place for me to be. I'd like to say thanks to the Irish in particular. They opened their arms and hearts to me and accepted me as one of their own. I pinch myself that the road 'more travelled' took me to this wonderful country and to the people who make it special.

Thanks to those most important in my life – far too many to mention – but who include my family, my partners, those in RTÉ, Clontarf and St Mary's. To all the many friends in the worlds of rugby, art and television, I can't thank you enough for your support and love. I will be forever in your debt.

Most importantly, I owe a debt of gratitude to those people who dare to be different in life, to push the boundaries, to, "fill the unforgiving minute with sixty seconds of distance run". I applaud your spirit to, "keep on trucking".

Even if this book does not sell one copy, it's been an honour to end up where I feel safe in my own skin. Finally, I feel it's now okay to be Popey. No more, no less.

Thank you, thank you, thank you!

Brent Pope
Dublin, 2012.

Contents

Foreword

Popey and I met in the mid-'80s in Dunedin, where we were teammates in the Otago rugby team. We immediately forged a strong friendship in what I would describe as the start of a 'golden era' in Otago rugby. Otago had been struggling in previous seasons and the arrival of talented players like Mike Brewer, Arthur Stone, Popey and others, mixed in with a bunch of hard-working lads with good character, initiated the change in fortune that would last for over a decade.

Popey enjoyed a distinguished career with Otago and it must be said that he was one of the unluckiest players not to have worn the All Black jersey. In fact, it was only timing, not talent, that stopped him wearing the black jersey with the silver fern. Standing in his way were two of New Zealand's greatest-ever players – Buck Shelford and Zinzan Brooke. But even allowing for those two players, he experienced another unlucky blow when he dislocated his elbow in a trial match, just as he was on the edge of selection. I'm sure, with the form he was in, that selection was a formality.

It didn't happen. But I will always remember a conversation between us which epitomised Popey's career and brought home to me the importance of earning respect. I was offering my support to him on missing out on All Black selection and he replied that, yes, he was disappointed, but it was very important to him that when he ran out of the tunnel at Carisbrook and looked at the packed terrace (as it was in those days!) he saw people whose respect he had won.

That was never in doubt and anyone who knows Popey will understand that he was never your everyday, rough, tough New Zealand forward from the '80s. Yes, he was rough and tough when he needed to be, but he had many other sides to his make-up. Talents, you might say. Humour was one of them: practical jokes were part of his weaponry and those unfortunate enough to be on the receiving end learned very quickly to stay alert and to never take things for what they seemed to be when he was around. When we were low as a team, you could always rely on Popey to lighten the mood, normally it centred around him mocking himself or some poor, unfortunate teammate. Coaching and management staff weren't exempt either!

Throw in author, TV personality, businessman, and you start to understand that Brent Pope is not your run-of-the-mill rugby personality. As a professional rugby coach for the last twelve years, I've developed an understanding of the importance of 'character versus ability' in the selection process of any team I'm involved with. Ability without character will lead to inconsistency and, eventually, failure in terms of team dynamics. Surround a player possessing marginal character with a team of players who work hard and act professionally, on and off the field, then that player has no option but to conform. Popey was one of the many players in that 'golden era' of Otago rugby who was strong in character. That character, added to his talent, allowed him to enjoy a very distinguished career.

However, my respect for him as a person crossed more than the normal strong bonds that are formed when teammates go to 'war' together year after year on the playing fields around the world. In 1991, my first child, Hannah, was born and my wife, Sam, and I were delighted when Popey agreed to be her Godfather. Despite being away from NZ, he has maintained regular contact and visited us whenever possible. Hannah has talked about spending a bit of time in Dublin, now that her university years have been completed, and I'm sure her Godfather will take great care of her! No doubt, the years at Otago University will assist in preparing her for the wonders of the Dublin entertainment scene.

Greg Cooper
Otago. Hawke's Bay. Auckland. Otago Highlanders Coach. All Blacks.

Prologue

Otago 1990

Worzal Earl is a tough bugger.

He's a legend in New Zealand rugby.

His real name is Andy but he picked up his nickname on account of his unruly mop of hair that resembled the scarecrow off kids' TV.

A hard sheep farmer with hands the size of shovels, Worzal was reputed to have once knocked out his own Canterbury out-half the night after a game because the guy refused to stop partying and he had to get up early the next morning for lambing season.

I could well believe it about him, it sounds just about right.

But this time Andy had caught me during our match with his Canterbury team.

By accident? On purpose?

I don't know. But he caught me with one of those size 11, old-style, high-cut boots of his, full force square in the kidneys.

I've never been stretchered from the pitch before but I made an exception in this case. It was embarrassing: leaving a game because of an injury is never an option in

New Zealand rugby. It's bloody soft.

But, Christ, this is sore. Even a week later, the pain is almost unbearable.

I've stopped urinating blood as heavily as I did that first night in Christchurch Hospital's emergency ward and, loaded up with anti-inflammatories and painkillers, I can walk now. That's got to be a good sign.

The doctors don't want me to play tomorrow. They've warned me against it, told me I'm risking a vital organ, my rugby future, my health. I listened to them and said nothing.

Laurie Mains, my coach at Otago, and our team doctor have interrogated me about the prognosis.

I lied to them, told them I couldn't train but that I'd be fine after a few days' rest. I won't be, but I'll still start that game.

My team stands on the brink of history and its greatest triumph. Tomorrow we play Auckland in the Ranfurly Shield Challenge. Our province has only won it once before, over 30 years ago in 1957. Victory in the Shield means everything to us, it's what we have been training for, what we have been building towards and we are good enough to do it.

Two years ago we lost to these guys at this stage. We weren't given a chance, but we'd been leading them with only a few minutes to go. Thousands of Otago supporters were even making their way to the Dunedin airport in anticipation of us creating Otago history. The bitterness of defeat lasts long in the mouth.

We're a much better team now. They know it and so do we. We've just beaten Canterbury, Worzal and all on their home patch, our preparation has been perfect.

Mains, or 'Funeral Face' as we know him, has built a special team in Otago. We are not a collection of disparate players vying to win a trophy. We are now the top South Island team. We have All Blacks scattered amongst us, but many of us are also drawn from the ranks of the overlooked and unrecognised – players like Crazy Dave Latta – unlucky because of a perceived rugby hierarchy in New Zealand: we are on a crusade to explode the Ancien Régime.

Tomorrow, we can achieve that.

Deep down, I know it will be another step for me. My story will not end tomorrow, even if we win. My ambitions are deeper, much deeper, than that. I still have unfinished business from 1987 and tomorrow will be one more step towards what I crave most – the black jersey with the silver fern.

That's all I think about. It's everything to me. I dream, breathe, live to be an All Black.

My doubts, the self-doubts which are my constant companion, crowd in around me as ever, edging the positive aside.

"Am I good enough? Will I ever be good enough? Am I just always unlucky?"

I push them away. Tonight, there can be no place for the weaknesses in my mind. I must focus, stay positive, and stay strong. I am good enough, I always have been.

My captain, Mike Brewer, has arranged for a doctor to come to the hotel tonight. Laurie doesn't know, he'd be furious. The doc stabs about fifteen pain-killing injections into my lower back. They've numbed the pain on the surface, but they haven't dulled the real hurt coming from deeper in my kidneys. Worryingly, I am still passing blood, the toilet is splattered with it.

I can't even touch the area directly above my kidney, but I've patched hard foam around it as best I can. I can't sleep for the pain. It's immense.

Mike has faith in me. I've made an agreement with my friend and Otago replacement, Arran Pene, that I will at least start the game, play as hard as I can for ten minutes and then come off. Arran's a good guy but he wants my place, I know that. If our roles were reversed we'd be doing exactly the same thing, just in a different order. Any sub who tells you he's happy to be on the bench is either a fool or an outright liar. I've never trusted any replacement who wished me well before a game – I always wanted the guy whose place I coveted to have a terrible game. Arran knows that he feels the same: we're bred to compete.

I'm being stupid. I'm being selfish. I know that. I'm not thinking of my coach, of my team, of the supporters, of my family.

I'm thinking only of myself. I'm putting my ambition ahead of my physical health. If I get hit in the kidneys again, I could be risking everything.

But that's okay with me. The risk is acceptable.

Tomorrow we make history. Tomorrow we join the the elite provinces like Auckland and Canterbury. We're going to win the Shield tomorrow and, along with it, we'll win a little bit of immortality for ourselves.

I won't miss that for anything. I have fought too hard and too long to get here to be denied by a stupid injury. I want that piece of immortality and, come what may, I will be on that pitch tomorrow.

I am still young enough. Surely my greatest rugby years still lie ahead of me?

And though I don't know it, so too does a rollercoaster adventure of the body and mind which will take me across the world to Ireland and turn my life upside down.

But, right now, in this hotel room in Auckland that is not a future I'm contemplating. The only future I care about begins tomorrow at 3pm when the referee blows his whistle and the oval ball is kicked hard and high.

Behind that ball will charge the Auckland team and almost fifteen All Blacks who make up their First XV. Their ranks will be filled with star players and All Black legends, current and future, including the likes of Zinzan Brooke, John Kirwan, Grant Fox, Sean Fitzpatrick and Michael Jones. They are the thoroughbreds in this sport and they will be hard to beat, innovative, sleek and experienced in the backs and hard as nails up front. They will be ferocious and relentless and will seek to impose their will on us from the start of the game.

But we will not bend for them.

We will stand up and fight.

We are Otago.

We are proud, Southern men.

We are the blue and gold.

We are Laurie Mains' men and we are here to win, to turn the tables on Auckland and write a new chapter in Otago rugby.

We will not be denied.

I will not be denied.

Not if takes pain, sweat, tears and blood.

This is Otago.

This is rugby.

This is my life.

1

Irish Blood, Kiwi Heart

My family heritage is far from being a unique Irish story.

In common with the tales of so many other Irish families spread across the world, it's a tale of emigration, hardship and battles against local opposition.

But, as I say, that's nothing new for the Irish. Down through the centuries, the Irish have been on the move, undertaking spasmodic nomadic journeys in a bid to find greener pastures. They've left for various reasons, forced out by the famine, the Depression, various recessions and now another, calamitous, economic crash.

When viewed through the prism of a post-Celtic Tiger Ireland, it's easy to see just how history keeps repeating itself. Within the first dozen years of the new millennium, we have already witnessed wave after wave of young people leaving the s in search of opportunity, prosperity or maybe just survival.

In the 1980s, the destination of choice was usually London, Boston or New York. But, today, a bold new generation of Irish explorers has emerged, seeking new lives in the more distant lands of Australia and New Zealand. Student gap years are no longer limited by an eight-hour flight to the United States, with trips to the other side of the world where the bath water goes down the wrong way proving most popular.

Modern Irish students and backpackers seem happier spending a couple of years frequenting some of Sydney's many Irish bars, or sporting their milk-bottle tans and GAA jerseys on Bondi Beach for Christmas Day. Tales of old broken down Ford V8 cars crossing the Australian Outback, full of modern Irish explorers, are commonplace.

There's an understandable tendency here to view Australia and New Zealand as lands of adventure and wealth, where you eat your Christmas turkey on the beach and sink a few tinnies before bungee jumping or waxing up your surfboard and catching a wave.

The reality of course, is – and always was – different, although there's no doubt things were much tougher for the first Irish emigrants who landed in Australia and New Zealand. For my parents' generation – those who were the children and grandchildren of older Irish emigrants – the lands Down Under, and the lifestyles they led there, were full of war, poverty and incredibly hard graft.

While today's young European backpackers look at Australasia as a place of adventure and freedom, the children of those first emigrants spent the early 1900s looking at the exotic pictures of Dublin, London and Paris on their biscuit tin lids. They dreamt of escaping the harsh realities of immigrant life by returning to their grandparents' home across the waves. But it was an impossible dream for the majority of them. Europe was an inaccessible world: travel was expensive and a preserve of the wealthy and the elite. Moreover, even if you could afford the fare, trips to the other side of the world were arduous and dangerous in those days. Few New Zealanders ever left their islands.

Even for the early All Blacks, Tours meant almost half a year off work. Players trained on the decks of boats as it took months to travel, and it was the same for players travelling in the other direction. In 1950, the Lions, featuring the late, great Karl Mullen as Captain and including the likes of the outstanding Jackie Kyle, endured months of sea travel. By 1959, when the Lions travelled back Down Under, this time with the likes of Sir Tony O'Reilly (who scored an amazing 22 tries), they saw a marked change in travel time because the team travelled by plane.

Technology now means the two ends of the world aren't quite as far apart as they once were. Thankfully, my dad, Mick, has now managed to achieve something his parents and grandparents could only ever have dreamt about: return to see Ireland. My dad has visited Ireland on numerous occasions over the years, though the trip has now become too long and tiring for a man in his 80s. My mother, sadly, has only managed to make it back to the land of her forefathers and foremothers once: a broken neck, cancer and a nasty leg injury frustrating her plans to do so more often. Still, despite not making the trip back to the 'Auld Sod', she remains fiercely proud of her good Irish stock.

I always wished, for her sake, that I had approached RTÉ in an effort to appear on their fascinating heritage programme Who Do You Think You Are? or a similar type of programme that searched out people's roots and traced their family trees back over the generations. I'd love to have been able to hand my mum a DVD and say: "There you go, Mum. There's my … your … our Irish history." It would mean the world to her to know the who, what, when and where of the events that shaped her life.

Certainly, it'd have been a good story, if I say so myself.

The tale of my family tree – the Popes, Noonans, Connors, Shanahans, Haydens, Doyles and O'Briens – goes back mostly to Ireland, to Dublin, Tipperary and Limerick, and in part to Scotland. It's a story that illustrates the similar traits between the Irish and the Kiwis. Both are homebirds (the Kiwi is supposed to be flightless!) in many regards, but both are known for their nomadic explorations and their propensity to spread their wings and search for fresh beginnings.

In fact, as many as 15 per cent of Kiwis can lay claim to Irish ancestry. In the mid-19th century there were several waves of Irish immigration to New Zealand, starting with the arrival of British imperial regiments after the signing of the Treaty of Waitangi, in 1840, which resulted in large-scale Irish settlement. Many of the soldiers in those regiments were Irish and taking their discharge in New Zealand. The Royal New Zealand Fencibles were pensioned soldiers from Ireland and Britain who enlisted in Britain and Ireland as a defence force for the protection of Auckland. They emigrated, often with their families and, between 1847 and 1852 alone, over 2,500 men, women and children, many of whom were Irish, arrived and settled across Auckland. By the early 1990s, it was estimated that 250,000 New Zealanders were descended from a Fencible family. By 1851, one third of Auckland's population was of Irish background, and the thriving Irish community continued to be fuelled by the gold rush period of the 1860s.

In the many years since my forebears first left Ireland, their physical journey has become a social journey. From humble beginnings in Ireland, they became cattlemen and farmers, builders and hoteliers, and built up business and farming empires which, at one point, encompassed thousands of acres on Canterbury plains' rich and fertile farm land. Along the way, one of them helped solve a notorious payroll robbery and catch a double murderer while another founded his own town.

But at the centre of it all, down through all those years that they've been in New Zealand, has been their love of horses. Their devotion to the 'sport of kings' and their genius for breeding and training horses – a skill they brought with them from Ireland – has served my family well.

It's a different kind of story to the one most Irish people know about what happened to their kinsmen Down Under. While the history of the convicts in Australia is well documented, much less is known about the Irish influence in New Zealand. Certainly, the trip there was as terrifying, maybe more so, than the notorious trans-Atlantic trade plied by the Famine's coffin ships. Similar conditions persisted in the New Zealand-bound boats – overcrowded, timber ships riddled with death and disease, sailing months in dangerous waters to perhaps the most remote place on the planet.

Once there, the Irish encountered similar problems to those they faced back home. In many instances, those early Irish pioneers were probably regarded as social lepers by the ruling English class who, under British explorer Captain James Cook, had registered New Zealand as an English colony and part of the empire's global Commonwealth.

When I was growing up we sang 'God Save the Queen' every morning at school assembly. To a young Kiwi schoolboy, it seemed a strange choice of song given that none of us, or anybody we knew, had ever seen the Queen. Like everything else, that too has changed in the years since I was a boy. These days the improvements in travel have meant that the royals are regular visitors to New Zealand.

Maybe it was their early exclusion from 'genteel society', or maybe it was their shared history of oppression, tradition and clan that led the Irish to strike up a strong bond of friendship with New Zealand's indigenous Maori population. No doubt, both tribes felt themselves alienated from the ruling English elite, and often found themselves working in menial, labour-intensive jobs. The old cliché of "No blacks, dogs or Irish" was probably just as applicable for the early Irish emigrants in New Zealand as it was in places like 1950s London or the United States.

But, despite the exclusion and the hardship, the Irish contrived to help shape the future of a small island in the Pacific that, in so many ways – culturally and in terms of population makeup – is very similar to Ireland. In fact, the history of mixed marriages between the Irish and the Maori, and the respect they hold for each other, is a fascinating story and something I would like to learn more of.

A perfect example of the merging of the two cultures is the current 'Irish' Maori leader, Tipene O'Regan. He's a South Island New Zealander who, in recent times, has worked alongside my family and friends in helping to lead the rebuilding effort in earthquake-hit Christchurch.

But Tipene, as most Kiwis know him, has been at the forefront of the battle for Maori rights and social rights for more than four decades. And this 72-year-old was knighted in 1994, quite an honour for a native who can trace the heritage of two of his grandparents back to Ireland. His grandfather was the son of an illiterate emigrant called O'Regan who left Cork in 1869. One of his sons, Patrick Joseph, was born on the beach at Charleston and, though he didn't go to school until the age of 12, PJ went on to become a celebrated lawyer and judge of NZ's Supreme Court. He was Tipene's grandfather, and the Maori leader credits much of his passion for battling social injustice to his grandfather's fight against conscription in New Zealand and his support for the Irish Home Rule movement.

It's not an uncommon story. The Irish and the Maoris share a similar sense of humour, a great zest for life, family and tradition, but at the base of it all is a shared, common experience of knowing what it's like to be oppressed by much bigger and stronger countries.

Tipene has been quoted as saying, "My father used to say the Maori are very Irish, but the Irish are not very Maori". According to Jamie Ball, an Irish writer based in Christchurch, O'Reagan, " was really saying two things. The Irish are Europeans – they belong in Europe – but they have a whole lot of characteristics, in terms of family and extended family and region and place that are also very characteristic of Maori. The tendency [of Maori] to retain a view of myth in places and place names and stories and traditions is very comparable to the Irish tendency to the same thing." It seems, therefore, that when Irish players do face the famous New Zealand Haka, they can take solace from the fact that they may well have more in common with their opponents in battle than anyone would have thought.

But times change and so do people. Many Irish men and women have become extremely rich and influential in NZ society. Their astute land owning and property development skills, coupled with a focused work ethic, have combined to propel many of them into the Kiwi rich lists.

A prime example of this is the recently departed, Eamon Cleary, the Irish-Kiwi property magnate who was born in 1960 in County Monaghan. A regular fixture in the Top 10 of New Zealand's Rich List, it's been estimated that, at one point, Cleary was worth in excess of NZ$1.2billion, with a range of assets across four continents. Sadly, Cleary passed away at his Kentucky horse stud at just 52 years of age.

It is also a little-known fact that 21 per cent of New Zealand's thirty-eight Prime Ministers have Irish ancestry, including Robert (Rob) Muldoon, James (Jim) Bolger and Helen Clark. In fact, Irish immigrants have had great success in achieving political influence, with 28 per cent of Australian Prime Ministers being of Irish descent and 27 per cent of American Presidents. Other notable early New Zealanders who can proudly claim Irish ancestry include: Lieutenant Governor William Hobson, born in Waterford in 1792, he signed the Treaty of Waitangi on behalf of the Crown in February 1840. Thomas Bracken born at Clonee in County Meath, in 1843, he wrote the words to the national anthem "God Defend New Zealand" and Sir Edmund Percival Hillary was the conqueror of Mt Everest whose grandmother, Annie Clementina Fleming, was born in Dublin, in 1856.

Meanwhile, the Finn brothers – Tim and Neil – who front one of the most iconic bands of the '90s, Crowded House, can also trace first-generation roots back to Ireland, their mother being Irish.

From a sporting perspective, and in modern times, one Irishman who has made his name in New Zealand is Barney McCahill. Barney had the unique and proud opportunity of seeing both his sons play International rugby – for two different countries. Cahill, along with fellow Donegal emigrant, Hugh Green, founded one of New Zealand's biggest construction firms, Green and Cahill, and made his fortune in earth-moving and infrastructure before successfully moving on to horse breeding.

Barney's sons, Bernie and Sean, were born in Auckland and educated, in books and rugby, at St Peter's College. But Bernie went on to play for the All Blacks while Sean played for Sunday's Well in Cork and won an Ireland cap. I was lucky enough to play against both brothers on many occasions and toured with Sean in the mid-1990's.

Perhaps the best-known of the Irish sporting success stories is that of Dave Gallaher. Along with his family, Gallaher left his Donegal hills to become one of New Zealand's most famous rugby sons, even claiming the captaincy of the mighty All Blacks. This great sporting icon's efforts in a black jersey are still remembered by All Black teams who regularly make the pilgrimage to visit his birthplace in Ramelton, County Donegal, when they are in Ireland.

A prop and a wing-forward, Gallaher is credited with being one of the game's deepest thinkers back then. His development of the game – in particular his revolutionary roving wing forward play – ensured his place in the pantheon of All Black heroes. Maybe less well-known is the fact that Gallaher was killed in the First World War. As a young man, he had already fought in the Boer War, having altered his official birthdate, 30 October, 1873, to 30 October, 1876 to allow him to enlist. When the Great War broke out in 1914, his age exempted him from conscription but, after his younger brother, Douglas, was killed in action, the former All Black captain decided to join up. He fought in Ypres and survived the hellish battle there, but in the Passchendaele offensive, in the attack on Gravenstafel Spur on October 4, 1917, Gallaher was caught in a shell burst and died later that same day, aged 41, at No. 3 Australian Casualty Clearing Station. His body lies at Nine Elms Cemetery near Poperinge, Belgium. A silver fern adorns the grave, which inaccurately records his age as 44. By the end of the war, five of the nine Gallaher brothers, including twins Charles and Henry, had fought in the war. Three were killed: Douglas, Dave and, lastly, one of the twins, Henry.

Gallaher was typical of the kind of men the Irish contributed to New Zealand and, despite his extraordinary prowess, he was no Irish flash in the sporting pan. Another Irishman who made his name in his adopted New Zealand was world champion bare knuckle boxer Bob Fitzsimmons. Fitzsimmons, whose father hailed from Armagh, was regarded as one of the greatest, if not the greatest, bare knuckle fighters of all time. Aged only nine years old, Fitzsimmons first emigrated to Timaru, just an hour's drive from my birthtown, where he later became a

blacksmith before entering the world of pugilism. Fitzsimmons fought in New Zealand, Australia and eventually in the country where he took up citizenship, the USA. Interestingly, Fitzsimmons once won a fight despite being knocked to the canvas by Edward 'Starlight' Robbins. Starlight broke his hand in the process and could not continue so, despite being knocked out himself, Fitzsimmons was hauled to his feet and declared the winner by knockout. Fitzsimmons won his first world title when he knocked out Jack Dempsey (from whom the later heavyweight champion would take his name) in the 13th round to become the World Middleweight Champion in 1891. Fitzsimmons knocked Dempsey down at least 13 times and, by the finish, left him in such a pitiable condition that he begged Dempsey to quit. Dempsey refused, so Fitzsimmons knocked him out again and then carried him over his shoulder back to his corner. In another twist of history, no less a personage than the legendary lawman, Wyatt Earp, officiated as referee in a Fitzsimmons fight. Earp was later accused of being on the take and fixing the fight. Whether there was any truth in the latter story remains lost in the fog of history, but Bob Fitzsimmons' life was certainly full of stories that could script any Hollywood movie.

And, while there haven't been many men with as colourful a sporting life as Bob, the Irish name has survived in the New Zealand pantheon of sporting greats courtesy of such All Black greats as Sean Fitzpatrick and scrum-half, Byron Kelleher, to name but two.

• • • • •

On the subject of my own family, it might sound strange but, when I was growing up, I had no real sense of really being Irish. We had Irish connections but my own relationship with my heritage was complicated and, even when I arrived in Ireland, I had no real inclination to pull an 'American' and immediately claim my Irish roots. Truth be told, when I arrived here more than 20 years ago, I wasn't really aware of my Irish heritage at all. I hadn't really been brought up as Irish. Growing up in Ashburton, the only Irish person I knew was our parish priest, Fr Duggan, from Cork.

I guess, after nearly 22 years – half my adult life – in this wonderful country, I can consider myself a 'plastic paddy' or a 'blow-in' that never left. But, since looking into my family history, I like to think that my return to Ireland is balancing the books in some small way: recompense for so many Irish family members heading the other way – though I think New Zealand probably got the best of that particular deal.

So, despite my early ignorance of my heritage, my Irish roots run deep. On my dad's side of the family, we know his mother was Irish and that her maiden name was Hayden, possibly from Cork, but that's, unfortunately, about it.

More was known about my mother, Helen's, Irish connections. The family was Irish – it had to be, given names like Doyle, Noonan, Connors, Shanahan and O'Brien – and its tentacles reached back, on both her parents' sides, to the areas of Limerick and Tipperary. I always knew I had some Munster blood in me and not just Francis Brosnahan's from Young Munster RFC.

My maternal grandmother, also named Helen, was an O'Brien, and her father Morgan was one of a long line of generations of Morgan O'Brien's from Limerick, she married my grandfather, William John Doyle. It seems that my grandfather originally hailed from the family of John Doyle, whose birthplace is listed as Dublin, while Helen O'Brien's family originated in a small rural area in Castleton, Ballingarry, County Tipperary. It was my grandmother's forefather, Morgan, who emigrated to New Zealand with his wife Mary (née Shanahan) from Castleton, Ballingarry. Mary was one of eight sisters while Morgan had one brother, named Jeremiah.

The love of horses ran deep in the O'Brien side of the family. Indeed, my mum often likes to claim a family connection to the late, great Vincent O'Brien. No amount of argument from me about how many O'Brien's there are in Ireland, and how remote the chances of being connected to the great man actually are, will dissuade her from hanging on to her pipe dream. She dines out on that connection regularly, telling anyone who will listen about her famous distant Irish relative – who knows, maybe she's actually right.

Certainly, the O'Brien's displayed the kind of work ethic and talent for horses and business that made Vincent the greatest influence in Irish horseracing history. After Morgan O'Brien arrived in New Zealand, he went on to become a well-known businessman, a prominent hotelier and a very successful owner and breeder of racehorses. After a stint serving in the Permanent Artillery base in Christchurch, Morgan went on to become one of the best known individuals in the New Zealand licensing trade. He also took a huge interest in racing administration and, for two years, was president of the Canterbury Park Racing Club and was a steward for many years after that. He was also a prominent member of the Canterbury Jockey Club and Metropolitan Trotting Clubs.

Morgan built and owned numerous important hotels in Christchurch, including the Railway Hotel and later the trendy-sounding Café de Paris, one of Christchurch's most prominent downtown bars. But it was while he was the owner of another hostelry, called The Empire Hotel, that Morgan gained national notoriety when he helped solve a famous murder and robbery.

These days, sadly, death by foul means is not uncommon but, back in my grandfather's days, it was front-page national news. The incident he was caught up in revolved around the case of a man by the name of Frederick William Eggers, who had arrived in Christchurch from Greymouth. Though he wasn't staying at the hotel, he was supposedly married to a former Empire barmaid called McMahon, and called to the hotel asking if he could leave his suitcase there.

When my grandfather tried to move the suitcase to the hotel safe, it was so heavy he became suspicious. When police detectives began to enquire about the barmaid, he became even more suspicious. That evening, he spotted Eggers coming back to the hotel to meet up with the McMahon woman, he alerted the detectives who arrested Eggers. On searching his bags, they found a loaded revolver, 100 cartridges and more than £3,600 – a huge amount of money in those days. The money was the proceeds of a notorious coal mine payroll robbery on the West Coast in which one employee was murdered and two others shot, and left for dead. Eggers was tried and convicted for robbery, murder and attempted murder, and later executed.

Morgan's position as organiser of the annual Canterbury race week would also have meant he was in the middle of the infamous 'Flu deaths in New Zealand.

According to one report of the time: "Hundreds of racegoers from the North Island had come south to Christchurch for the races, inadvertently bringing a serious infection with them. At least the city had some warning, from the sudden worsening of the epidemic in Auckland and Wellington but, apart from a useless atomised zinc sulphate spray, the health authorities had no answer to the killer 'flu."

"Friday, 8 November, was People's Day at the Show, and this was probably the point of maximum spread of the infection, and over that weekend, half the city seemed to fall ill with the 'flu. Hotels crowded with visitors began to look like hospitals. Doctors and nurses were run off their feet. This 'flu struck suddenly, and some victims died within days, or even hours. Most of those who developed pneumonia were dead within a week. Yet, amazingly, Christchurch went ahead with long-laid out plans for a procession and rally in the City Square. The Cathedral bells [now no longer there, after the earthquake of 2011] rang out in cheer and celebration, yet people were dying in hotels nearby.

"For a fortnight after the outbreak, normal life was suspended in Christchurch. Many shops and factories closed as staff fell ill, or to release the able-bodied for relief work. Banks were shut by government decree for a week, and all hotels, billiard rooms and theatres were closed to prevent further spread of infection. The streets were left empty, except for the odd ambulance or relief car. Fourteen tramcars were stationed at suburban termini to serve as inhalation chambers. The worst day of the epidemic was 19 November, when forty-eight victims died. Thereafter, the death toll declined as quickly as it had soared. Over five hundred people died in Christchurch during the terrible 'Spanish Influenza' of that era."

• • • • •

Morgan has certainly left his mark on my family's history but, interestingly, it's his wife Mary – a Shanahan from Castleton, Ballingarry – who has provided me with most of my 'living' relatives in Ireland.

A few years ago, I received a letter from a local parish priest in New Zealand, saying that if I was ever in and around Adare, Ballingarry and Tipperary to look up the O'Grady and the Chawke families for a free pint, as they were all relatives of mine. It seems Mary O'Brien, née Shanahan, came from a family of ten children – eight sisters – one of these sisters married a man called Chawke. They, in turn, had 10 children of their own, one being a daughter named Kitty who married into the O'Gradys. Obviously, all the boys in the family would have retained the name Chawke, although I am not sure how many boys there were. I also haven't been able to find out much about the other seven sisters but, if they run true to form like the first two, I could see out the rest of my life full of complementary pints.

Every time I bump into famous hotelier and businessman, Charlie Chawke, I claim him as my 'adopted' cousin and, given that Adare and Ballingarry are not huge areas, maybe claiming Charlie as a relative is not too far off the mark. Regardless, when we meet up the craic is great: Charlie and his family are lovely, warm, generous people so, if the Charlie Chawke connection is true, then I'm delighted to be related to them, however distant that connection might be.

On the O'Grady side of the family, I was approached a few years ago at a Munster match by a distant relative, Meta O'Grady. The O'Grady family own a large garage on the main road into Ballingarry town and I've managed, on a rare occasion, to pop in to say hello. They're a GAA family so I am told, so they're probably a bit disgusted to have a grey-haired old Kiwi rugby player snooping around their premises, but I try not to disturb them too much!

The old O'Brien homestead is still standing, though these days it serves as a farmer's shed in Castleton, and I've only managed to get a look at it from the other side of a hedge. One day, I'll piece the entire story together but, in the meantime, if there are any Noonans, Connors, Chawkes or Shanahans out there who still count Mary and her husband Morgan among the branches of their family tree, I'd love to hear from them.

• • • • •

On my maternal grandfather's side, the Doyle's were also very successful land-owners and horsemen. They had originally emigrated from Ireland and Scotland, all sons and daughters of John Doyle and Elizabeth McKean of Dublin. Family legend states that the Scottish connection on the Doyle side came about when an Irish Catholic priest (or bishop, even?) ran off with a young Scottish woman he was tutoring. That was bad enough, but he then turned Protestant which would have been scandalous in any era!

A total of seven Doyle children emigrated to New Zealand and one of them, Joseph Hastings Doyle, even founded Doyleston, a small rural community not too far from the birth-place of a certain famous All Black, Dan Carter. At one time, Doyleston promised to be one of the main townships in the Ellesmere area, with a hall on the main street, vibrant businesses, and a school. These days, Doyleston is best known for Osborne Park, which has been the centre of junior soccer in Ellesmere for a number of years.

Among the next generation of Doyles, and more significant to me, was my grandfather, William John Doyle. Known throughout New Zealand as a horse breeder, WJ, or Bill as he was also known, also became a very successful landowner and stockman. But, while he might have bred and raced gallopers – winning many prominent races including the New Zealand Grand National – WJ's real expertise was in trotting or harness horseracing, a sport that is reasonably small here in modern Ireland but huge in Australasia, America and parts of Europe.

WJ was known throughout the sport as the 'King of the Square Gaiters' and, over many years, he captured most if not all of New Zealand's most prestigious races. He also bred and trained some of New Zealand's best ever harness horses and created bloodlines that still produce champions today.

One of his most famous horses was a champion NZ race mare named When, and it was his ownership of this horse that brought him into contact with one of the world's most famous race men of the era, Martin Tananbaum. Tananbaum, the wealthy owner of Yonkers Raceway in New York, wanted to create a world harness racing series in the early 1960s, he cast his net wide in a bid to attract the best international horses. The Tananbaum line-up would not have been complete without the incomparable When, and so Tananbaum's quest brought him to New Zealand and to the doorstep of WJ Doyle.

My grandfather was a shrewd businessman. He knew Tananbaum had money to spend and was determined to get as much of it as he could. So, he conducted negotiations with Tananbaum in a small tin shed in the middle of a field at the height of the baking hot Canterbury summer. My grandmother was instructed to keep refilling Tananbaum's hot drink, as WJ turned up the heat in the negotiations. Tananbaum's standard deal was to pay for the horse and owners to travel to New York, and any winnings after that were split 50/50. Doyle's tactics ensured that Tananbaum made further concessions – WJ got to keep 100 per cent of any winnings in When's first race, which carried a first prize of US$65,000 an amazing amount of money at that time.

Mr and Mrs Doyle brought their two youngest daughters, my aunts Lynn and Denise, on what proved to be an eventful trip. Family history has it that one New

York trip ended in an aggressive car chase through Manhattan Island as one of my aunts' husbands chased some lusty Italian racegoer who had dared to flirt with his glamorous wife!

On the racecourse, things didn't go as planned. When didn't come first in that initial race but she did finish second, and her subsequent successes in Yonkers ensured a steady stream of race invitations from around the globe.

WJ's success was built on iron discipline and a ferocious work ethic. When he was just a lad of 14 years old, his father took him to a racetrack almost half a day's drive away and warned him that if he didn't win the race he was entered for, he needn't bother coming home.

WJ's horse won by 20 lengths.

When he had his own family, he was determined to pass on this harsh approach to educating his children. My mother believes her own success in becoming a strong, independent woman at a young age, was down to her father's 'University of Life' attitude. Among the lessons he administered were trips to various train stations where he would abandon his terrified daughter on the platform, warning her that she would have to find her own way home.

Tough as it might sound, WJ brought his children up to be successful in the world. When he became too old to look after the huge cattle and sheep station in the fertile lands of Rakaia, on the Canterbury plains – at one time he owned 6000 acres – he turned to his family. My Aunty Lynn and her family still farm some of that land.

If a WJ-inspired education sounds tough for daughters, maybe it's because life was tough back then.

His older sister, Laurel Doyle (who later married a Campbell), was born in 1902, and was only seven years old when her mother, Mathilda, died in 1909. An accomplished young rider from an early age, Laurel suffered extreme personal hardships in her determination to succeed in a male-dominated sport, and a similarly inequitable world. She worked in her father's racing stables and trained her first thoroughbred horse at just 20 years old. By 1927, she had become only the second woman professional racehorse trainer in New Zealand's history.

Her career began with one of the greatest 'near misses' in racing history. The legendary racehorse, Phar Lap, a horse that is often ranked alongside the likes of Secretariat as the greatest racehorse of all time, was bred at Seadown Stud in

Timaru. In 1928, just after she had won her trainer's license, Laurel was offered the training duties for the owner's best two yearlings, traditionally kept back by the breeder. She accepted one yearling, but she declined the other, named Phar Lap, which was sent off to be sold at the 1928 national yearling sales for a pittance. Eventually, Phar Lap ended up in Australia where, affectionately known as 'Big Red', he went on to dominate racing for the next four years, winning the Melbourne Cup and capturing the Australian public's imagination during the Great Depression, in much the same way that Seabiscuit did in the United States. After surviving an assassination attempt by gangsters, the great Phar Lap died in 1932 after a sudden and mysterious illness. His heart – said to be much larger than an ordinary horse's heart – is still on display at the National Museum of Australia in Canberra, while his skeleton is exhibited in Te Papa Museum in New Zealand, both countries claiming the great horse as they their own. Under different circumstances, it might have been Laurel's destiny to have trained the legendary horse, but it was not to be. She was given charge of two other foals from that 'crop' and, though one of them won a few minor races under her care, it didn't compare even remotely with Phar Lap's career.

But, if missing out on Phar Lap was disappointing it was nothing to the personal difficulties she encountered that same year. Admired for her good looks, sense of fashion and respectable upbringing, Laurel's low-key wedding to a Scottish-born jockey by the name of James Campbell, attracted the dismay of both her family and Canterbury racing circles. The Doyles were highly respected and Jim Campbell, despite being charming and talented, had a severe drinking problem. His behaviour had prompted many official warnings and disqualifications and, at the time of their marriage, his jockey's licence had been cancelled. Five months after their marriage, their daughter, Shirley Janet, (Wee Janny) was born.

Laurel continued to train for many prominent owners and, even in those days, was regarded as head of the household and the main breadwinner. The family moved to a spacious house near the Riccarton Racecourse, which was almost certainly financed by Laurel. Among the owners she trained horses for was her brother Bill, my grandfather, and it was one of his horses, Thurina, which gave Laurel her first major race victory by winning the New Zealand Grand National Steeplechase at Riccarton.

That season, listed as 'Mrs J. Campbell', Laurel placed highly on the trainer's winners' list, ahead of the vast majority of her male rivals, even training Vintage to win the Wellington Cup, while Willie Win ran second in the Melbourne Cup after a string of major victories in New Zealand. But, because of her gender and the nature of the race game, this remarkable woman continued to be excluded from the inner circle of the Victoria Racing Club.

Professional triumph turned to personal tragedy: less than a year after winning the 1935 Wellington Cup, Laurel faced the heartbreak of her daughter's death. Aged just six years old, Wee Janny was hit by a truck outside their home and died hours later. Laurel's marriage, already in trouble, eventually foundered as her jockey husband sank deeper into alcoholism.

Although they didn't divorce until 1950, my great-aunt left her husband in the '40s, sold the family home and moved to Hastings in the North Island, where she went into partnership with Jack Jefferd, an English-born trainer. The duo enjoyed great success: they jointly headed the 1947-'48 trainers' table, and Campbell won her second Grand National Steeplechase in 1951 with Bandmaster.

But their business relationship became a personal one and the affair caused huge distress to Jefferd's wife and family. Laurel, once again, packed her bags and returned to Christchurch, this time for good.

Jim Campbell died in Porirua Hospital, a mental asylum, in 1956.

My great-aunt, after years six years of depression, died of a heart attack in Sunnyside Hospital, another mental asylum, on January 3, 1971.

• • • • •

Despite the ups and downs, the ins and outs, the Doyle and O'Brien legacies live on.

My mother and her two sisters, Lynn and Denise, still form part of a great racing dynasty in New Zealand.

All three women became noted horsewomen and 'trotters' in their own right and Mum was the first woman to be inducted into the New Zealand Trotting Hall of Fame, as well as being voted Ashburton Sportsperson of the Year, in 2011, for her years of dedication to racing. She was one of the first – if not the first – woman presidents of a racing club in Australasia, and is a well-respected owner and breeder of racehorses, claiming numerous national awards and races both in New Zealand and Australia.

Her sisters, hewn from the same stuff, have also continued to fly the Doyle flag in the years since Bill passed away. Along with my nieces, Kim and Margo, and my nephew, Justin, my mum and my aunts continue to work hard for their success on the racecourse. Denise – a pioneering racing woman in her own right – married Denis Nyan, from a well-respected horse family in New Zealand. Lynn still owns and runs most of Grandad's original farm with her husband, Gerard Smith, and continues to breed and train racehorses. Their son, Justin, is now one of the country's up and coming horsemen, so it really does seem as if the apple doesn't fall too far from the tree.

Well… Maybe I'm the exception to that rule.

No doubt, my mother has some regrets that I was more interested in picking up a rugby or cricket ball rather than a horse's reins. But, then again, Mum, maybe if I'd continued my promising equestrian career, in my little brown riding boots, jodhpurs and tweed jacket, then I would not be writing this book from your family's homeland.

As they say in Ireland … swings and roundabouts.

Small in stature, growth was to happen in late teens.
A mass of freckles on a perfectly round face. Incredibly
funny with most of the humour always poked at himself.
Excellent cartoonist, even at a young age. Wild but
generally well behaved, due to a strict upbringing. Spent
hundreds of hours horseriding or clearing horse manure
from their paddocks. One of the only advantages of the
horse scene was the girls who also rode. Kicked out of
movies for throwing ice creams from level one – a huge
event in Ashburton. Grassed on by his brother and then
thrashed by his father. Strapped at Netherby Primary
School for sucking a lolly in class. Couldn't tell parents
as they would hit him worse than the teacher.
In retribution, he stole one of the Maori Poi the teacher
had painstakingly made to teach the class Poi and
burned it in the class's pot-belly stove. He should have
burned them both because he was soon identified as
the culprit and strapped, yet again!

Richard Taylor.
Friend. Netherby Primary School.

2

Early Days

I arrived into this world black and blue, without oxygen, and with my umbilical cord wrapped tightly around my neck.

My near-strangulation, added to the simultaneous combination of double pneumonia and bronchitis from which I was suffering, led the medical staff to speculate that the following twenty-four hours would tell the tale of whether I would live or die. A priest was called, ready to baptise me and anoint me with the last rites, if it looked as though I wasn't going to make it.

It had been an eventful birth, mainly because it was unexpected. I was well over a month premature (I've tried to be more punctual ever since) and, in those days, a baby arriving four weeks or more early, was deemed highly unusual and very serious. On examination, the doctors informed my mother that I was lying in a dangerous, life-threatening position in her womb and the surgeon was rushed in to perform an emergency C-section.

Following the surgery, I was immediately taken from my mother's arms, and put into a plastic bubble at Karitane Hospital, where I spent the first few weeks of my newborn life. A worrying time for my mother and father, it must have been especially tough on my mother – she'd had to endure a traumatic delivery and was then forced to miss out on the crucial opportunity to bond with her baby.

The problems surrounding my birth continued to haunt me for the first few years of my life. I suffered countless health problems, to such an extent that, until my health improved at around four years old, the doctors thought that I might have leukaemia.

I have vivid memories of those early years: memories of my father awake in the middle of the night in the sunroom of our old house … wrapped in a blanket to keep warm … watching over me. While it's a beautiful memory – a souvenir of the unconditional love and support my family gave me in those early days when I was most vulnerable – it's also a sad reminder of more tragic events. Because of my difficult birth and the surgical intervention that went with it, Mum never got to have the girl she so desperately wanted. To this day, my mother bares a large scar from that C-section birth – the mark, not only of the operation, but also of the fact that it prevented her from having any more children.

Instead, my parents had to settle for two boys: my brother Mark, who was the eldest by 18 months, and me. We almost had a sister. A few years after I was born, my parents went to the last stages of adopting a little girl, but it wasn't to be, much to our regret. I often wonder where that little girl is now, and think about how she could have been my sister and a huge part of our lives.

So, my entry into this world – more precisely, to Ashburton, New Zealand in October, 1961 – was a rough event for all concerned. It had a lasting effect on everyone, not least me. Growing up in the small rural, farming township, about fifty miles south of Christchurch, my mother would constantly tell me that I was lucky just to be alive and that I was destined to do something with my life.

Not that, for large parts of my youth, I was much preoccupied with thoughts of greatness. I'd trouble getting the local girls to notice me, never mind the rest of the world. I was a fairly shy kid who lacked confidence in that department, and it didn't help that the few girlfriends I invited over to my house had eyes for someone else!

On the rare occasion, even as a teenager, when I managed to invite a girl to my home, their attention would often be drawn to the old black and white sporting photographs that were dotted around the house. Who, they would enquire, was the dark-haired, brooding James Dean-type in the back row of the photograph of the rugby team?

And why shouldn't they ask about the good-looking bloke with the movie star looks? With his collar up, his jet-black hair slicked back, this Mr Dean, even in a photograph, carried about him an air of arrogance and cheekiness. It was the kind of bad boy, rebellious combination that most women find irresistible.

Unfortunately for me, it wasn't a snapshot of yours truly. It wasn't even my older brother, which would have been bad enough. No, worst of all, the young 'rebel without a cause' that my girlfriends were drooling over was my father, Michael Bernard Pope.

Born into a working class family in a pretty unspectacular suburb of Auckland called Otahuhu, Dad was actually born on April Fool's day, but he claims the family stowed him under the blankets so they could release him on the more appropriate date of April 2. His neighbourhood was later made infamous as one of the settings for the tough New Zealand gangland movie, 'Once Were Warriors', and today it still remains a large working class, state housing area of Auckland, with its fair share of socio economic problems, a bit like those you might find around Dublin.

Dad's father, Cecil, was a Post Office worker and, as a result, the family moved around a lot, at one time living in Post Office quarters on Karangahape Road, which has been known for years as the red light capital of New Zealand, full of prostitution and drugs.

Like poorer areas in most cities around the world, Otahuhu was a melting pot of cultures and people, as subsequent waves immigrants poured in for the cheap housing. Chief among those waves was the influx of Asian immigrants, cruelly later called the Asian Invasion. For my dad, at least, the arrival of these Asians was a blessing – his first girlfriend was the daughter of the Chinese man who owned the local fruit stall. Back then, mixed relationships were unusual in New Zealand and, as a reward for walking hand-in-hand to school with his daughter, the stall-owner bestowed a dowry of free fruit upon my father. No doubt her father was just pleased that a nice young Kiwi lad had taken an interest in his foreign-born daughter.

Before long, the Popes were on the move again, a final move to the South Island's biggest City, Christchurch, and to another largely working class suburb, called New Brighton. The family lived in a small, two-bedroom house just 100 metres from the crashing sound of the Pacific Ocean. My grandfather, Cecil, carried the nicknamed 'Popey' and, like my father, was a dark-skinned, handsome man who certainly looked as though he had a little Maori blood somewhere in the family line.

The nickname, Popey, stuck – not just for my grandfather, but for my father, and for me. In fact, so common was the usage of the nickname, that my dad didn't actually know his father's first name until he was a teenager. He always believed 'Popey Pope' was Cecil's actual name.

I got it a lot, too. In my early days playing rugby in New Zealand, someone was always inquiring: "Popey, what the hell's your real name?" And moving to Ireland hasn't spared me, even today most people know me as Popey, as in Hook and Popey.

Though my dad grew up close to the beach, in those days it wasn't a particularly trendy place to live. It was only in later years that beach suburbs with sea views became the place to live. It's amazing to think that his family's lack of money was the reason he got to spend his early years crashing in the waves at New Brighton beach, eating and digging for raw muscles and pipis directly from the sand, sucking them down as though they were oysters. It's a practice that's extremely dangerous if your pallet is not used to raw seafood, but Dad still loves it to this day.

My grandparents made huge financial sacrifices to send him to a good Catholic Boys' school, St Bede's College.

St Bede's is one of Canterbury's leading producers of young rugby and sporting talent, and Dad was always more interested in sport than studies. As a result, he ended up as a speedy, lean winger in the St Bede's First XV. More significantly, he became an outstanding schoolboy sprinter and long jumper, eventually going on to win a national title as a long jumper, and represent Canterbury in the 100 metres at the New Zealand Sprint Championships.

But a lack of diligence at his schoolwork caused him problems and only the intervention from the sports rector at the exclusive school saved Dad from expulsion on several occasions, though he was lucky enough to make it to his final year.

Despite graduating from St Bede's he found it tough, like many Irish people in those days, to secure work. His constant, negative, encounters with the school authorities and an eye for the ladies ruled out the priesthood. So, in the end, it was either Post Office work like his father or a job in the bank. Dad chose the latter.

But his weekend activities were deemed a bit wild, particularly after several run-ins with the police. He and a few mates were charged with after-hours drinking, when a friend's cigarette smoke, billowing from the back of their van, led the cops straight to the culprits' hideout. But the writing was already on the wall at the bank. My dad's easy-going approach to life clearly didn't fit in with the conservative nature of the work and, by mutual agreement with management, he surrendered all ambitions of a career in banking.

Instead, he and three friends moved to Wellington in the North Island with the eventual goal of reaching Australia. It's a well-worn path, trodden by many young guys from Christchurch and one that, years later, I would follow myself, as I made my way to the other side of the world.

As a way of earning quick money for the trip, Dad took a job as a Freezing worker in the meat export industry. It was hard, dirty, manual labour and in those days often attracted the more unruly elements of society all looking, like my father, for the fast bucks the job offered. But, though he was lured to the job by the prospect of quick money, he wound up finding a career that would support him and his family for the rest of his life, eventually moving to Ashburton Freezing Works and working there until his retirement at 65, the last twenty-nine years spent as a full-time union official of the NZ Meat Workers' Union.

It was decent, honest, hard work but being a Freezing worker carried a social stigma. It was, after all, seasonal work, viewed to be the preserve of working class men with relatively little education and few prospects.

And that was exactly how WJ Doyle viewed the job and viewed my father. It didn't sit well with WJ, more commonly known as Bill, that his daughter was stepping out with a Freezing worker.

Bill was a self-made man who had pulled himself up by the bootstraps to become a successful businessman and horse breeder, and he didn't welcome the idea of his precious daughter, Helen, taking a backwards social step.

So, he didn't exactly roll out the red carpet when Michael 'Popey' Pope eventually asked for Helen's hand in marriage. The prospect of being the father-in-law of a Freezing worker didn't fill him with joy. The happy couple's engagement ring cost just £75, half of which was won on a poker bet from one of dad's drinking buddies.

To be fair to Bill, the young couple's love affair was an unlikely one. Dad came from a working class part of town, while Mum was brought up at the opposite end of the social spectrum – in Leeston, Canterbury. Her parents were Bill and Helen (Nell) Doyle, both of Irish extraction. Bill Doyle was a proud man who was forced to take on the mantel of breadwinner after his own father died young.

With little prospects of his own, Bill knuckled down and worked hard. The most precious thing his family had given him was a love of livestock, especially horses, and an 'Irish way' with them. He developed that 'Irish way' with animals and went on to build a reputation for breeding and training some of the nation's greatest racehorses, which still stands in New Zealand racing circles. He also accrued large tracts of land in and around Leeston and further afield, in the Canterbury plains, at one point owning 6000 acres. A tough taskmaster, he passed on his strong work ethic to my mother and her two sisters. No doubt, he'd have liked a son to follow him onto the family farms but, when life dealt him three girls, he didn't hold back on passing on to them his twin passions for farming and horses.

As a result of her driven father and the farming life, my mum found school to her liking. She was sent to an elite, Catholic girls' school, called St Patrick's Teschemakers, run by the Dominican nuns, where she excelled in sport and studies.

She also became something of an adventurer in her own right. Though both my parents aspired to travel after leaving school, it was my mum who managed to accomplish her goal. While Dad went to work in an abattoir, Mum and a school friend actually made it to Australia, where they worked for 18 months.

As part of the trip, the friends hitchhiked from deep in Aboriginal country, high above Cairns, all the way to Melbourne, a hell of a distance for two young ladies. She also worked as head-waitress on the Hayman Islands, off the Great Barrier Reef, hobnobbing with future sports stars like cricketer Ritchie Benaud (whom she had earlier met and briefly dated in Wellington). Mum was even given personal responsibility for looking after Hollywood movie star, Katharine Hepburn, who was holidaying on the Islands.

After that, she spent six weeks as a governess on an Outback cattle station, miles from anywhere, and took part in rodeos at Mount Isa. She even had a stint as a truck driver, driving the utility trucks from Geelong to Melbourne.

Pretty unusual stuff for a woman, in those days.

When she eventually came back to New Zealand, she worked in various fashion houses until she met Dad. By that stage, she was scholar, horsewoman, rodeo rider, truck driver and fashion guru all rolled into one.

She was never shy about rolling her sleeves up and mucking in, no matter how hard and how dirty the job, a trait she still carries with her today.

In today's, supposedly, more equal world, my parents' incompatibility – at least to the outside world – would probably mean they'd never even have met, let alone get married. They came from two different worlds and, as a couple, they could not have been more different. My mother was obviously attracted to my father's good looks and wild side, while my dad fell in love with a beautiful, driven and self-possessed convent girl.

Life wasn't easy for them.

My father was, and remains, a proud man and never accepted a handout from anybody in his life. He turned down his new father-in-law's offer to set him up in his own butchery business, insisting he would make his own way in the world.

He did and, though we never went short of the essentials of life, we never had the high life. Dad had a cleaning business which he operated in the off-season from the Freezing Works and I remember helping him on the weekends. One of his clients was the grandfather of Oscar-winning actress, Anna Paquin, who won Best Supporting Actress for her role in The Piano and stars in the vampire series, True Blood. He worked all the time. I don't even remember seeing him much as a kid, but I do recall staying up late at night to greet him when he came home – he always brought us a chocolate bomb ice cream.

Even as a youngster, keeping up a sharp image was important to me. At one point, Mum was working in a women's clothes shop when I announced to her that I absolutely had to have a denim jacket. They were the fashion at that stage and, while I longed for a designer one, I knew it would be beyond our financial capabilities so implored Mum to use her fashion contacts to get me one.

Imagine my delight when she came home one evening and handed me my very own denim jacket. Looking and acting the part, I proudly sported my tough new denim jacket look around the mean streets of Ashburton, until a girl down the road taunted me about my girl's jeans jacket.

"What do you mean?" I asked.

"It's got the buttons on the left-hand side, you idiot."

As if?

Of course, I stuck up for my tough new look until I got home and saw that the label on the inside read 'Jennifer Jean Jacket'.

I was mortified, although, with hindsight, I'm pretty sure my JJ Jacket wasn't the first, nor the only, piece of woman's clothes I wore.

Despite missing out on some things, like flashy clothes, I was lucky as a kid, and remember my childhood as full of fun and fights. I shared a room with Mark, who, like all older brothers, was happiest when he was terrorising his younger sibling. I remember, as a youngster, being terrified after glimpsing the highlights of 'The Exorcist' movie on the TV in the lounge. I was horrified – religion was a large part of our lives – but my loving brother made the most of my terror by, every night, shaking the legs on the bed. I was convinced that I was about to be possessed by demons and, to this day, I can't bear to watch that movie, it still scares the bejaysus out of me. Just writing about it now makes me worry my head is about to revolve through 360 degrees.

Religion was an integral part of our young lives. Dad was head of the parish council for years and Mark and I took an active part in the church every Sunday, either with the readings from the Gospel or the offerings and, on a Monday night, we attended extra religious studies, CCD or Catechism.

Dad and Mum both remain good church-going people, and my father in particular has a true faith. I, however, have strayed from the faith a bit and, regrettably, I am no longer a regular church-goer.

I do believe I'm a good, kind person who tries to always treat others in God's way. But Catholicism? I'm not sure any more, and my doubts have increased in the wake of the last few years' revelations about the involvement of priests in child abuse scandals. On occasion, I argue with my father on the issue. I still cannot get over the fact that, as a young religious child, I was told, and believed, that God was everywhere, looking after us and watching over us. I would drop to my knees every night beside my bed and pray to God that he would watch over me and my family. Yet, despite his all-seeing, all-knowing presence he allowed some of his own beautiful children to be raped and molested by his ambassadors on earth.

I still can't understand that. I know people will explain it by claiming God gave humans freedom of choice but, somewhere deep inside of me, I always trusted that God would protect the innocent. I can grasp the biblical concepts of natural disasters and loss of life, but the painful death of those who have hardly committed sin, while murderers and rapists walk free is a tough one to comprehend, even for the most devout Christian. I know there are many good, well-meaning priests and clergymen out there – I've met many of them – and most do a wonderful job. But I'm sure that I'm not alone in being disillusioned, and in my doubts about what true faith really is.

So, the question remains – do I have a faith? I guess the answer is I do … of sorts. Do I want to think there is a God or something spiritual waiting for us after we die? Definitely. But I feel neither the need, nor the desire, to go about the business of God in a formal way, bound up by the rules and expectations of any religion. I hope that, come Judgement Day, God will look at my actions rather than the fact that I didn't attend Mass as often as I should as an indicator of my faith. I guess I will never know what God thinks of me until I meet him. In the meantime, I simply intend to carry on with what I've been doing these last few years, trying to make God happy in the way I treat other people in my life.

● ● ● ● ●

But it hasn't always been easy.

I've battled a long time to overcome many of my own failings and I haven't always succeeded in that struggle.

My conscience still pricks me that, in one of the most important relationships of my life, I fell well short of living up to that simplest rule in life – treat others as you'd like to be treated yourself.

I knew my brother Mark was gay from an early age.

Like many of his contemporaries, Mark was wracked by fear and guilt about his sexuality and didn't come out to my mother and father until he was in his early 20s. I can only guess how hard it must have been for him in those early years. Growing up, dealing with adolescence and learning about oneself and one's sexuality is a tough experience for most teenagers and young people, even if they're heterosexual. To try and grapple with the problems of being gay – in a world which represses and oppresses homosexuality – is harder again.

At the exact time that these young, gay teenagers most need love and understanding, just as their heterosexual friends, they are exiled to a world of secret pain and exclusion.

For a lot of his early teenage years, Mark was angry and confused. Like a lot of gay men, he didn't want to be gay. He grew up like me, probably had the same hopes and dreams of a 'normal' family life, replete with wife and kids. But life, his life, didn't turn out that way and it was as much to his surprise as everyone else's. He didn't fill out a form, requesting to be gay, nor did he suddenly decide he wanted to be gay because it was the trendy thing to do.

The world is full of ignorant speculation over homosexuality and lesbianism. Are you born gay or are you converted? Nature versus nurture. There are many people who believe that it's a lifestyle choice, the implication being that if you can choose to go one way, then you can also choose to 'go back' to being straight again.

I don't agree.

In my brother's case he was simply born that way. Who knows why? Maybe a difference in his genetic blueprint, maybe not... That's a very cold way of looking at a very human issue. But, in the end, nature decided the issue for Mark, not nurture. He just wasn't physically attracted to women – it's as simple as that.

Still, growing up was difficult. We lived in a small, rural area which required men to be rugged, hard-working and self-sufficient to survive. It was a very macho environment where the closest a bloke got to having feelings was the pain he felt after being clobbered on the chin during an obstreperous night out on the beer. Weekends usually meant young, and old, bucks out on the lash and happy to square off against each other as they measured their entry into, or exit from, manhood. As full of piss and vinegar as any of them, it was a world I understood and liked. I, too, was aggressive, macho and ready to fight at the drop of a hat.

Unfortunately, as well as being a macho environment, it was also homophobic. The two went hand in hand (if you'll forgive the irony) and that was tough for Mark.

A strapping bloke with his father's good looks and his mother's zest for life, Mark could easily have blended in to one of those nights out at the bar, though his 6 foot 4 inch frame would have been more than enough to discourage all but the drunkest of barroom brawlers.

But, from an early age, it was clear to me that Mark was different to me. Despite his size, Mark was very sensitive, very emotional for a young man. While I dealt with hurt and pain by trying to inflict them in equal measure on some unsuspecting rugby forward, Mark would take things to heart.

Growing up in our homophobic, New Zealand world, gays were regularly ostracised and bullied with the result that Mark and I had very different experiences. He put up with knowing people viewed him and other gays as 'faggots' and 'queers', while I hung out with many of the so-called tough guys who were often behind the name-calling. It was difficult for me – a rugby team's dressing room is not the place to defend or empathise with gays, lest you be called one yourself.

And so, while some of my teammates and friends, indirectly and unwittingly, laughed at or insulted my brother – whom I knew was just another man making his way in life the best way he could – I gutlessly kept quiet. I was trying to be accepted as well, and while I didn't join in the taunting as much as the others I still didn't stop it. I didn't say, "Look guys, my brother is gay. Some of you know him so if you want to ridicule him then please have enough respect to do it away from earshot. Better still, not at all."

But I didn't and, like the worst kind of coward, I went along with the pack. Remaining silent was as bad as joining in, worse in many ways. I'd find excuses for myself by considering how the others would view me – an aspiring young All Black – and whether they would think me gay by association. My teammates knew no better. But I did. I denied my own, and only, brother whom I loved – love – very much. My only excuse was that I was young and ignorant and I didn't want to be associated with gay men, let alone admit to having one in my own small family.

But I'll always feel guilty and ashamed about my actions back then. I laboured under the misapprehension that Mark's homosexuality was a difficult problem for both of us. But that was the ignorance of youth. I wish now that I could have seen how tough it was for him to face his battles alone, and I wish that I could have been there for him. That, when the guys in the changing room started shouting about 'queers' and 'faggots', I could have stood up and told them about my brother and who he was, about how great he was and how they didn't know what they were talking about.

But I didn't. Deep down, I probably wanted him to be straight. I wanted a brother that I could meet in a bar, have a beer and talk about woman with. Maybe he'd have wanted that for himself – it might have made life easier for him. It would have made life easier for me.

Even when Mark visited Ireland nearly 16 years ago his sexuality, or rather my view of its impact on my life, caused a huge row between us. One evening during his trip, he indicated he might like to go to The George for a drink. The George was, and is, a well-known Dublin gay bar, one of only a few back then.

I begged him not to go. I'd just started a new career with RTÉ television as a rugby pundit. I was worried that, since Mark and I looked so alike – we're almost twins in how we look – people would mistake him for me and I'd be labelled as gay, something that could reflect badly on me as I tried to develop my TV career. I was worried that the thought of a gay rugby commentator would not have sat well with many sections of rugby society – who knows, maybe I was right. History is full of people who've been denied jobs and opportunities because of their colour, appearance, accent, sexuality or whatever. Irish people know better than most what it's like to suffer at the hands of racists and bigots.

But Mark couldn't see my point of view. He just thought I was ashamed of him.

I wasn't. In fact, I was, and am, immensely proud of him. But I was being selfish, thinking only of myself. I've often run through that row in my own mind, examining my own actions and questioning myself and my motives. I've talked to other people about it and they've reassured me that they can understand my motives, and many of them agree they would have done the same thing. Rugby is the same the world over, they point out, it's a sport for men's men and, sixteen years ago, Irish society may not have been ready for a rugby pundit who was 'gay' – mistakenly or otherwise.

Still… Mark didn't go to The George, so we'll never know.

Instead, I'm left wondering if I was right or wrong that evening.

Maybe, if I'd approached things differently, then I could have avoided that row. Maybe, I shouldn't have been so worried about Mark being mistaken for me in a gay bar in Dublin.

Maybe…

What if…?

To a degree, I'm still paying the price for my actions that night, and further back. Mark and I are brothers and friends but, while we are blood, we still live different lives. We are, perhaps, not as close as many brothers, and I guess both of us have lived our lives as slight loners.

I'm fine with that, I respect that.

I'm proud of who Mark has become as a man, as a gay man. I'm proud of the fact that he now helps so many young people with similar, troubled and confused backgrounds. His work is a credit to a kind and loving human being and I love him dearly.

And I believe that life is too short for 'maybes' and 'what ifs'.

But that doesn't mean that I don't have regrets.

Looking back, it's easy to see which of us was the braver brother, which of us had the stomach for life's real battles.

● ● ● ● ●

It's ironic then that, having denied my own brother's homosexuality, I've been the subject of some speculation that I might also be gay.

Once you hit a certain age in Ireland without getting married, or having children, then you are conferred with the (dubious) honorary title of 'confirmed bachelor'.

It's gas: the breakup of first-time marriages in the likes of the UK and the US is fast approaching 50 per cent, meaning half of all those loving couples who walk down the aisle will not end up with their 'happily ever after' dream.

Yet, despite such pessimistic statistics, simply mentioning that you are single and fifty years old you are labelled a freak.

It'd be easier for me to tell people I've been married and divorced, three times, and have eight or nine kids strewn all around the world, than it is to admit I'm unmarried. Most people wouldn't react to the former statement but, "He's fifty, unwed and without kids? Go ahead and burn him at the stake!" or "He must be gay."

In the past, I haven't really felt the need to address the question of my own sexuality. My private life is just that. But, in the context of talking about the mistakes I made with Mark, it's maybe time to say that I'm not gay. I'm as proud to be 100 per cent heterosexual as others are to be gay. Whatever floats your boat.

Just because I am not married does not mean I'm a confirmed bachelor. It doesn't mean that I'm gay. It doesn't mean I want to be alone. It doesn't mean I'm a commitment-phobe.

It just means, I'm me.

I've been lucky enough to have had a few, long-term, relationships with wonderful, beautiful, caring women, including one that lasted a long number of years here in Ireland. I've admired, respected and adored them on many levels and, out of respect, I won't mention them by name here. A gentleman never tells that sort of thing.

But they've all been part of a lifelong, and often traumatic, journey of love and acceptance for me. I've always struggled with relationships because of anxiety-based issues and lack of self confidence. In some ways, I have an inability to feel that I deserve real love, despite knowing in my heart of hearts that I am a good life-partner.

Every serious relationship I've had has been sabotaged by my own failings. They are killed by my inability to avoid "paralysis by analysis".

But I am working hard on changing that.

In the meantime, I continue to appreciate women. Many of my best friends are women and, in many ways, I prefer their company to a man's. I have always been like that, since school, through university, in the life I've made in Ireland. I've met, studied with and worked with some women whom I regard as my really good friends. I feel I can talk to them about anything.

That ability to open up about our feelings is something that a lot of Irish men have trouble with, regardless of their sexuality. Instead, they are told that real men don't cry, they bottle their feelings up, tough it out and just get on with things. That macho propaganda we're feeding to our children is forcing many young men to take their own lives in this country.

Why?

Men don't know what they are meant to be these days. Sensitive but strong is often the women's magazine ideal of a perfect man – able to cry at a sad movie but also capable of knocking out the guy who's eyeing up his girlfriend. Caveman with soft hands.

Against such a backdrop some young men don't, can't, reach out for help.

They feel their only option is to end their lives. If there are some men out there who are worried about debt, love, loss – whatever – they need to understand that reaching out for help is a strength, not a weakness. That a problem shared is a problem solved.

Rather than trying to convince someone who feels down or depressed to tough it out, we need to help them understand that they are not alone, that we all experience times like that. More than most, life has taught me the value of reaching out to a loved one, family member, priest, counselor, whoever. Help is there.

It's worth pointing out that having a gay brother doesn't qualify me to hand out advice on sexuality in sport to people, but I'm regularly asked about the issue of gay players in rugby. There must, people insist, be a lot of secret, gay, rugby players.

My answer is no, I don't think there are many undeclared gays playing rugby. Despite the law of averages, during my rugby career I've only ever known two gays playing the game, one in my university days and another, a prominent Irish provincial player, from a few years ago.

Some time ago, I penned a rugby comedy movie script that I hoped would attract the attention of some of Ireland's Hollywood movie stars or producers.

'Coming Out to Play' is centred on the story of a young Irish rugby star who, courtesy of his selfish and arrogant attitudes, faces the prospect of losing his rugby scholarship and, along with it, his idyllic Trinity College lifestyle. To avoid this disaster he's forced to infiltrate the Irish gay rugby team and convince the players he's 'just like them'. En route to competing in the Bingham Cup, the story takes many twists and turns before reaching its conclusion.

A kind of 'Billy Elliot' meets 'The Full Monty', what I wanted to achieve with 'Coming Out to Play' was less a sporting movie and more a story about what it takes to be a man. I want to pass on the lessons I've learned in life and in sport. While the project is still in its infancy, the script has already received some good responses from a number of film companies, such as Parallel Films which was behind movies like 'The Wind that Shakes the Barley' and 'The Guard'.

Like all aspiring movie makers, my dream is to see my work up on the silver screen. But, like all aspiring movie makers, I first need to secure funding and the backing of some guardian angel in the movie industry. That's the hard part. So far, as they say in Hollywood, the heavy hitters are not exactly banging down my door just yet.

But the very fact that I can get a positive response to a movie which involves gay rugby players is a good indication that the modern game isn't as homophobic as it once was. A number of gay players have sought to change attitudes, among them Ian Roberts, one of the hardest men to ever grace Australian Rugby League. About twenty-five years ago, the Australian Rugby League world was rocked when Roberts, a muscle-bound, 6 foot 5 inch scrapper few people would dare to call a 'fag', publicly revealed he was gay. Even now, almost three decades later, his autobiography, 'My Life', is a fascinating read, regardless of your sexuality. No one messed with Roberts and his book is littered with instances of his having to face abuse from a country and sport that could not accept that one of their favorite genuine Aussie hard cases fancied men.

More recently, of course, Welsh Captain Gareth Thomas talked about being gay and coming out, I remember reading Thomas' comments about how Ireland's Trevor Brennan was a rock of support to him as he faced coming out.

Doesn't that say something about Brennan the man, about how a man that epitomises the machismo of rugby can be such a kind-hearted friend that he will support his mates, and not give a damn about what others think? That, to me, said more about Trev's heart than anything he had done on the rugby pitch – he was there when a friend needed him most.

It seems to me, though I missed the message earlier in life, that the game of rugby is as much about making the whole man as it is about making a sportsman.

I feel I failed my brother three decades ago but, if someone like Trevor can lend support to his gay friends, then, maybe, the world is finally moving in the right direction.

• • • • •

As a footnote to this chapter, I'd like to correct another serious disservice I did to my brother, Mark.

Earlier, I pretty much rubbished all notion that he had any success on the field of rugby endeavour. I may have intimated that, despite his size, my brother Mark was no Gareth Thomas or Ian Roberts. I may also have given the impression that he was, emotionally, too soft for a sport as aggressive as rugby.

Actually, Mark did have one moment of rugby glory.

Well … almost.

It came during a season in which he played for the local First XV. On one notable occasion, and much to his own delight, he managed to score a try.

His only try.

Ever.

Sad to report then that, as he lay there on the line, bathing in the afterglow of his own sporting glory, the only person to approach him was the referee, who duly looked down upon Mark's beaming face and informed him that he had, in point of fact, just dotted down on the 22 line, not the try line.

Life can be cruel sometimes.

First memories of rugby: trial for a Town team to play Country. Playing 2nd 5/8 he put up a bomb [Garryowen] that went 30m backwards and bounced kindly for the opposition who scored under the posts. Did not make the team. Fancied all the best looking girls but the adoration was not generally reciprocated. Wasted most of his misspent youth with Playboy magazines. As a cricket player, Brent was very talented but not very interested. Would often bowl pace then revert to spin in the middle of an over. Was once making a daisy chain while bored and standing about gully when the ball was edged into his unsuspecting hand. It stuck. When playing for Mid Canterbury against Canterbury, he came up against Mark Priest. Priest was an excellent player and ended up playing for NZ. Brent said to Mark, "I'll be better than you because you're only a Priest but I'm a Pope!" At a local party on a farm, he had an altercation with another guy and decided to urinate in the other guy's motorbike fuel tank so that it would seize up and break down. In the dark, he got petrol on his pecker much to the burning delight of those watching. At the same party he tried his chat-up lines on a girl he had his eye on. Things progressed to his VW. The seats were reclined a bit, causing one to come in contact with the car battery which then fused, setting the entire back of Popey's old rust bucket on fire. Two lipstick-smudged, clothes-adjusting teens escaped to the hilarity of all those watching.

Richard Taylor
Friend. Ashburton College.

3

A Farewell to Mullets

It might come as a shock, but one of my first fist fights at my primary school, Netherby, was in defence of the British and Irish Lions, though back then they were still somewhat arrogantly known as just the British Lions.

As a kid, I used to get up early in the morning with Dad to watch black and white TV images beamed in from the United Kingdom of the old Five Nations tournaments and the English FA Cup. Although I played soccer a bit at school, it was the game of rugby that always captivated me most, mainly because Dad had played it, plus, like GAA in Ireland, it was drilled into you from the pram.

But, on one particular occasion in my childhood, I was lucky enough to go along to the Ashburton Showgrounds to watch the British and Irish Lions players in action. I was amazed at the skill of the likes of Gareth Edwards, David Duckham, and Irishman Mike Gibson, though my favourites were Barry John, the twinkle-toed Welsh out-half, and the big Welsh winger, John Bevan – players who were a million miles from the burly, cauliflower-eared forwards I later soldiered with at the back of countless scrums.

We actually cheered for the Lions that day, as we feasted on lukewarm mince pies and sugary soft drinks, but within twenty-four hours my willingness to embrace these foreign Lions earned me a fight in the Netherby school playground as I defended Welsh wizard, Barry John, against his local detractors.

In the midst of the conflagration, one schoolboy who was not involved picked on my friend, Peter. As a last resort to help my mate from getting pummelled by this much bigger kid, I grabbed the bully's hand and stuck it under the strong spring of my bike carrier, before releasing it and seeing him reel back in pain. He ran off but threatened to kill me the next time he saw me at school, and at that age I had every reason to believe him. He was, after all, a bully who towered above the rest of us.

Funnily enough, he steered clear of me after that, but standing up to him was the beginning of a lifelong inclination to at least try to stand up for the underdog. As a kid, I despised bullies... Still do. I often found myself sticking up for kids who were weaker or even a bit different. My ability at sport meant that, for most of my young life, I was usually 'in' with the so-called A-crowd at school, but I always had a lot of friends who were the opposite. Many of them didn't like sport at all, and were the type of 'nerds' whom the sports-jocks liked to pick on. I'd like to think that I was the type of person who stuck up for them, and defended them. I'm not sure where that trait came from – most likely my dad – but I've always felt that it's important to look after people who aren't mainstream, or who are a little different or eccentric.

My quick and fiery temper wasn't always appreciated, though, and I can't honestly say I only ever deployed my little, balled fists in the role of UN peacekeeper with special responsibility for Kiwis. After one particular schoolyard encounter when I was about six years old, my dad received a visit from my primary school teacher. It soon became clear that this was no social call as my teacher proceeded to tell Dad of his disapproval of my playground dust-ups and of his suspicion that I might have psychological problems.

If the teacher thought he'd find a sympathetic ear in my father, he was sorely disappointed. Dad marched him off the property in short order, but not before he informed him that it was he, the teacher, who had "the problem".

My physicality found an outlet on the rugby pitch and I got my first real taste of rugby action in a green Celtic jersey when I was about four years old. Wearing a green Celtic, or Dooleys, jersey favoured by most Marist Brothers clubs throughout New Zealand, was an interesting development for a kid who began school every day with a full rendition of 'God Save the Queen'. As part of the Commonwealth, the British anthem was piped across the school assembly yard via a crackly old sound system, followed by the New Zealand national anthem, ironically written by an Irish immigrant.

At times, it must have sounded a bit like a throwback to old WWII German war propaganda, certainly to some of the Maori kids whose parents may not have had the same allegiance to a British flag. The Maori have a mixed view of allegiance to the Queen and crown. In recent decades, they've been trying, with some success, to claw back the land and fishing rights that they felt their forefathers signed away, in what many Maoris may regard as unfair treaties.

But, as a schoolboy, I didn't really understand or care about politics. Even the Irish heritage that lay behind a green Celtics jersey was lost on me. All I knew was that I wanted to get on the pitch and start playing football. Man, was I excited about playing rugby! I was actually unable to sleep the night before my first big game. I got up every hour, on the hour, dressed in my little green jersey, white shorts, green socks and black plastic boots.

"Is it morning yet?"

"No. Go back to bed."

And so it continued, all night long. Not exactly great preparation for my first big game for the Celtic U-5s, but I suspect it was more of a trial for my parents than for me.

Finally, my bleary-eyed folks got to see me – green jersey stretched tight across my little frame – roaring out onto the pitch, the Celtic teams' very own fast, chubby, freckle-faced, curly-haired winger.

Even back then, at U-5 level, there was no pussyfooting around. Tag rugby was unheard of – football among those ankle-biters was all-action, big-tackling stuff. Having your elbows and knees cut to ribbons on rough, frequently frosty, pitches like Ashburton's Showgrounds was a rite of passage for many a youngster. And, on many playing fields, it required a fair amount of dexterity to pick a path through the sheep dung that littered the ground. New Zealand was a bit like Ireland in those days, it wasn't unusual for play to be held up until a couple of stray sheep could be herded off the pitch.

But, complex and painful as our playing conditions might have been, the game itself was straightforward. My coach's only instruction was the definition of simplicity itself: "Pin your ears back and head for the corner, son!"

So I did. I loved the game and I loved scoring tries.

Some Saturdays I would come home in the late afternoon after scoring four or five tries and playing for teams in a couple of different age groups, just to make up the numbers. Of course, as I got older and my love of rugby grew into an obsession, my mother was a little disappointed that I was eschewing the chance to follow in the family tradition and become a horseman – something, if you'll excuse the pun, she had been grooming me for. Her love of all things equine was evident from an early age, and keeping horses meant we were the envy of the local school.

But keeping horses was hard work for a young boy. You had to be very disciplined, and that meant getting up early each day, cycling to the horse paddocks to feed, water and exercise them, come rain or snow. I was a decent enough rider and, at the local pony club, I was one of a small, select band of boys amongst fifty jodhpur-wearing hotties. God, what I would give to be able to say that now!

After pony clubs, I was moved on to various agricultural horse shows, hunts and gymkhanas. Admittedly, I absolutely loved the thrill of horse riding, the exhilaration of riding over jumps or at hunts at extreme speed. There is nothing more frightening, or exciting, than trying to control a powerful horse which bolts on you. You don't know if you'll be pitched into, through or over a wall or hedge or fence, and I had plenty of serious spills in my time. On many occasions, I wound up on my arse, tangled in barbed wire or being dragged, western-style, behind the horses because I couldn't get my feet free of the stirrups. I've been kicked, bitten and stomped on by those wonderful animals.

But I was the grandson of WJ Doyle and, every time I took a fall, my mother repeated the mantra which had been taught to her many years before: "Get straight back on the horse and never show fear."

Even the injuries meant I was carrying on a noble, family tradition. We Pope boys, Doyles and O'Briens, have enjoyed being physically abused by horses for generations. My cousin, Margo Nyan, still bears a huge crescent-shaped scar on her head, marking the spot where a horse kicked her as a child, almost killing her. My Aunty Lynn was also seriously injured by the foot of a horse.

But, perhaps the worst injury of all was suffered by my mother who, twenty years ago, was thrown by her mount. She landed on her head, breaking her neck. She hyperextended her neck and received a horrendous injury known by the sinister name of a 'hangman's break'. It's the same injury that befell former Superman actor, Christopher Reeve, in 1995 when he tumbled from his horse in a point-to-point race. Reeve survived his fall but was paralysed from the neck down for the remainder of his life. Despite a heroic campaign on behalf of spinal injury victims and fighting to recover from his own spinal injuries, he eventually died in 2004, nine years after his initial fall, from an allergic reaction to an antibiotic he was taking.

Mum was luckier. God must have been watching out for her that day and, while she broke her neck and had to have a halo brace screwed to her head for a long while, she managed to avoid death or paralysis by inches. Still, her fall marked the end of her days on a horse, though I suspect that, even now in her late 70s, there are many times she'd still love to climb back into the saddle. Horses are in her blood, they are in my brother Mark's and, according to Mum, they should have been in my blood, too. They were, and still are, but rugby was becoming my real love and my new focus. While Mark took some of the heat off me by concentrating his athletic talents on following the equestrian path, I broadened my sporting horizons.

From an outdoors point of view, New Zealand is an idyllic country to grow up in and I couldn't get enough of all kinds of sports. Back then, my long, hot, dry summers were filled with running, ocean swimming, softball, tennis, soccer … whatever. A gang of us roamed across the countryside without fear of boundaries or rules. One of our favourite pastimes was floating on large inflated tractor tyres for miles downstream, to where the Ashburton River met the ocean. The absence of lifejackets as we hurtled along swollen rivers and dangerous currents only added to the thrill of the ride. There was cricket and athletics in the summer and rugby and skiing in the winter and my best friend, Richard Taylor's, home even had its own swimming pool and all-weather cricket pitch, just around the corner from my house.

From early in the morning until the cock crowed at night, we played cricket during the summer months. The rules were dead simple: into the swimming pool was an automatic out and so, too, was breaking the neighbour's windows, something we did almost every weekend. We would put our protective pads on in a little shed and then walk into Richard's nets, assuming the identities of the world's greatest cricketers. I was a leg-spin bowler at that time, so I became one of the great Australian or Indian spin bowlers, while Richard's fast-swing bowling meant he played the role of New Zealand's Richard Hadlee or an Aussie great, like Dennis Lillee or Jeff Thompson. We could remain batting for weeks at a time, resuming our game each weekend if you weren't out, and often scoring runs into the thousands before eventually being bowled or caught out, or putting one into the pool or through the neighbour's plate-glass window.

In those days, cricket in New Zealand was hugely popular, and we often went up to Lancaster Park in Christchurch to watch the Australians or West Indians when they came to town. It was a time when the likes of Lillee and Thompson would walk back almost to the boundary in their run-up and then hurl the ball down at over 100 miles an hour, directly at some poor tail-order batsman, who would await this hurtling meteorite, trembling in his boots and filled with trepidation.

It was not uncommon for bouncers or beamers to strike players and almost cause death. There were no helmets in those days, just a pair of good batting gloves, a thigh pad and the necessary protective box that covered your crown jewels. A couple of players were nearly killed through being hit with these rocket balls, while many more risked missing out on a full, family life in the future.

Later, at university, the thought of spending an entire weekend chasing a small red ball in the hot afternoon sun would bore me. Rugby was a short game at least, done and dusted in just over an hour. But, in my school years, I loved the game and was a reasonably talented schoolboy cricketer, opening the bowling and batting at No. 3 for Ashburton's First XI.

I was good enough to play in the senior grade in the local Ashburton Saturday competition and I represented my province, Mid Canterbury, on many occasions at underage level, even being selected one year in the tournament trial team for the South Island Under-18s.

Probably the greatest honour bestowed on our cricketing group of teenage friends came when one of the gang was selected for a Representative team.

Getting selected to play for a local Rep team was a challenge for any Ashburton cricketer, but markedly tougher for a player who never actually existed in the first place and whom Richard Taylor and I had conjured up out of our fertile imaginations.

In those days, the local cricket or sports reporter was meant to cover all of the Saturday cricket matches for the local newspaper. But attending every game was a logistical nightmare and, often, there were better ways for a journalist to spend a hot summer's afternoon than by doing his job.

As a result, some of these absentee hacks would while away the workday by sinking a beer or two down the local, and depend on the players or team managers from each team to fill out a press card, detailing the scores and major events of their match. Cricket, unlike rugby, was an easy sport to report on and the press cards would contain the details of who played well, who scored the runs, who caught whom out and who claimed all the wickets. These press cards were deposited into a small box after the match, which the reporter would duly collect and base his Monday morning's sports report on.

To spice things up, Richard and I invented a player called Peter Muldoon – named after the then New Zealand Prime Minister, Rob 'Piggy' Muldoon. Postgame we would tally up a few of the insignificant scores, wickets or catches and attribute them to the fictitious Pete Muldoon. This continued for a few months until, much to our own surprise, young Muldoon hit the sporting headlines in the local rag. A promising young player, and rising star of the future, Peter Muldoon had been selected to attend an underage Mid Canterbury Rep training session – a rare honour. Even more impressive was the fact that our ghostly friend had made it in a sport where no one had ever met him.

Mysteriously, the media clamour for young Muldoon to be picked for the Rep team fizzled out as rapidly as it began. Presumably the reporter, and then his apoplectic editor, discovered they'd been had. Richard and I didn't ask. After considering our options, we reckoned discretion was the better part of valour and decided to keep our heads down.

We didn't find out what happened to the reporter but, suffice to say, he disappeared from the cricketing scene as effectively as Peter Muldoon.

• • • • •

On leaving primary school, I didn't follow in my father's – or mother's – footsteps by attending one of the South Island's top schools. My dad had gone to St Bede's, one of the island's top rugby breeding schools, but I opted to stay at my local school, Ashburton College, a large, co-ed public school of about 1500 pupils.

My brother, Mark, was already there so it made sense – or so it initially seemed. But it soon became clear that, like a lot of teenage boys, our personalities were different and this often led to conflict. Problems arose because Mum and Dad both worked particularly long hours and, as a consequence, there was often no one at home to greet Mark and I when we finished the school day. Familiarity can breed contempt amongst siblings and, having no one to say hello to Mark and I when we came home also meant there was no referee to separate us when we clashed. No-holds barred fights became common and, for their entertainment value alone, they eventually achieved legendary status in the local area. Mark was older than me by around eighteen months, and considerably bigger. But he'd also matured much quicker than me and, by nature, was a gentler, more emotional kid – traits which combined to mean that he often had the wit to hold back during a fight, regardless of how angry he might become.

On the other hand, I was younger and very immature which translated – in our fights at least – into my being rougher, far more aggressive and much dirtier. When I look back now, my temper at times was uncontrollable and I'd attack Mark with just about anything I could lay my hands on. On one unfortunate occasion, unable to let go of one particular fight, I waited until he got into the bath and then ran in, grabbed his foot and held it against the scalding hot tap, burning it.

I saw Mark as a 'do-gooder', especially in the earlier days of both primary and secondary school. He was always immaculately dressed, got 'A's on his report card and was involved in countless activities like class committees. As a youngster, he even set up the 'Ooky Spooky Club' in which he and his mates would go on exciting Famous Five and Secret Seven-type adventures. Mark organised everything: the club cards, secret codes and invisible ink and the Club would meet weekly in an official clubhouse that Dad had made. I desperately wanted to be a member of the that darn Ooky Spooky Club, and being left out of it just made me all the more jealous.

While Mark was high achieving in most areas of school life, I had more in common with Denis the Menace (Bart Simpson nowadays, I guess). Mum was always sewing up my school pants, the pockets – into which I constantly thrust my hands – were always ripped and my knees were always skinned. I was forever getting up to some sort of mischief.

One time, Richard Taylor and I decided to play polo on our pushbikes using Dad's brand new golf woods. I broke one almost immediately but, thinking on our feet, we Sellotaped it together and put it back in his bag. We were miles away the next weekend when Dad took out his brand new wood at the golf course and teed off. He was furious when it broke in two but, having missed the Sellotape, he instead put the break down to the power of his drive or dodgy craftsmanship.

Sorry, Dad.

Perhaps unsurprisingly, my main interest at school was sport, where I excelled at almost everything I tried. I was a decent sprinter, a good 800 and 1500 metre track runner and a promising cross-country runner. I represented Ashburton College at various South Island athletics tournaments and, at different stages, represented the school in cricket, soccer, table tennis, softball, basketball, skiing, swimming, horse riding and, of course, rugby.

Sadly, I was less adept at studying, and academia – Mrs Stapleton's English class aside – held little appeal. As a result I cultivated a less enviable reputation in that area of my life. End of term, especially until the 4th or 5th form, was always the worst part of the year for me. My report card was due at that point and mine was always the same – 'C's or 'D's, followed by comments such as, "Brent disrupts the class", or "Brent is far too easily distracted and distracts others".

Things got to the point where I would even try to convince my parents that I'd lost my report card on the way home or, for some reason, my report had been delayed. They swallowed none of it.

I suppose the truth was that, in those early years at least, I was just too impatient for schoolbooks or anything that required me to sit still for a period of time. If I got a model aeroplane as a birthday or Christmas present, I couldn't wait for the glue to set before taking it for a test spin. As a result, many of my creations crashed and burned, falling apart into a thousand tiny balsa wood pieces on their maiden flights.

That was disappointing enough, but what made it infinitely harder to take was the fact that Mark was the exact opposite. While my models were slapped together in double-quick time and 'rushed to the front' before they were ready, Mark would lay his models out perfectly with pins and follow the instructions to a 'T'. Needless to say, his planes would glide effortlessly and without disintegrating. It was like living with a German car manufacturer.

So, it came as much as a surprise to me as to everyone else when, years later, I earned a bursary scholarship to university by finishing in the top percentile of New Zealand students. I was an intelligent kid, but a complete messer. I was the person most likely to screw around all year, skip classes or lectures in favour of riding motorbikes or playing rugby. I would be the type of student, even at university, that would photocopy the class swat's notes a month before the exams and then cram a whole year's work into a couple of weeks. But I did like English, especially Mrs Stapleton's class. She was unusual in that she encouraged me just to write and be creative. Her simple instruction was, "Use your imagination and we can worry about the spelling and grammar later". She fired my imagination and I discovered that, not only could I write children's stories, but it was something I loved doing. Years later, that love of writing, drawing and story-telling found expression in my children's books but, while at school, it is safe to say that academia always – without exception – came a distant third behind sport and having the craic.

Things were different when it came to sport. I was different. I was comfortable on a rugby pitch and my interest in the game was rewarded with onfield success. By my fifth year at Ashburton College, I was still a reasonably talented midfield back, representing my province Mid Canterbury at most underage levels. I didn't play rugby to the exclusion of all else, but that changed in Year Six, my second-last year at secondary school.

In the space of twelve months, I suddenly spurted, shooting up and out like a bean sprout. Out of the blue I was tall and, due to a summer lifting weights at the school gym with Richard Taylor, Parry Jones and Richard Smith, I was also fairly muscular. Our school rugby coach, Bevan Bain took me aside preseason and informed me that, henceforth, I was to be a second-row for the First XV that year. SECOND BLOODY ROW!

I bitterly protested. I was a centre – everybody knew that. I even had the shoulder-length, mullet hairstyle and the headband to go with the centre's image. Second rows, or locks as they are called in New Zealand, were considered the donkeys of the team – big mulluckers whose main image centred around a pair of cauliflower ears. Locks with banged-up ears were certainly not a woman's choice of player: girls liked the flashy types, the lads who ran in tries and made scintillating breaks. Centres, and backs in general, held infinitely more romantic appeal than blokes who stuck their heads between squat props' legs and grabbed their groins during scrums. And, like all young, testosterone-riddled adolescent males, meeting girls was important to me in those days.

That very summer, I had forgone a very promising cricket career as a leg-spin bowler, where I could tweak the ball a country mile, in order to become the First XI's opening fast bowler.

Why?

Because it was cooler. Australian speedsters Thomson and Lillee were where the girls were at. They loved you as you sauntered in from a long run-up, medallion swinging off your tanned, hairless chest, cricket whites open from the stomach up and long hair flying in the breeze, terrifying the bejaysus out of some poor batsman with the speed of the ball. As a fast bowler, I wasn't too accurate or successful, but I could throw the ball down with fury. Each year the students played the teachers in a match watched by all the school and I took great pleasure in pelting the teachers at bat. Once, I even managed to sneak a ball into the testicles of a rather unpopular member of staff, much to the delight of all of the pupils and more than a few of his co-workers. He hated the fact that I had embarrassed him in front of the whole school.

So, I cursed Coach Bain's decision to demote me from my starring role in the centre of the rugby pitch. I cursed him all the harder when I had to start taping up my ears, jumping in the lineout and pushing in the scrum.

Ireland legend, Moss Keane, always said he preferred doing the opposite, namely pushing in the lineout and jumping in the scrum and I wish now I'd done the same thing. I'd come home after a match with a pair of ears that were black and blue and screaming with pain, after the new experience of being sandwiched between two big props' arses.

The one, saving grace that year was the fact that, my ruined ears notwithstanding, we had an incredible team – still the most successful our school has ever known. We were very unfashionable, a small, unknown, rural rugby school, but we took on and beat some of the Christchurch teams that traditionally made up the elite of New Zealand's top rugby schools.

After a string of unexpected results against the 'better' schools, the rugby system had to suddenly sit up and pay attention to us. Two players from our First XV, prop Ken Rogers and hooker Andrew Beattie, made the New Zealand schools and U-19 teams respectively, an honour never before, or since, achieved at my old school. The majority of that particular school team also went on to play at U-18 level for Mid Canterbury and did well in the national South Island Championships, beating highly-ranked Otago and running Canterbury to within a point in the final.

A lot of us, myself included, won South Island and New Zealand underage and youth trials. During one of those South Island U-18 trials, I was pitted at second-row against a huge, but soft-looking, lock from Southland. Even at that age he was a freak, standing about 6 foot 7 and weighing in at around 16 stone, while I measured a mere 6 foot 3 and boasted a pair of chicken-sized legs.

I needed to develop a strategy to deal with him so I tried to stand on his toes at lineout time.

It worked, too … for a while. But, generally, I wasn't a spring-heeled jumper and that was always my Achilles heel as a player. Later, as a six foot three player who couldn't get far off the ground I was always competing for a No. 8 position dominated by guys who were, on average, two or three inches taller and able to jump. I was a shorter, more powerful type of ball carrying player, much in the mould of current Irish International, Sean O'Brien. In the modern game I would still play at No. 8 but would have the job of lifting a taller player at the lineout. In fact, it would have been easy to lift me as all my weight was in my upper body. I had good hands and strength, but my chicken legs just couldn't get the necessary spring and I had virtually no vertical jump.

Fortunately, I had a unique ability to run ugly. As one reporter put it, I ran "like a reverse hovercraft" which may have looked stupid but made me difficult to tackle. It meant that I would lead into the tackle with my barrel chested body. That was the last thing an opposition defender wanted, they would have preferred to target those darn chicken scratchers.

The success of that Bevan Bain-coached school team had long-term consequences for my playing career, in particular copperfastening my transition from centre to lock. But Bevan has much to answer for in terms of his crimes against fashion. Thanks to him, the Brent Pope mullet-haired, headband look was lost forever to the sports world, replaced by taped-up ears and a pair of underdeveloped pins.

Still, I suppose I should grudgingly, and gratefully, acknowledge just how massive an influence Bevan had on my rugby career. He took a long look at me that summer and figured I had more chance of making a decent second row than a flashy centre. He obviously had vision because he went on to represent New Zealand Schools Rugby as an administrator. He was a wonderful, warm-hearted man who had a passion for the sport of rugby and wanted to give something back to the game that had given him so much.

Not surprisingly, he was also the school's career guidance counsellor, though you could never get much advice from him on anything but rugby. When the door of Bevan's office closed, it was a case of, "let's talk rugby". If he eventually got around to discussing your non-rugby future, he would open a big, black book and start at the As: Aeronautical engineer? Astronaut? On and on through the alphabet he would move until some kind of employment option struck a chord (however discordant) with the pupil before him. My brother Mark had a particularly long encounter with him: though Mark now works as a counsellor himself, he did, at one stage, aspire to be a vet, a job that meant the only person queuing outside Bevan's office was the wannabe zoo-keeper.

All rugby schools need enthusiasts like Bevan Bain. Times have changed a bit, but every local rugby player of my generation can recount stories of wonderful Marist Brothers who went down the line of potential players, deciding, "you're a lock, you're a winger..." and so on.

That's the beauty of rugby there's a position for every type of body shape. Very few, if any, other sports are like that.

Similarly, players of my vintage can also remember the days when your studies counted for less than your ability to make training on time. I'm not suggesting that academia isn't equally important – it is. But it strikes me that those wonderful old rugby priests, brothers and coaches were a special breed of mentor who understood the importance of developing qualities beyond academic skills. They valued sportsmanship, teamwork and camaraderie, things I regard as vital in a young man or woman's passage through life and which cannot be imparted via books or computers on their own. There is surely room for both.

●●●●●

My last year at secondary school was a breeze.

In my time, the education system in New Zealand allowed you to qualify for university in your second-last year of school – so long as you performed exceptionally well in your top four subjects in the national exams. Not only was I accredited my University Entrance Exams for my work over the year in the mock exams, but I also finished in the top few percent of my year. Thus, my results were good enough to guarantee me not only a spot in any course at any university, but also the bursary scholarship to pay for much of it.

Effectively, it meant that my last year at school was redundant, apart from a set of Leaving Certificate exams at the very end, and even those couldn't really affect me. While I could, and maybe should, have gone straight to university I couldn't leave my friends or lifestyle. So, in that last, wasteful, year at Ashburton College, I took subjects like art history just for the craic. I didn't attend class very much, and instead played rugby, cricket, hung out in the common room or took off on my motorbike, with Jeff McLay and Craig Niven, riding the various trails that cut through the Ashburton riverbeds.

Unsurprisingly, it was the best year of my school life with nothing to do but just have fun and enjoy the great weather. Along with mates like Richard Taylor, Richard Smith, Parry Jones, Gerard Prendergast, Craig and Jeff, we'd jump the school fence on Friday nights and go swimming with our then girlfriends. Often diving off the high boards in the nude, much to the dismay of the neighbours, the only thing I can say was that the water was always so cold, they'd have needed a telescopic lens to see the cause of their offence.

At the weekends, we'd cruise the Ashburton party scene in my old Volkswagen Beetle, taking with us the customary dozen bottles of Dominion Brewery's (DB) beer. We used to drive everywhere in that old 1950s Beetle which sported swept-up chrome pipes, fat tyres and a painted mural on its back, courtesy of my mate Parry's artistic flair. Parry was the son of one of New Zealand's foremost sculptors, Morgan Jones, and later illustrated one of my children's books. Recently, Parry won a national film contest run by no less a figure than Peter Jackson of 'Lord of the Rings' fame.

That year was a bit like living in a John Hughes movie – a long hot summer spent with beer, cars, motorcycles, girls, parties, the beach, rugby and fun.

I never wanted it to end.

But at some stage, even the credits in a movie have to roll.

By the end of that last, lazy, idyllic year I still had no clue about what I wanted to do with my life, despite the urgings of my parents. Rugby was great fun and I was good at it – I was a decent provincial schoolboy and youth player who was already in the national system, due to my recognition at South Island U-18 level.

Still, regardless of what others said, I didn't regard myself as a future All Black prospect and, in that amateur era, I certainly didn't consider the game as something which offered long-term security. It was just a pastime, a hobby.

For me, as for many school-leavers, it was a case of just, "go to university and see what happens". I'd looked at various careers and thought seriously about sports physiotherapy and I'd even looked at applying for a degree in criminology at Wellington University.

But nothing seemed to fit. It was the same for my friends Jeff and Gerard, so, in one final tilt at a great adventure, we decided to take a year – maybe a few years – out from education and hit the yellow brick road that led all the way to Australia, and beyond.

Unable to play rugby for University A due to a massive boil on his neck, he decided to ask a flatmate to squeeze it. It was going to be very painful so he put some leather between his teeth. The violence of the do-it-yourself surgery squirted puss over the walls but allowed him to play. Brent owed $10 for the weekly rent: a $10 note was put on the pinboard with a note that said, "Popey does this remind you of anything?" He took the $10, went to the Cook Tavern and drank nine jugs at $1.10 a jug. Came home pissed having also missed his cooking night!

Richard Taylor.
Friend.

4

Home, Convicts and Personal Heroes

Admittedly, the three of us didn't exactly slum it on our arrival in Australia.

My university bursary, already assured, kick-started things for me and, courtesy of Jeff's wealthy older brother, our first home was a luxury yacht moored in a flash part of Sydney called Hunter's Hill. The area has been home to a number of celebs, including Cate Blanchett, Delta Goodrem and, at one time, Ireland's own Brian McFadden.

The daily trip on the ferry across Sydney Harbour was stunning, but us three Kiwi lads were innocents abroad and it became evident, early on, that trying to sell encyclopedias door-to-door or washing cars was not going to fulfill my dreams of a prosperous future.

We may have started out big but, pretty quickly, market reality set in and we had to trade down from our 'rich and famous' lifestyle in Hunter's Hill to a dingy caravan park in a dodgy area of South Ryde. We wasted all of our earnings and the best part of our savings on cans of fly spray to combat the local insect infestation. Each morning we'd greet the huge spiders and creepy crawlies on our curtains with a newspaper bashing, and each evening we'd spend a considerable amount of time searching under the toilet seat for the infamous red back spider that lurks in such filthy confines.

It didn't take long before we reached crunch time. Living on a yacht in a plush suburb had been fun, squeezing into a banged up caravan with a plague of flies and deadly spiders was no fun at all. Jeff wanted to stay and, I suppose, if I'd wanted I could have made more of an effort to make a go of it. I should have tried to join a local Sydney rugby club and develop a few work contacts from there, but I didn't. At the time, Rugby Union was a bit of a minority sport in Sydney – the city was all about Rugby League. I loved league, it was a great game and, to be honest, it would have suited my strengths as a player: I was fast, aggressive, tackled hard and loved to take the ball into contact. A forward's job in league football was to cart the ball up time and again, take the hits and just keep going. The best thing was no lineouts, so I would have enjoyed that. Later in my career, after playing on a tour of Australia, I had a couple of serious enquiries to play for top Australian League teams like the Canberra Raiders. While I didn't consider the potentially big money on offer, I still thought I would have made a good league player if I'd chosen to take that route.

But, back then, in our post-school year, Gerard and I decided we had no future in Sydney. Soon after we ran out of cash, we decided to forsake our Aussie adventure and head home.

Of course, on our departure from New Zealand, we'd told everyone that we may never come back, so our return to Ashburton was with tails tucked firmly between legs. I'd blown a lot of my university money in Australia, so, once the ribbing had died down, I took the decision to work for a year and raise some more funds before starting varsity the following year.

Over the next few months I had a couple of what can only be described as menial jobs. For a while, I worked as a scrub cutter for the Forestry Board which entailed cutting access trails in dense, prickly gorse, so that forestry workers could walk behind, planting new trees for future regeneration. It was tough, hard, manual work which left your hands and body in bits at the end of the working day. Days were spent swinging timber machetes, often blazing trails uphill, while nights were spent in the bath, picking inch-long splinters and prickles out of blistered hands.

But, as in most jobs I ever had, I met some real characters there. There was one old guy who would always go to the toilet in the very same place at the very same time every day. He was so regular you could set your watch by him. He'd crouch down and hold onto a couple of tussocks to do his business.

In fact, he was so reliable and relaxed about it all that the rest of us couldn't possibly allow him to go on, unmolested. So, one day, one of the lads took a long handled shovel and, before the old fella stood back up, secretly removed what he had done and chucked it a good distance away. The bloke duly got up, fastened his pants and turned to admire his handiwork. But, to his amazement, there was no sign of it. He knew he had done something, but it had mysteriously disappeared. We watched in tears of laughter as first he lifted both of his feet, and then hunted high and low in the brush, searching for his lost deposit. He eventually found it, about fifteen feet away, but he was damned if he could figure out how he'd shot this projectile so far in one sitting. To this day, he's probably still out there, wondering out loud over a beer, how he ever exerted the necessary force.

Not all my temporary jobs that year were quite so glamorous, but the disappointment of my failed Australian odyssey was offset by the experience gained in being involved with two areas of Ashburton life, intrinsically connected to my dad.

The first was the Celtic Rugby Football Club. Celtic was the local Marist club Dad had played for when he first came to Ashburton, an obvious choice given Dad was a Catholic and had attended St Bede's in Christchurch. Celtic was also where I had first started playing the game as a little kid. Over the years, I'd drifted away from Celtic, instead playing for my school but, when I got back from Australia, I rejoined the club mainly because my good friend Gerard Prendergast was already there.

The club was a lot different from my high school teams: it was full of tough, hardworking guys with not a runny-nosed schoolboy in sight. Around town, many of the Celtic players had tough reputations, none more so in that era than the O'Grady brothers. The O'Gradys, as the name suggests, were a tough, Irish boxing family whose father, Des, had coached me as a Celtic youngster and was a good boxing coach as well. The O'Gradys doubled up as fine rugby players and even better scrappers. There were five brothers in all, but I really only knew three of them well, Shane (Sog), Chris and Mark (Fly). The remaining two bothers were twins, one of whom was nicknamed The General. Both Sog and Fly would end up having long and distinguished rugby careers with Celtic, and both were good enough to play Representative rugby for Mid Canterbury.

As a prospective university nerd, even knowing one of the O'Grady's was a huge advantage when you were out late on the town on a Friday or Saturday night. Chris O'Grady, despite his smaller stature, was one of the toughest buggers I've ever met. Aggressive, quick with his fists, and with a fierce reputation, you messed with Chris at your peril. But I liked Chris, Sog and Fly immensely, and was lucky enough that, at times, they all overlooked my university 'flaws' long enough to develop a mutual respect for me, too. Most of the Celtic boys would occupy the back seats of the Catholic Church on Sunday, watching the girls coming back from communion and discussing the weekend's activities.

It might seem a million miles from rugby in Ireland, and no doubt things have changed dramatically in Ashburton over the intervening years but, back then, there wasn't much to do on a Friday or Saturday night except for young men to cruise the streets in old British cars, like Mark 4 Zephyrs and Cortinas, looking for parties, drink and a quite often a fight. And not necessarily in that order.

Every Saturday night, somewhere in town, you could bet that some of the Celtic boys would eventually clash with some other group, usually a crowd from just over the bridge called Tinwald, who had their own tough team. As a student, I often found myself and my mates at the wrong sort of parties, but I was always lucky enough to have one of my Celtic teammates vouch for me and get me out of trouble, if need be.

And if, for some reason, the Celtics couldn't bail me out, I could count on help from an even rougher, tougher part of my extended family – the lads who worked with me at the Freezing Works.

Soon after I returned from Sydney, my dad found work for myself and Gerard at the Works, the same local meat-killing plant he'd worked at for most of his life. He'd been promoted from a 'butcher on the chain' to union delegate and with his advancement came respect and a certain amount of 'pull'. It was a bit like being the son of an Irish cop in New York but, after failing so spectacularly in Australia, I was relieved that I could turn to him for work. I was lucky, it could have been hard going into a job more or less as the "son of" or teacher's pet, but Dad had so much respect from almost everyone at the Works that it was easy.

My jobs at the abattoir were, in a word, 'varied' but always uninspiring, boring and often mind-numbing. Dressed in big white overalls, a paper hat and heavy white gumboots, I would stand in one place for hours on end as the dead sheep made their way slowly along the overhead chain. When the sheep reached me, hanging upside down, still warm and dripping with blood, my job was to trim the eyebrows off the beasts' heads. This was accomplished by perfecting the little-known, and even less-appreciated, fine art of putting your fingers into the eyes of the sheep as you tried to snip the wool off their eye brows. After that, I was expected to pull the dead sheep's tongue from its skull and then wash it.

Some days I would work on the chain trimming eyebrows but at other times I went downstairs and worked in the laundry store with John Scammel, a role that entailed dispensing the butchers their knives and gear.

I saw some nasty injuries in my time at the Works, especially involving razor sharp knives. I even had a couple myself.

But they were nothing compared to what befell one unfortunate butcher. At one point, this particular bloke, who was working on the legging table, lifted up one leg of the sheep to strip the meat but managed to run the knife all the way up the inside of his own calf, slicing it away from the bone and hitting a main artery. Within seconds, his gumboots filled up with blood as the blood squirted everywhere. An ambulance was called and he was transported to hospital.

Most days someone cut themselves, some even deliberately so they could get off work and attend rugby matches, race meetings or weekend-long concerts. That kind of skill was beyond a novice like me, but some of the lads became experts at the art of knicking themselves badly enough to get a couple of days off, though not severely enough to maim themselves.

Against that kind of backdrop – difficult work and ever-present danger – workers frequently turned to practical jokes to lighten the load. Being a complete messer, I was among the worst or best, depending on your point of view, of the practical jokers. I won enough of a reputation for it that, instead of having a work number printed on my white overalls like everyone else, I had the word 'Loon' – short for lunatic – printed on mine.

At one stage, myself and 'Doc' – medical student and friend, Malcolm Ward – decided to wind up one particular new employee. Doc, now one of Christchurch's most respected surgeons, and I confided in the guy that we'd been entrusted with the vital job of preparing for the visit of the 'Lift Inspector' from Christchurch who would randomly call in to inspect the efficiency and safety of the lifts. While outwardly playing down the importance of the visit, we gave the guy the impression that it was a big deal and, the more we tried to play it down, the more he demanded to be involved in such an important task. The trap was set.

On the given day, I met up with the two others and reported that rumour had it the inspector was on his way. We had to get ready immediately and make sure the inspector was impressed with the state of the company's lifts and its plans for the safe evacuation of the workers, should disaster strike. The new guy pushed his way in, demanding a role and brushing aside our objections that persuading the lift inspector of the preparedness of the Freezing Works for any crisis, was simply too important a job for a novice.

He was having none of it.

In the end, we dressed him up like Darth Vader, and gave him an explanation for every piece of equipment we dressed him in: He had a welder's mask, a metal apron, big heavy gloves, knee-high fishing boots and carried what looked like pair of normal garden hedge clippers (which they were) which we convinced him were to be used to prise open the lift doors in the event of an emergency. The entire look was finished off with a set of fluffy orange ear-muffs.

So armed, we sent him up to walk along 'the chain' in front of his tough workmates. Amazingly, he did. Work had to stop as everybody howled with laughter at our Darth Vader lookalike shuffling across the Works floor. I understand the Loon and the Doc are still remembered with fondness at the Works, any time someone recalls the Day the Lift Inspector Came to Visit.

It's hard to believe now, but I did that foot-killing, back-breaking work eight hours a day. Even harder to believe, it was great fun and I loved working there. Not so much because I had to pull tongues out of sheep's heads, but because it introduced me to a whole new group of friends.

Like it had done in my dad's day, the Freezing Works often attracted what many saw as the elements of society who didn't have many career options. Obviously, there were good jobs at the Works – such as meat inspectors – that involved higher levels of education and many of the men working there were like Dad – decent, hardworking family men. But, in common with the wharfs, shearing and similar sources of employment in New Zealand at that time, the Freezing Works' good money, seasonal work and lack of required qualifications attracted not only the usual, hard workers looking for a decent start but also some of the town's wild young element looking for a fast buck. A lot of Ashburton's young troublemakers found some sort of work there at some stage in their lives, and quite often it was my dad who had played a part in getting them a start. Most Mondays a lot of the stories in the smoko room – or morning tea room – would centre on who was arrested the previous weekend or who got in a fight with whom.

During my time in the Freezing Works I met some hard men, men that would possibly go on to join gangs or end up in prison. A few wound up dead and many lived tough lives to extreme excesses. In hindsight, some of my university-bound friends and I could have wound up in serious trouble if we'd found ourselves included in some of their illegal after-hours activities. They were motivated by different things: boredom, hard lives, cruel treatment or lack of opportunity. It's hard to say, and I don't view it as my right to judge.

Crazy though it may sound, a couple of the better, but rougher, rugby players I met at the Works actually committed petty crimes in the off-season so that they could spend some time in jail. There they could give up the drink, or whatever, and get fit for the coming season. It was a hell of a boot camp and a million miles from the middle and upper class image of rugby in these islands, but that's how it was.

I'll say one thing about the majority of the hard, uncompromising characters that I encountered and befriended there – they had a code of ethics all of their own and were, at least according to that code, honest and true with each other. They respected that I wanted to go to university eventually and, in their own way, they kept me on the straight and narrow.

Most importantly, they looked after their own, and I was lucky enough to be able to count on the extended Freezing Works family.

I rocked up one night to the local club with a bandage on my hand – I'd cut myself fairly seriously with a knife at work and, as a result, was stitched up and bandaged by the doctors. For reasons unknown to me, some massive Maori guy from out of town took a dislike to me in a dancehall. He kept looking over at me, clearly unhappy with my being in the same place as him. I was getting nervous – it was clear something was going to happen but impossible to figure when or what. Sometimes, the best option with someone who's trying to intimidate you is to confront them, but this guy was huge, covered in tattoos and looked like a gang member.

In the end he came over, grabbed my hand and started squeezing it, breaking open the stitches, and taunting me for a fight. He kept asking me did I, "think I was a boxer?" and demanded that I come outside where he described, in no uncertain terms, how he would, "mess me up".

Already bleeding profusely from the re-opened wound, I didn't fancy visiting the hospital a second time in twenty-four hours. But, out of the corner of my eye, I spotted one of my co-workers from the Freezing Works gesturing to me that I should take him outside for a fight.

By the time we spilled onto the street, there was a welcoming committee of a couple of my Freezing Works mates already waiting for the guy. A flurry of punches and head butts settled the issue fairly quickly and the lads delivered a Mafia-style message, that if anyone messed with young Pope, they messed with them. Like most bullies, the guy broke down when confronted and pleaded with them not to hurt him.

• • • • •

One of the guys I became especially tight with at the Works was a young guy called Phillip (Pip) Kavanagh. Pip was a wild guy. His arms were covered in tattoos and he and his brothers were a tough crew. Pip needed a chance to get back on the straight and narrow, and my father helped to give him that chance by influencing the powers that be to give him a job at the Freezing Works. After working side-by-side each day, Pip and I became really good friends. Like most of the others I appreciated the fact that he was always very respectful of me and seemed to enjoy my company, too.

So, when he invited me to his wedding I said yes without thinking too much about it. When the big day rolled around, I was one of the only guys on Pip's side of the aisle who didn't much look like an enforcer. I felt out of place but Pip's brothers, tough men that they were, recognised my discomfort. The Kavanagh family showered me and my date, Catherine, with courtesy and kindness: "Could they get us this, could they get us that?"

They were so polite, they even asked my permission to dance with my girlfriend. The Kavanagh boys displayed a depth of feeling and kindness that went much deeper than in many of the shallow types I've met who live in big houses and wear flashy suits. Pip and his people didn't judge anyone, least of all me.

But that's how it went at the Freezing Works.

Many of the guys there kicked around in large groups, not gangs as New Zealanders would know them. But, they were bound by strong ties. It was a different form of respect or friendship than most of us are used too, but was very powerful.

Some of the people I liked most at the Works didn't have much of a start in life for several reasons but, in my experience at least, many of those guys – like their more privileged counterparts – just wanted a chance in life. They wanted people to look past their tattoos or police record and see that they could be productive members of society. My father gave many of them that chance in life: he never judged them and often looked far past what they had done, or where they had come from.

He'd never admit doing it – his own humility and his self-effacing character meant he'd sooner claim that helping to hire or putting in a good word for these men who may elsewhere have been deemed society's rejects, was just part of his job.

But it wasn't.

Giving people a second chance ran much deeper for him than any job. He was firm but fair, my dad. He figured that if these young men – maybe just out of jail or in trouble with drugs and life – could keep their noses clean at the Freezing Works, then they could make some good money and maybe give themselves a chance for a better future.I know that he made a huge difference to some of their lives. Not all of them, though. Some of the lads he may have vouched or gone on the line for may have failed and made mistakes, ending up back in trouble or, in some circumstances, even dead. But in the midst of it all, my dad never, ever, judged them. Never once did he treat them with disrespect or talk down to them and, as a result, many of them treated him, and his son, with the same respect.

As a student, I once dropped my wallet in Christchurch's Square which was a favourite hang-out for some of the patch-wearing street gangs. As I bent over to pick it up, I came eyeball-to-toe with a pair of the hobnailed boots much favoured by the gangs. I didn't know what to do. One of the boots planted itself on top of my hand while a blue, heavily tattooed hand retrieved my wallet. Another, unseen, hand pulled me roughly to my feet and I found myself standing face-to-face with a gang member.

He examined my wallet and fixed with me with a stare.

"You're Mick's boy, huh?"

"Yes," I stammered, not knowing if that was a good thing or not.

Luckily for me, it was. Years before, my dad had helped the guy find work.

"He's sound, mate, always tried to help me," concluded the guy, handing back my wallet and bestowing upon me a big, toothless grin.

In that one, single moment my dad was summed up.

Respect is a lesson I learned firsthand from him. I never speak down to anyone, regardless of their background or appearance, and I try to give everyone the respect they are due as human beings. Only God has the ability to judge us and, while I know that people can be evil and do bad or stupid things at different times, I learned – from my father and from life – that most people are neither all good, nor all bad. Usually, they're a bit of both.

• • • • •

So, whatever became of the O'Gradys? Shane and Mark are great family guys and have done well and I often have a beer with Shane when I'm back home in Ashburton. He's a good mate. Though I have not seen him in years, I understand Chris runs a successful scaffolding business and is also a good family man. I'm proud to know them all.

As for Pip Kavanagh?

Unfortunately, I don't know.

I've no idea where Pip is today and I worry that, somewhere along the line, he maybe slipped through life's cracks again.

But I think about him often.

About how kind he was to me.

• • • • •

On the first day of new university life, one particular hard bugger I'd worked with at the Works – who shall remain nameless – arrived at the door of my Christchurch flat. Accompanied by a few of his dubious friends, their arms were full of gifts and their mouths full of offers of free TVs, a car and other things to give me a start at university.

I looked at the presents and asked the obvious question.

"Guys, are these stolen?"

The bloke just rolled his eyes, smiled and replied, "Argh, Popey, you don't want to know."

Receiving stolen goods would not have read too well on my university application so I politely declined. But I recognised that the offer was just his token of friendship.

The final act of my transition from Freezing Works employee to university student was played out, fittingly, at the college's rugby pitch.

I'd been unable to catch a lift to my first university rugby trial, I knew nobody at university and could get to the grounds about 10 miles out of town. As I stood waiting by the side of the road, one of my old work buddies and a gang of his Harley and Triumph motorbiking mates thundered past. They saw me, swung around and offered me a lift. To this day, I've no idea what the coach and the team made of this wannabe university flanker climbing off the back of a Harley Davidson, kitbag over his shoulder, saying cheerio to a group of leathered patch-wearing bikers, but it still makes me smile.

• • • • •

Looking back on it all, I recognise that, for that year between school and university, my own future hung in the balance.

It would have been easy for me to go off the rails a bit, stay on at the Works and end up with a much different future.

But, at the end of my year there, I realised I wanted something more than that. Sure, I liked running with a rougher crowd and I enjoyed the excitement of cruising around town, the parties and the fights. At times it was an adrenaline rush. But, after that year at the Freezing Works, I was ready to move on.

The year had taught me real-life lessons about what's important. The way some of the Celtic boys and my Freezing Works mates had looked after me made me more determined than ever to stick up for the underdog and to make a stand for things I believed in, no matter how much my convictions ran counter to the mainstream.

Within a few months I got an opportunity to test my mettle. Soon after I started at Lincoln College in Christchurch, then part of Canterbury University, I was forced to take a stand against my teammates. It was 1981 and New Zealand was hosting the controversial Springbok tour. People argued bitterly for and against it, but I was completely anti-Tour and so was my father. South Africa promoted Apartheid and, as far as the Popes were concerned, that was that.

It wasn't a popular stance by any means. I was just a first year student without many friends at that stage, and a member of a rugby fraternity that was almost 100 per cent pro-Tour. Rugby people, nonsensically, tried to argue that sport and politics don't mix – ignoring the fact that hosting a team from an Apartheid state was, on its own, making a political statement of support for South African government policy. The anti-Tour camp was ridiculed and harassed and, on one protest march in Christchurch, we had eggs thrown at us, I was spat on and abused and my teammates did not think too much of my stance.

But I believed what I believed. My father had given me an example of what it meant to stand up for people, and the 'School of Hard Knocks' run by my pals at Celtic and the Freezing Works had given me the steel and strength of character to see it through.

That period was a remarkable time in my life.

At the end of it all, I was lucky enough to get a chance at changing things for the better. University would send me in a new direction in life and in rugby.

When I went down as a youngster to play for Otago, Popey was a senior member of the Otago team, he played No. 8 and I was half-back. To me, he was one of the most under-rated players ever and should have been an All Black – he was so explosive off the back of the scrum, was very mobile and as tough as they come. He scored many tries using his strength and speed, and was a great defender and a terrific link player. But Popey's greatest strength was as a team man, he was one of the funniest guys around. He was the centre of attention after a win and always lifted the boys' spirits after a loss, which is very hard to do. Every team needs a guy like this. One of my lasting memories is of Popey having to put two pairs of rugby socks along with shin guards on his 'chicken legs' to make them look bigger. He didn't need to as he had the heart of a lion.

Stu Forster.
Hawke's Bay. Otago. All Black.

5

Of Men
and Baby
Giraffes

Time and tide wait for no man, or woman, and, if my own life had moved on during that year out at the Freezing Works, then the same was true for many of my old school friends. They had gone directly to university after school and, as a result, had made new friends and moved on in their lives. By hitting university twelve months later, I was faced with the prospect of a lonely start to academic life.

And, despite the lessons I'd learned at the Freezing Works' 'University of Life', I was still struggling with my actual degree choice. I'd always enjoyed psychology, so I thought about applying to Wellington University to study criminology, though why I didn't just apply for a straight psychology degree is still beyond me.

But, after talking to my brother Mark's best friend, Brent Spicer, who was, by association, also a friend of mine, I decided to follow in his footsteps. Brent was a great guy who, tragically, took his own life a few years back. He'd studied Valuation and Property Management at Lincoln College, located in a beautiful semi-rural setting about twenty minutes outside Christchurch City and that seemed a good plan to me.

The fact that my old schoolmate and fellow 'Aussie Adventure' survivor, Gerard Prendergast, had enrolled there further sweetened the deal. I desperately wanted to get into the halls of residence in an effort to make new friends, but I missed out. Gerard had got in and, because of the university's somewhat remote location, he was suddenly immersed in campus life, while I was forced to go flatting in the city, albeit with two friends from school, Bernadette O'Connell and Al Bain.

I was lucky to hook up with Bernie and Al and we had great craic in the flat. But they had an established set of friends in Canterbury University that they could enjoy cups of coffee with in the Student Union buildings or meet through the many clubs that the university had to offer. By contrast, I was extremely shy and I was making no friends of my own.

That first week, Fresher's Week, I felt very isolated. I lived off-campus, hadn't started any classes or rugby as yet, and was a bystander to student life compared to Gerard who was already building a great network of mates in the halls. My confident, gregarious personality belied a kid who, deep down, was shy and painfully self-conscious.

Lincoln College was populated by a particular type of student. Many of its students, especially those deemed to be the so-called 'in crowd', were rich kids from prestigious schools who liked to mask their wealthy farming backgrounds by 'dressing down'. Their 'scruffy Merivale (a suburb of Christchurch, something akin to D4) look' was typically made up of brown riding boots, cream moleskin trousers and a blue and white striped shirt. The 'just right' level of scruffiness was achieved by leaving the shirt hanging out. For their part, the girls and girlfriends of this set dressed almost the same, save for a set of cultured pearls or a knotted jumper slung, casually, around the neck.

It was an expensive image to achieve. But, no matter what they were dressed in, they exuded an air of confidence, attending all of the best parties or sitting about in large groups laughing and having fun.

It was a big social leap for a small-town boy from Ashburton who'd just spent his year out in the local abattoir socialising with ex-cons, and tough but genuine, working class men. While my best mates from school had moved on – two Richards, Taylor and Smith, were at Otago University, Parry, Craig and Jeff had gone travelling – and Gerard was having a ball up in the Halls of Residence, I was out on a limb. I missed being part of the old gang where I was accepted and in which I felt comfortable being myself. In that first year in Lincoln, I was in no one's gang. Too shy to force myself on any group or individual, it took time for me to meet new people and try to fit in.

I loved clothes – still do – but I was too trendy to fit the university look at all. My personal image involved wearing a pair of rolled up trousers, white sandshoes or blue slip-on boat shoes and an array of fashionable tops. And in a college, where cool cars were the rule, driving to campus in an old, pimped-up VW Beetle with chrome pipes, fat tyres and murals didn't do me any favours.

It was hard to avoid the obvious conclusion that I was different, too different for some. Even when I made the university rugby team, I was still slagged off for being too trendy. For about a year, my dress sense cost me a lot of money – I'd be fined at every kangaroo court session for my fashion crimes, until the team finally accepted I wasn't going to conform and start wearing stripy shirts. My look was more band member from Dexy's Midnight Runners than D4, private school, rugby type.

The conformists did force me to join their ranks at one point. I'd been invited to a posh party at a farmhouse out of town and had accepted a lift in the backseat of a friend's car. While self-praise is no praise, I reckoned I looked pretty good in my trendy new outfit and was looking forward to trying to impress the many classy ladies who were reputed to be frequenting the party from a posh girls' school, called Rangi Ruru. The weather was miserable as it had been raining on and off for days and, as we approached a ford, even in the dark it looked a little deep to me. But, we were on a tight schedule and the driver, who had driven that way for years, told us to relax – the water was no more than a foot deep.

He was right about the first foot, but wrong about the nine feet above it. As the car began to fill with muddy water and then sink, everybody scrambled to the bank. Most of the gang somehow stayed reasonably dry but, typical back row that I am, I was mucked to the eyeballs in mud and silt. Worse, we were stranded and, to cap it all, the rain began again. In the distance we could see the lights of the farmhouse and hear the strains of the party's music but, in between, were acres of unidentified farmland, bathed in pitch darkness.

As the others cowered beneath the trees I had a Scott of the Antarctic moment and volunteered to go in search of a phone and a lift. By the end of the first field, my shoes, trousers and shirt were soaked and heavy with water. My heroic trek was beginning to look like a suicidal Captain 'Titus' Oates mission. Despite the rain, it was a warm night, so I stripped to my boxers and shoes and ploughed on, eventually reaching the nearest farmhouse where, through the windows, I could see the lady of the house watching TV.

I repeatedly banged on the door but she was obviously engrossed with whatever she was watching and completely oblivious to my knocking. So, I tried a different approach, tapping at the window of the front room.

I've done smarter things…

The lady heard my tap, tap, tap all right, but when she looked up all she could see at her rain-hammered window was a face belonging to a bedraggled, near-naked stranger staring back at her in the pitch dark.

Not unreasonably, she screamed.

Very loudly.

Within seconds, my hands were in the air as I stared down the twin barrels of a shotgun, held by a burly agricultural type who seemed more than capable of handing out a buckshot lesson in life to the peeping Tom who'd scared his young wife.

Over the sound of my knocking knees, I rapidly explained my predicament and waited for the sound of a gun being cocked…

But my luck was in. As an ex-Lincoln College man himself, not only did he take my word for it, but he fired up the tractor and dragged our car out of the raging ford, before giving us a lift to his neighbour's daugther's party. If that wasn't enough, he presented me with a dry set of clothes to wear to the night's social event. It was an offer I couldn't refuse, so I cast my designer jeans and trendy shirt into his wife's washing machine and donned the worst-fitting set of clothes imaginable. At five foot five, and weighing in at around 20 stone, the farmer had a different physique to myself – what a sight I looked.

Suffice to say, the beautiful out-of-reach ladies of Rangi Ruru remained just that, beautiful and out of reach. Out of my reach, at least. I couldn't get anyone to talk to me, let alone dance with me. The socialites took one look at the three inches of shin that separated the bottom of my brown corduroys from my black shoes and gave me a very wide berth. Maybe, if it had been a Hallowe'en bash I'd have stood a chance but, as it was, I went from fashionista to fashion disaster in less than two hours.

So, aided by disasters like that, for the first three months in Lincoln I knocked around with the sole friend from class who liked rugby and a beer. Ian McGowan and I got on instantly: he rode a big motorcycle and was an all-round fun guy. All through my stay at Lincoln he was my best mate and, years later, I was proud to be the best man at his wedding.

Things got better. After few months I met another guy who became a lifelong friend, Gerald (Ged) Hay. Birds of a feather flock together – especially when they're an endangered species – and Ged was like me, a bit different. But, unlike me, who was blasé about other people's opinions on the outside but desperately self-conscious on the inside, Ged really didn't give a toss about what people thought. This surfer dude was extremely confident with the ladies and knew how to best employ his muscular, tanned physique and long, blond ponytail. As well as his good looks, Ged was a tough, talented rugby player whose late father, Colin, had been a player, coach and administrator with Hawke's Bay. Truly fearless, Ged later moved to Queenstown where he ran a number of high-octane, adrenaline-fuelled leisure companies. One of his firms offered thrill-seeking, river boarders the opportunity to navigate the Grade 4 whitewater rapids of the Kawarau river, using only a bodyboard and fins, a practice described in one US paper as, "one of the most dangerous things you could do on water".

Ged also had the distinction of being Robert De Niro's stunt-double in a movie called 'Midnight Run', in which Ged starred in many of the dangerous river rapids scenes.

At one point at Lincoln College, I shared a flat with Ged, Janet Aitken and another great friend, Liz Jarmey. Each year, we held an annual dinner at which we were expected to invite someone you'd never met before.

This caused Ged no problems as he was already fairly confident talking to the opposite sex. There were even occasions when, as we drove to university in my beat up VW, he'd spot some attractive lady going to work down the Riccarton high street and immediately ask me to stop the car before jumping out and disappearing. Nine times out of ten, he'd be a no-show for that day's lectures and, when I got home, he'd have secured a number and a date.

There was a strict set of rules around the whole dinner event. There was a time limit of two minutes set for convincing the stranger to come for dinner and, on the evening itself, each of the hosts had to cook an entire course for the meal – the course randomly dictated with help of a hat. If you couldn't find a date then you'd have to cook all the courses yourself. Although Ged would always end up chatting up my date as well as his own, often leaving me high and dry, the dinners were great fun and a brilliant way to meet new people.

Another student event, which most students attended, combined two of my favourite pastimes, food and rugby. The annual 'Chunder Mile' was a dash around Rugby Park with the athletes expected to down a jug, which was equivalent to three pints, of warm beer and eat a pie en route. The last man standing was adjudged the winner. But the Chunder Mile was only one of a series in the annual 'Drinking Games', which were a popular way for hundreds of students to spend a day. Alongside that middle-distance event, there were the sprints – quick skulls – and the helicopter heave, in which the competitor was judged on his, or her, ability to vomit in a perfect 360 degrees. Nice!

Tragically, the Drinking Games came to grief after the intervention of a red-top tabloid. Exhibiting a hypocritical disregard for their own profession's notorious abuse of alcohol, the red-top published photos of the student event bearing the caption: "Is this your son?"

Inexplicably, the Games lost their attraction after that but, for a while, it was very much part of the annual sporting calendar and, no doubt, is still mourned by a special breed of student athlete.

Now happily married to Nadia, with two fun-loving kids, along with his other two kids from a previous marriage, Ged remains a great and valued friend. Visiting him in Queenstown remains one of life's great adventures: I spent Christmas 2011 bouncing off numerous rocks on the Kawarau River as Ged powered us up the rapids on a dangerously souped-up aluminium jet-ski of his own design. I survived, obviously, but was bloodied and battered from head to toe by the time I arrived upriver.

But that's Ged. The original kind of bloke who, when he brings you skiing, takes you to the top of the steepest, iciest, blackest run he can find, points you straight down the slope and simply let's go! There's a metaphor for life somewhere in Ged's fun but I'm usually far too terrified to figure out what the hell it is.

I supplemented my university income by doing a bit of roadie work for bands that came to Christchurch as part of their world tour. It was simple enough work: loading and unloading the bands' gear and, on the night of the gig, throwing any over-eager fans off the stage.

I worked for George Thorogood and the Destroyers (think 'Bad to the Bone'), The Cure ('Friday I'm in Love') and even worked at a small gig for Herman's Hermits ('I'm Henry the Eighth, I am, I am'). Herman – Peter Noone – brought his hermits to do a small event at a regular student haunt called The Bush Inn. After playing their set, the Hermits triggered a great session by asking me and my mates, "So, what's there to do in Christchurch on Sunday night?"

I still remember piling into a bar somewhere in Christchurch, hammering out a drunken version of, 'Mrs Brown, You've Got a Lovely Daughter', I recommend you Google it!

So, gradually, life at Lincoln got better and less lonely. I began to find my feet, and some friends. Rag weeks were great fun: filling up rooms with pieces of scrunched-up newspaper, or lowering a sheep with a bucket of water and bales of hay into the room of a student who was away – the sheep was quite happy, after he ran out of hay he chewed his way through the student's notes.

We disassembled a lecturer's Mini and, after transporting all the bits in the lift, reassembled it on top of the Student Union building.

We even managed to marry one student off to an Indian mail-order bride which was funny until we received a telegram from the new wife requesting to be picked up at the airport. Though we tried to let her down gently, she took the marriage break-up badly. Wedding pranks became a bit of a theme. At one point, we had a friend who decided to leave uni after just a few weeks and move to Australia. On the appointed day, a group of us rushed to the airport dressed as though we'd come straight from a wedding, with a pregnant-looking, and very distraught, bride in full regalia and a bloke (one of our dads) dressed as a disgruntled priest, in tow.

As the student waited in line for his boarding pass, the entire wedding entourage descended en masse to complain about his doing a runner. The jilted, pregnant bride-to-be broke down in floods of tears, the priest begged the student to reconsider his callousness in leaving his expectant betrothed at the altar and the rest of us moaned and wrung our hands on the sidelines.

As luck would have it, there were two big Maori guys in the queue right in front of the dumbstruck student. The harder our friend protested his innocence and tried to explain it was all a hoax, the more the two Maori blokes told him he was a gutless coward. Warning him to accept his responsibilities like a man, they collared him and frog-marched him out of the queue and stood him in front of the baying crowd – which now included most of the plane's passengers and its ground staff – and made him 'take his oil'.

The abuse got so bad that we ended up feeling sorry the guy and spending a considerable amount of time trying to explain to the otherwise-convinced crowd that the whole thing was merely a wind-up. Fortunately, they saw the funny side of it, though the two Maori guys looked disappointed when they had to let our friend go.

In another prank, we took a drunk student out to Sunnyside Hospital, dressed him in hospital pyjamas and left him propped up near the fence, it took him nearly half a day to explain he was not a patient but rather the victim of another student prank.

If we'd put as much creativity into our studies as we did our pranks, we'd all have whizzed through the university system.

As I settled more into Lincoln life, my sporting life improved.

Just like at Ashburton College where my years there coincided with the development of the school's greatest ever team, I was lucky enough to be at Lincoln during its best-ever rugby era. The University won the senior competition during my first year, though I only played a small substitutes role in a team that included future All Black World Cup winners, Bruce Deans, Craig Green and Albie Anderson.

Lincoln presented me with a whole new set of rugby challenges.

While I had been a good schoolboy player attracting national attention, the Lincoln College side played in the senior Canterbury competition, one of the strongest in the country.

Like anywhere else – UCD, Queen's, UCC or Trinity – playing with a university team against 'normal' sides is a different kind of experience. To non-academic competitors, university teams often play with what appears to be 'wild abandon'. In working class areas, where there may already be a chip on one or two (or all fifteen) shoulders, this type of play can come across as arrogant so, in a game where our oldest player was likely to be the age of our rivals' youngest, the Canterbury League was a place where you grew up and toughened up fairly quickly.

My debut game for Lincoln College First XV was a double celebration for me. It was the first time I'd made the A-side and was my first-ever senior club game. I was young, confident and fancied myself as a bit of an enforcer for the college team.

I reckoned I could handle most situations. In many of the fights I'd encountered alongside the Celtics and the Freezing Works gang, I'd been targeted by older, bigger blokes but I was strong and aggressive and had acquitted myself well. Moreover, the hard manual labour I'd survived while working for the Forestry Board had toughed me up. So, by the time my first Lincoln game against a local Marist team rolled around, I was ready and confident about the challenge ahead. The Marist Bothers' club, was full of so-called Paddies and Dooleys – Kiwi shorthand for Irish Catholics. So, it was no great surprise when my opposite number, who was in his 30s, turned out to be a bloke of Irish extraction by the name of, I think, O'Byrne. I knew the guy had played a couple of Representative games for Canterbury but to me, a young whippersnapper, he seemed ancient and ready to be shown a thing or two.

In the first lineout, I jumped on his shoulder, basically holding him down so that he couldn't compete for the ball. I was brutally effective, winning the ball so easily that I even brought a smile to the face my coach, who had selected me ahead of several other players with bigger reputations.

Buoyed by my success, and thinking how easy senior rugby was, I strutted to the next lineout. O'Byrne, however, was less than impressed by my youthful cockiness. Getting right into my face, he cocked his fist and warned me: "Right, son, if you weren't just a young student playing your first senior game I would have broken your nose by now."

Who was this old guy trying to kid? Did he honestly think he could intimidate me with a few verbals after failing so miserably in the last lineout? Remaining staunch, I replied something to the effect of, "Well, there's no good just talking about it, old man."

You learn a lot at university and O'Byrne gave me a valuable lesson that day about knowing when to keep my mouth shut.

He didn't say anything after my outburst. He just waited for the lineout. Then he whacked me, right on the nose, breaking it.

I left the field of play, nose smashed and streaming blood.

'Old' O'Byrne had kept his word.

Years later, in one of my first games in Ireland, we played a team from Limerick in a friendly (which they never were). I felt I had to make my presence felt, I guess I believed I still owed Byrne and the Irish a thing or two.

By a quirk of fate, my opposite number on the Limerick team did exactly the same thing to me as I had done to O'Byrne all those years before, he held me down in the lineout. So, remembering what had been done to me in the same situation, I unleashed a punch and floored the big second row.

As I loomed large over the stricken player in my best gladiator stance, admiring my handiwork, the guy looked up at me and sheepishly demanded: "For God's sake, Pope, I'm a Kiwi as well. Why don't you whack an Irish bastard instead?"

"Sorry, mate." My hand was proferred, I pulled him up and on we went.

That was how things were. Players wanted to see what the opposition was made of. The omni-presence of TV cameras at games has, along with yellow and red cards and suspensions, all but spelled the end of punch-ups in the modern game. But in those days a thump was often the way troublesome players were sorted out on the field of play, especially if that player carried the tag of being 'dirty'. Such players lived and died by the sword and they almost always found there was someone harder, tougher or dirtier out there.

The golden rule was that you never, ever went down, unless you were knocked out stone cold. The law regarding punching or softening up players in New Zealand in those days was simple: If you took a punch – in many ways a rite of passage for young forwards – then you had to give one back at the next break of play, regardless of how groggy or how weak the blow was. It was all about respect and, as barbaric as it may seem now, it was how the game was played.

At Lincoln our biggest rivalry was with Varsity A. In my fresher year, Lincoln College was still a part of Canterbury University – the two formally separating in 1990 – but, because of its location, it had its own rugby team. Lincoln's student numbers were much smaller than Canterbury Uni, so the pool of available rugby talent was also much smaller and, as a consequence, the team was generally less successful than the more illustrious Varsity A squad.

Every year, the A team were there or thereabouts at the top of the Canterbury League. In my time, the Varsity A team featured players like All Blacks Warwick Taylor and Victor Simpson, and a big, thunder-thighed Maori All Black named Dale Atkins. The toughest opponent I ever faced on a rugby pitch, and that includes the likes of Buck Shelford and Zinzan Brooke, how Atkins never made All Black remains a mystery. His playing career was ended in 1988 as a result of a terrible cruciate ligament injury but, before that, he was a key part of Alex Wyllie's remarkable Canterbury Ranfurly Shield side.

Atkins' Varsity A side were so good that one year, in the final of the senior competition, they arrived on the pitch with their hair dyed pink then stood around like statues. When the opposition kicked off, these pink-haired players stood stock still as their rivals picked up the ball and strolled over the line for the opening try. What's more, they refused to move as the opposing out-half booted over the conversion and trotted back to the halfway line, along with his teammates, in utter bewilderment.

Then the As began to play.

At the end of the 80 minutes, Varsity A had won the final by about 30 points.

The press rioted, claiming these disrespectful, arrogant, pinko students had made a mockery of the competition… But the hacks were missing the point. The students were just being, well, students. Having fun. Taking the proverbial.

During my time in the Canterbury area I, along with my fellow Lincoln College players, got our big opportunity to show off our flexibility. At that time there was a medical symposium for physios, and the event attracted some of the best practitioners from all over New Zealand and Australia. Part of the programme was a live experiment to test which group of sportsmen – rugby players versus the martial arts lads – was the most flexible.

These days the result would be a forgone conclusion but, back then, we fancied our chances and agreed three rugby guys would allow themselves to be put through a series of onstage tests to gauge our suppleness. Myself and Jock Fulton signed up and, after struggling to attract a third team member, we eventually prevailed upon Jock's mate, Chris Stiven to volunteer. Stivey was the walking definition of an uncoordinated Southland farmer. A big 6 foot 6 inch second row, he was all arms and legs with a hairstyle that defied descriptive analysis.

On the day of the physio tests, we agreed to pick Stivey up en route. He'd finished his exams the day before and had been on all-nighter, so we had trouble rousing him from his bed. He came-to like a moth seeking the light, his top lip curled up and stuck to his nose, hair going in thirteen different directions, and peering at us through a pair of bloodshot eyes. We looked reasonably professional and athletic, but after Stivey had looked around his messy pile of unwashed and unironed garments for something to wear, he arrived out front resplendent in a pair of runners, old track pants still caked in mud from the previous week's rugby training, a manky old T-shirt covered in … whatever. Unshaven, unkempt and definitely unfragrant, we bundled Stivey out of his flat and into the car.

The tests were being conducted in a large room at the Russell Hotel, which was quite a swanky place. The room itself was packed with physios – the front row was all female – and the lecture was being directed by a professor who was controlling the overhead projector at the front of the stage.

The martial arts guys were ready and one of them, a 5th Dan black belt by the name of John Boniface, was limbering up with high kicks. On the other side of the stage we were going through our own, particular set of warm-ups. Jock and I stretched while a half-unconscious Stivey leaned against the wall and dragged on a cigarette. By the time we were introduced to our fans, Stivey had begun to sober up and voice his reluctance to show off his skills. It was too late, though, and he was unceremoniously pushed into the centre of the stage.

There was an audible gasp as the physios compared the cut of Stivey's dishevelled jib to the crisply starched, brilliant whites of the karate boys. So, with the six of us facing off, Jock got us going with a simple forward roll. It was basic stuff, but, as I prepared to do my roll, I felt a tug.

It was a terrified, sickly, Stivey.

"Popey, I can't do one."

"Of course you can, Stivey. Everybody can do a forward roll."

"Not me. I've never done one before in my life."

"Take it easy, Stivey. It's simple. Just watch me and do it. You'll be fine. Trust me."

And he did. Trust me, that is. Which was a bad move for Stivey. When his turn came, he did a fair-to-middling impression of a newborn, baby giraffe. When he tried to roll he went everywhere in a move which I'd never seen before, nor since. Pandemonium ensued with Southland farmer limbs seemingly everywhere, all at once. As his long legs splayed outwards, one of them caught the end of the professor's projector and sent it crashing to the floor. Worse, as he tumbled out of control around the stage, the badly hung over Stivey let rip with a Richter-scale fart. The sound of the blast rumbled off the sides of the room, ricocheted off the back wall and washed over the heads of the assembled physios before meeting us all again on the stage.

The result was chaos. Though I don't think any of the ladies in the front row actually fainted, some bolted for the door while the rest pulled faces, conveying either disapproval or pain – I couldn't be sure which.

Stivey was mortified but Jock, seizing the moment, turned to a disgusted John Boniface and threw down the ultimate gauntlet: "Fight that one off!"

It was a shame that the tests were abandoned because Jock and I were rolling around the place and laughing so hard that, if anyone had been able to measure our abilities, we'd have broken every flexibility record in history. We laughed until our bellies hurt and, even after we'd been ejected from the hotel and sent home, Jock had to pull the car over so he could actually be physically sick with laughter.

Certainly, the sight of that unkempt, leg-spreading, hall-clearing, 6 foot 6 inch, Southland-farming, baby giraffe was a first for Jock and me. And, I believe, for the physios.

• • • • •

I was exceptionally lucky in having Roger Lough as my rugby coach at Lincoln College. He probably influenced my rugby career more than anyone, and was the man who gave me the confidence to set goals and, even more importantly, the confidence to achieve them. It was Roger who set me on my way, pushing me hard, but he was a good enough coach to know how to encourage his players rather than just bark at them. A strict disciplinarian, he was approachable and fair, explaining why he'd dropped you and providing you with a route or a plan for how to get back into the team. Despite being a top rugby man, Roger never got the chance to coach at a higher level – something, I think, didn't bother him. He was happy with his students and had plenty of other things going on in his life. Rugby was a passion for him more than a job.

He was a great example for any player and, in my later coaching career, I drew heavily on his example, particularly the emphasis he placed on encouragement, loyalty and friendship. Under Roger's guiding hand, I went on to represent Lincoln College in all the years that I studied there, ultimately winning a prestigious University Blue for services to university rugby. I also represented the South Island and New Zealand University sides along the way.

Fittingly, among the lessons in life and rugby I learned in Lincoln, was the importance of motivation – how to instill in oneself a sense of drive and purpose and combine it with discipline and work ethic in order to achieve.

What most people don't appreciate is that there's a very fine line between motivation, inspiration and provocation.

Some players – leaders in their own right – can motivate themselves: the mere thought of victory or glory is enough to spur these self-driven competitors to new heights.

Other players rely on inspiration from others to achieve the same results. They need their teammates or captain or coach to lead by word or deed but, once inspired, they too can perform to ever-higher levels.

Then there are the others, the players who find it impossible to rouse themselves from their torpor. These are the players who make up the numbers, who spend much of the game playing well within their own abilities, either unaware of their hidden reserves of greatness or, more likely, unwilling to get the finger out and push themselves. This latter type of character populates teams around the world and is familiar to anyone who has played sport at school. Many coaches, captains and teammates give up on these players as a lost cause, figuring that motivating them will be more trouble than it's worth.

At Lincoln, we took a different approach. Knowing that we would win very little unless every man in a jersey was playing at his optimum, we strategised and theorised about how we could inspire our 'one gear only' players.

Being university rugby players, we decided to combine our love of sport and learning and developed a complicated rugby concept known as 'tickling'.

At one stage in Lincoln, as captain of the college team, it fell to me to implement this new concept and so I lined up the perfect guinea pig for our experiment.

One of our forwards at the time was a player from deep in Southland farm country, who shall remain anonymous.

Suffice to say he was a tough bastard, a rugged farmer's son who ploughed a second furrow as a useful amateur boxer. But despite being rugged and talented, the player had a knack of mentally drifting in and out of games which could make the difference between winning and losing in a tight game.

He was the perfect candidate to be 'tickled'.

So, in the next game, I waited for the first signs that the bloke was drifting off into happy land and immediately went into action. I waited for a scrum and, from behind, landed a sweet left hook to the side of my teammate's skull.

"Jesus!" screamed the suddenly alert forward. "Which one of you bastards punched me in the head?"

"Dunno, mate," I replied, captain-like. "But, to me, it looked like their hooker," pinpointing one of the opposition's key players.

For the next ten minutes, the player was a like a prototype Trevor Brennan, going clean mad looking for the supposed perpetrator.

He climbed up on rucks, ferociously contested every kickoff, tackled like a demon, and, generally, terrorised the opposition.

Then he'd drift off again...

To get a full match out of him, I probably had to punch him about four times a game. But that presented me with a new problem – I constantly had to come up with new ways of disguising where the blow had come from. And changing the angle of attack sometimes had the undesired result of being too effective: I often connected too sweetly with his face, resulting in the odd black eye or broken nose. At those times, it was best to be behind the guy, not in front.

Luckily for me, he never copped what was going on. At least not while we were teammates.

Years later, at a team reunion, he confronted me as to why it was that, every time he played with me, he seemed to get injured. The mystery deepened when, after leaving university, he stopped getting injured during rugby games.

My ability to lie to his face evaporated and, in the spirit of comradeship, I confessed to being the culprit behind his woes.

"Mate," I said, "I'm sorry," hoping that we would be able to laugh about it. After all, it had happened years before.

I don't know if he ever forgave me because, almost as soon as my admission of guilt had left my mouth, he went for me and I spent the next hour of our reunion being chased around the car park. I found the kind of speed any All Black winger would pay money to have.

But my abiding memory of the same player was at a student party, where the young lad was tempted into a bedroom by an affable and attractive young lady. Not a great one for the ladies and very shy, he was delighted when the beauty asked him to strip naked, and then proceeded to tie his hands above the bed with a couple of rugby ties.

Farmer's boy he might have been, but he was cute enough to know that some kinky lovemaking was clearly in the offing. But his '50 Shades of Grey' moment turned to 50 Shades of Red as the young lady suddenly exited the room and the guy was left facing a room full of curious onlookers and the sadistic teammates who had set the whole thing up.

Worse, he was struck down by the Murphy's Law which dictates that, "When you want to get excited you can't, and when you don't, you can't get it to go back down!".

He spent many years extracting retribution in ways that made chasing me around a car park look like a stroll down memory lane.

But, if my rugby and social lives enjoyed an upward trajectory in my time at Lincoln College, the same couldn't be said of my rugby career outside university.

The obvious step after university rugby in the Canterbury area was progressing to the full No. 1 Canterbury provincial side. While it was an ambition of mine, I wasn't overly confident about ever being invited to join a team that was full of incredibly talented individuals and All Blacks, and managed by the legendary ex-All Black, and teak-tough trainer, Alex 'Grizz' Wyllie.

But late one night, after a Lincoln game, I got a phone call. It was short and sweet.

"Pope?" a voice barked out.

"Yes."

"Wyllie here. Be at Canterbury training. 6.30 tomorrow."

The phone was slammed down.

Was that really Grizz? It definitely sounded like him but I was certain it had to be a wind-up. Still, I couldn't afford to take the chance of missing out on training with the top province in New Zealand. So, the next day I sheepishly arrived an hour early at the Canterbury training ground.

If the invitation had been real then I wanted to make a good impression. As the Canterbury lads filed in, I didn't really know any of them, and had little to say for myself. They were all established Canterbury players, many were All Blacks, and I was just some young nobody from university.

Johnny No-mates.

Nobody really welcomed me or told me where to dress or what to do. In fact, nobody really looked in my direction. I grew paranoid. Was this, as I'd suspected all along, another student prank? I began to fret that all the other players were wondering who the strange kid was. I waited for someone to come up and enquire, "Are you lost?"

In a bid to do something – anything – rather than just sit around, I quickly got changed and pulled on my boots. I didn't want to force anyone to have to speak to me so I headed out and started doing laps.

Lap after lap after lap, on my own.

But I'd miscalculated. I did so many bloody laps before training that, by the time it started, I was already tired. There followed one of the hardest training sessions I've ever endured. At one point, I saw Wyllie arrive but I'm not sure he knew I was there. He certainly didn't take any notice of the new boy he'd wanted to attend training, he had other more important things to deal with. Canterbury had a big Shield game coming up and they'd not been very good on their last outing. So, understandably, he had little time for newcomers and fringe players. I began to feel like cannon fodder.

But, even if I hadn't already been painfully aware of my place on their rugby ladder, I was soon given the message.

I'd been so keen to vacate the dressing room earlier in the evening, I'd made the mistake of leaving my rugby kit, boots, socks and bag in a well-known All Black hard-man's dressing room space. When I got back to the changing room, there was no sign of my gear. After a brief search I found some of it… floating in the urinal where he'd tossed it. He'd clearly found my stuff in his sacred spot and so my fresh kit went into the bog.

It was all part of the rugby hierarchy that was prevalent back then. There was a pecking order which was based on earning respect, and that was achieved by knowing to shut up, keep your head down and speak only when you were spoken to. That was the message delivered to all young players when they arrived, as greenhorns, in a top provincial set-up. And that was an attitude that permeated right through all teams, from the players right up to the coach and management. Grizz Wyllie would never have stood for a newly arrived 'wannabe' making out he was better than he was.

So I learned, pretty quickly, how the system worked – for good or for bad. At times, I bought into the system myself and had no problem ribbing new players but not when you could see that, having just arrived alone and knowing no one, they were struggling to be accepted. I admired Grizz Wyllie and his Canterbury players: many of them were my idols, rugby men I wanted to emulate. But I didn't want to emulate the hard-man, 'earn your place, son' kind of attitude that ran right through rugby at that time.

After my experiences as a newbie I decided that, if I ever got to be a senior player in any team, I would go out of my way to welcome new players on board, even if they were directly competing for my position.

Otago rugby's later successes were built, in no small part, on their policy of developing the club and the team as a big, warm and welcoming family. During my very short and inconspicuous stint at Grizz's Canterbury team, I didn't even make it beyond the fringes. There was no shame in that: after all, he ran the best provincial side in the country back then. Holders of the Ranfurly Shield (known as the 'Log 'o Wood'), the Canterbury squad boasted a strength-in-depth no other team in the country at that time could hope to emulate. From a coach's point of view, that was a good thing but, when viewed from the perspective of an ambitious youngster who had yet to break into the team, it was a definite problem. I was, spasmodically, in the Canterbury second side – captained by future All Black coach, Steve Hansen – and my rugby CV, which included stints in many underage Representative teams, cut little ice in a team in which almost all the loose forwards were All Blacks, or All Blacks in the making. Up-and-coming players like myself might get a chance to make the first team, but only when the regulars were on national duty.

No matter how hotly my ambition to play top-flight rugby burned, at Canterbury I was at the end of a queue in which every player in front of me was clad in some sort of black jersey with a silver fern. My chances of ever making the full, starting XV were virtually nil.

I'd already been in the Canterbury area for most of my degree.

After a lonely start at Lincoln College I'd found some great friends and made some great memories at a university which was good for my rugby career.

But times were changing. My degree was coming to an end and it was clear that I didn't have much of a long-term future in Canterbury rugby. The press carried an annual review which stated: "Brent Pope, the young Lincoln College player, was possibly the best and most consistent forwards we saw all year." But nobody approached me and I began to worry about my rugby future.

John Lindsey, a former Otago player but then a university coach in Christchurch, came to my rescue. He'd seen me play for Lincoln and liked what he saw, so he mentioned to new Otago coach, Laurie Mains, that I was worth a look. Mains was just embarking on an ambitious rebuilding programme at Otago. He was carrying out a root and branch overhaul, at the end of which, he intended to make Otago a powerhouse in NZ rugby. The Mains era at Otago was unparalleled in the province's rugby history, before or since. Laurie was intent on building a team that would tear down the established walls of New Zealand domestic rugby. He wanted to take a failing Otago side, rich in tradition, and mould it into a weapon which could take on, and beat, the top provinces in the country.

I was a young player in search of an adventure and Mains was a coach at the start of an epic rugby quest, which would eventually span a number of seasons in the mid-'80s and early '90s and culminate in Otago winning its first-ever National Championship, in 1991.

Back then, I didn't know what Laurie Mains' future held for either him or me, but I knew enough about Mains to want to play for him. With Mains and his Otago team I had a chance, and that was good enough for me. So, when the opportunity of playing for Mains came up, I didn't hesitate.

• • • • •

My final swansong with Lincoln was when we won the DCL Shield and I picked up the 'Player of the Day' award. It was a fitting end to my time with a great team and a nice way to sign off from a college that had been very good to me.

I'd like to think that my legacy at Lincoln College was one of achievement – a tale of a young country lad who didn't think he would even finish secondary school, but who went on to win a great education on and off the rugby pitch.

Certainly my rugby time there had given me the change to rub shoulders with some of the best players in the country and realise they were only flesh and blood. My University Blue meant a huge amount to me because it was awarded for my services to university sport and, being based on the views of my peers and coaches, it recognised my 100 per cent dedication to my university team. Their respect and the realisation that someone believed in me, in turn ignited a self-belief that I might actually have the right stuff to go all the way in rugby.

So, as I said, I like to think that my Lincoln legacy was one of achievement.

Sadly, there's at least one former Lincoln lecturer, and a few generations of students, who know the full story. Those fellow Lincoln inmates know the truth about my ability to be the best – even when it comes to failing.

For, I hold one unfortunate record from my Lincoln sojourn, an unenviable achievement which, I'm led to believe, I still hold: the title of… Failing the Same Exam the Most Times in University History.

The exam was in maths and statistics and after getting an 'E' in my first year, things just snowballed from there. Because I passed everything else, the college authorities allowed me to re-sit it in a special exam over the summer months. Trouble was that, in my world, the summer was a time for the beach, girlfriends and parties, not spending hours indoors swatting for an exam…

So I failed it. Again and again. For four years.

Even with my poor maths, I know that adds up to 8 'E's, which isn't the best result for a student studying for a commerce degree in property valuation.

Still, it did guarantee me fame among the student body, though perhaps infamy would be a better word. At the outset of my fourth year, as I prepared for another tilt, my statistics lecturer stood in front of a hall full of frightened first year inductees and announced: "Everybody, can I have your attention, please? This is Brent Pope. He does exist, and he has failed this exam eight times."

The lecturer's attempt to make a point, and embarrass me at the same time, unfortunately failed as a number of impressed students (no doubt slackers like me) started a slow clap, which eventually erupted into cheering that filled the lecture theatre. I stood, proudly bowed to the madding crowd, and resumed my seat.

While I'm not proud of this particular accolade, as the years go by I find myself getting fonder of it, and hoping no one comes along to knock the crown off my head. I guess Oscar Wilde was right: "The only thing worse than being talked about is not being talked about."

•••••

In the end, the switch from Lincoln College to Otago University was swift. I was only trying to finish my maths and stats section anyway so I simply transferred my study program and enrolled part-time in Otago University, returning the following year to Lincoln to graduate, after eventually passing that darned exam with a mind-blowing 'C' grade.

The transfer from Canterbury to Otago rugby was even more rapid. One Saturday I was wearing the black and red of the Canterbury second team and, a few weeks later, I was scoring tries against the very same province at the South Island Sevens Tournament, only this time I was in the blue and gold of Otago. By that stage, I was a little wiser about where to sit in the dressing room and nobody threw my clothes in the urinal.

A few jaws dropped on the Canterbury sideline at the speed of it all, though I don't think they were too concerned as I hadn't really warranted their respect anyway. That was fine by me.

But I like to think that opinion of me as a player changed in the years that followed.

*There is, and can only be, one Brent Pope. A one-off,
brilliant guy with a great sense of humour, we've bought
houses together, travelled around the world and played for
the same club. His love of cheese sandwiches and Huntley
& Palmer cream-crackers was legendary. The guys would
just love to watch Popey munch his way through half
a dozen crackers loaded with cheese after dinner. Top
quality. The downside of owning the house together was
that Brent is not your DIY specialist, so I found myself
doing most of the repairs. Brent would assess possible
flatmates so I guess he had an important task. He was a
fantastic player with a great inner drive and determination
to succeed. He made me laugh as he could switch, in
seconds, from clowning about to playing a game and
having a blinder. Brent was an integral part of our time at
Otago. In fact, over those years, he was probably the most
popular player we had, and a great character to
have about the team. We spent time in LA and San Diego
with the OMBAC rugby club: going to the gym, then the
beach, more training, out for a pint and maybe trying,
often unsuccessfully, to chat up some American lass –
a pretty good time for a young Kiwi. We certainly had
some laughs along the way, which is as it should be.*

Gordy Macpherson.
Otago. All Blacks.

6

Hello World, I'm Bent Pipe

As part of my transfer from Canterbury to Otago or, geographically, from Christchurch to Dunedin, as well as enrolling at Otago University part-time in a post graduate diploma of management, I took a job as a property valuer with the housing corporation in Dunedin. This job formed part of a four-year registration period to qualify as a commercial property valuer.

Accomodation wasn't a problem as, luckily, I hooked up again with my old friend Richard Taylor in a flat which was aptly nicknamed, 'The Pigpen'. I was forced to live in the only spare room available, which was about the size of a closet and previously used as a telephone room. But at least I was with someone I knew so, unlike Lincoln, I was in a position to easily meet new people.

The Pigpen became a mecca for students. Over the years, because of its many rooms, a lot of scarfies aka scarf-draggers or students, passed through: At any stage there'd be six or seven of us in there, but then someone would fail an exam and be gone. Soon enough, the empty spot would be filled by some new flatmate.

At the beginning, I'd wonder where the hell all the new faces were coming from but, after a while, I learned to just go with the flow.

A cavernous flat, The Pigpen's old Victorian ceilings were so high that, on big-match days, we'd erect scaffolding like a grandstand and sell tickets to students who'd watch the game on our TV. Like those barroom stages in redneck states in the USA which are covered in chicken wire to protect performers, we'd shield the TV with a fireguard so spectators could fire their beer cans at it in disgust when the other team scored. One year there was even a fight in our makeshift stands.

Famous for the annual toga party for physical education students, during which we'd serve dodgy cocktails from our old agitator washing machine, The Pigpen was always full of unlikely characters, with the university rugby team providing many of the star attractions.

I made a lot of great friends during those years in the George Street flat, including Johnny McBreen who would pass away some years later, Davey Smith, Sean Synott Andrea McCone, Dianne Duncan, Donna Marris and the 'Nut', Matt Peters. Nut, who is now a top rugby referee in New Zealand, was one of the most honest men I ever met. He'd refuse to play touch rugby with any player that even looked like cheating and he stuck to that standard, insisting that, if he was to be involved in any sport from rugby to darts, then participants must always abide by the laws. A heavy metal music fan, Nut always kept a bottle of whiskey and 'Axe', his electric guitar, under his bed to entertain late night student revellers with some head-banging, shots and off-key chords.

We spent a lot of nights in the two campus bars around the university, The Gardens and The St George, great watering holes for decades of university rugby teams. Every Friday myself, Nut and a few of our friends would sit out on an old couch in front of the house, drinking beers and watching the local police set up a checkpoint for drunk drivers on that stretch of main road into town.

One Christmas break, I was the only resident left in The Pigpen, my flatmates having dispersed for the holidays to their homes in various parts of New Zealand. So, I invited a couple of my rugby mates to move in for a bit of company and some fun. Along with yet another VW, I had an old Vespa moped chained up outside The Pigpen. Late one night, a group of passing skinheads decided to steal my much-treasured transport, and proceeded to start cutting through the chains that kept the Vespa bound to the front fence. From the vantage point of his upstairs bedroom, one of my houseguests, a hard Maori winger by the name of Hugh Robson, heard the skinheads at work. Stopping only long enough to scavenge a length of tube from the washing machine, Hugh descended the stairs in two gigantic bounds and, dressed only in his underwear, reached the front door which he wrenched open. Brandishing the length of tube and yelling like a Banshee, he took off in search of the skinheads who had, by this stage, abandoned their attempt to steal the moped and were causing mayhem elsewhere down the street.

Hugh's yells were enough to stir the rest of us and we jumped up and ran after him. We didn't need to for, by the time we caught up, Hugh was already amongst the skinheads, administering his own brand of washing machine justice.

The skinheads didn't bother the Vespa again.

● ● ● ● ●

On the rugby front, I met with Laurie Mains as soon as I got down to Otago. Laurie was not a fan of student rugby players by any stretch of the imagination, in fact he had no time for them at all. Reluctant to select any student for his team, especially in the forwards, he viewed us as whispy, headless youths completely at odds with his favoured mould of hard, old-school, country men.

He took a fair bit of convincing about the potential value of the university players. After a few years, he not only came around to the idea of playing the scarfies, he embraced the idea. But in that first meeting, he made it clear that though he wanted me in his top Otago side it would only happen if I guaranteed not to play for the university side.

As I left the meeting I thought, "Stuff it. I want to play for the university. I want to play with my friends."

Over the years, I'd already had a bellyful of politics and the rules that came with playing for certain coaches and teams. I'd missed out on teams for all sorts of reasons, many of them nothing to do with my talent. On top of that, I loved the special kind of camaraderie that comes with playing university rugby. Even today, I still advise any young college players to make sure they play for their university if they get a chance, even if it's only for a year or two, and even if it's only for the thirds or the fourths. It will still give them some of the best experiences of their lives and memories they will carry with them forever.

So, I defied Laurie.

He wasn't happy and, like a lot of coaches at that time, he was the kind of man who never forgot. Players who disobeyed or disrespected coaches like Laurie or Grizz rarely got a second chance.

But I comforted myself with the thought that I wasn't disrespecting him. I genuinely believed I'd be a better player if I was happy in my new environment. I'd learned a lot from my time at Lincoln College, including a realisation that I didn't want to repeat the mistakes of my first year at university, when so much of my time was wasted just trying to fit in. I knew Laurie wouldn't be impressed with my decision to play for Otago University, but I reasoned with myself that, if I was good enough, I would make top-flight rugby regardless. On the other hand, running the risk of making myself friendless and miserable again could increase the risk of my game taking a downturn.

So, I settled into one of the best club sides in the country, Otago University. They had two sides in the senior club competition, the prestigious As and the B side. I made the As where I went on to form long-term partnerships, and friendships, with future stars like Mike Brewer (All Black) and Kevin Putt (Springbok scrum-half).

Otago University had always been a great breeding ground for All Black and Otago rugby and was a club steeped in rugby history. I was proud, still am, to have played for the Blues.

Within weeks of arriving in Otago I found myself lining out against some of my old Canterbury teammates. Otago were playing in the South Island Sevens Tournament and, after doing well in that, we qualified for the National Sevens. The game suited me in some respects – I was fast and reasonably powerful – but I was lacking in skills and the confidence to make decisions in the abbreviated game. For a rural boy like me with an aggressive, agricultural reading of the game, it was a case of either run through them or around them. Later on, players like Zinzan Brooke would make sevens an art form, showing deft changes in pace and ball skills but, more crucially, showing extreme confidence in his own abilities.

Still, in those first few weeks in Otago, my abilities caught the eye of the provincial side's scrum-half, Dean Kenny. An All Black himself, Dean had a huge influence on Otago rugby and, in some circles, was even referred to as 'son of

Laurie' because of his close relationship with the coach. Being seen as a teacher's pet didn't do Dean many favours, but he was good to me. Dean saw my potential, especially as a sevens player, and convinced Laurie that he had to select me.

Amazingly, despite my perceived disrespect, Laurie did. He was only marginally interested in the shorter version of the game at that stage, to him it was just a way of getting players fit for the fifteen-man game. But, for me, it was a way in.

During the South Island Sevens I played well, finishing as one of the leading try scorers, thus retaining my place for the National Sevens which was played over a weekend in the North Island. The Otago Sevens team was good, full of young university talent. My uni pal, Kevin Putt, was there: a cheeky scrumhalf who went on to play for the All Blacks Sevens side in Hong Kong and almost make the full All Black team itself, before shifting allegiance to Natal and eventually lining out for the Springboks. Later in life, Putty and I shared a house in Darglewood in Templeogue – he signed for Terenure while I was with St Mary's. A class player, who never shut up, Kevin asked me to be his best man at his first wedding, to Karen Palmer in New Zealand. The couple separated while I was in Ireland and Kevin went on to marry Louise, a daughter of popular Terenure RFC stalwart, Shay Connolly. The Putt family, which now includes a brood of great kids, lives back in New Zealand.

Progressing to the National Sevens was a big deal. They were due to be broadcast on national TV and I figured this was the chance to announce Brent Pope's rugby talents to the world. I was proud to be representing not just Otago but my friends and family who'd be watching it on TV back home, so running out there, wearing the famous blue and gold jersey, was a big moment for me.

This was my time, or so I thought.

We made the semi-final and I was informed by the coach he'd made the decision to rest me in case we made the final – an obvious piece of psychological BS I'd later employ on my own players when I wanted to let them down gently. More likely than not, he just dropped me because he reckoned I wasn't good enough. Either way, in the semi, an Otago player went down and I got the call to start warming up on the sideline.

This was it, I reckoned … my big moment. The game would be broadcast on Sunday TV and, in my mind's eye, the Brent Pope 'Boy's Own' success story would end with me, in the full glare of the TV cameras, coming on and running the entire length of the pitch to score the winning try to the sound of thunderous applause from the crowd. There'd hardly be a dry eye in the house.

As I awaited the substitution which would herald my TV appearance, the announcer took his place by my side. In those days, the guy with the microphone stood on the sideline, announcing the scorers, the injuries, the subs and so on – very much the role of today's pitch side sports reporters. This particular bloke was an older-looking man wearing a tweed jacket. He looked very officious, peering at me over the top of his half-moon spectacles.

Suddenly, I got the green light from the Otago management.

My chest puffed out with pride and I ran onto the pitch, ready to grab my big moment with both hands. It was my chance to shine, my future in the next five minutes.

But, as I ran past the elderly announcer with the specs, out of the corner of my eye I saw him look down at his programme, scratch his head and, via his microphone, blurt out to the waiting masses: "... and No. 7 for Otago is being replaced by erm... BENT PIPE... "

Noooo!

For feck's sake!

NOT BENT FECKING PIPE! BRENT POPE!

Who the hell had a name like Bent Pipe?

But it was too late. The watching world cracked up and, post-game, I was the subject of a horrendous kangaroo court session held by my teammates who finessed the announcer's gaffe into a new nickname – Copper, as in bent copper pipe.

It took me years to live it down and the name was kept alive by countless pub quizmasters who asked if anyone could recall the day a dodgy piece of plumbing played rugby in New Zealand.

It wasn't just my name that was causing me grief in those early years. My skinny legs were a constant source of embarrassment. In fact, they were so thin that, I'd often don two pairs of socks just to bulk them up, or put my shin-guards on back to front underneath my socks to make my legs look bigger.

But I came undone in one game which was played in muddy conditions. I couldn't afford enough studs for my boots, so I put the big tags, as studs were known back then, on the front of my boots making them high at the front and low at the back. Problem was, the ground was so mucky that my boots kept coming off every time I tried to get up a bit of speed. They would dig in and I would come out the back of them. I tried to borrow another pair at half time but size 12 boots were hard to get hold of.

Still, it was a crucial match so, with twenty minutes to go, I just threw away the boots as they were almost worse than useless and played the last quarter against Dunedin, a strong club team at that time, in my socks. Unfortunately, in the wet conditions, my two pairs of socks first became sodden and then elongated. In fact, so stretched did they become that, at one point, I had them trailing about five feet behind me. All the opposition had to do was step on my sock and I'd been tackled. In the end I had to throw away my socks and play à la South African runner Zola Budd, in my bare feet. This is not a tactic I'd advise any young player to copy, especially in a game full of blokes averaging over 15 stones in weight. From then until the end of game Tama Taita, Dunedin's tough Maori flanker, rejoiced in trying to jump on my toes every time there was a lineout. Even today, thanks to old Tama, whenever I have a bath I have to look at my black toenails.

It was great craic for everybody, except me. Watching this big, mud-caked No. 8 with skinny legs – so pale you could see their whiteness through the muck – trying to break off the back of the scrum with a pair of socks flapping behind him. Even funnier when he tried the same trick in bare feet. It must have looked like something from the Islands, where they do sometimes play without boots.

Mind you, there are worse things to play without in a game of rugby than a pair of boots.

Underwear, for one.

A good pair of underwear can save more than a player's blushes, it can protect his ego when it comes to playing a match in the rain, snow or frost while being watched by a girlfriend.

It's less of an issue in the modern game as many players favour tight Lycra shorts under their togs. But, back in the day, the crusty old jockstrap ruled the earth. And in those times of baggy shorts, forgetting your jockstrap was the stuff of nightmares, unless you were one of a rare breed of players…

I once suffered the humiliation of enduring eighty minutes of laughter from a group of women as they howled their way through a game in which I'd opted to go commando, having forgotten my jockstrap. Clearly, borrowing a substitute's would not have been an option, even under the most desperate circumstances.

Pinned to a ruck, with my hands held down and the wind flapping at my togs, this particular lady and her university friends were obviously getting an eyeful of a spectacle that underwhelmed them. The additional sight of 'builder's bum' when I was tackled from behind only fuelled their laughter.

From my own point of view, and without being too graphic, I'd advise any 'sporting commandos' out there that the swinging tackle approach is energy-sapping and not conducive to speed.

Perhaps the change to tight undershorts is for the best as, in truth, wearing the old jockstrap was a double-edged sword. The joke was that, if you wore them the wrong way round and nobody noticed, then perhaps you'd be better off with a G-string.

• • • • •

Truth, at least when it came to the media, was one of the first casualties of sporting warfare when I switched to Otago University in Dunedin.

I'd had a few scrapes with journalists in my school years, and the ghost of Peter Muldoon long outlived his fictional cricketing career. The trouble with the Muldoon experience, however, was that I was left with a bit of an arrogant attitude when it came to reporters. While at Otago University, I received a short, sharp lesson in media relations which, ever since, has influenced my approach to the Fourth Estate.

At one stage, when I was playing for the university in Dunedin, I was lucky enough to get a write-up in the Sunday edition of the *Otago Daily Times* news-paper. Even better, the reporter enthused about what a great game I'd had in the lineout.

I made sure to write a grateful note to the *ODT* editor, thanking him for the coverage and praising the individual sports reporter concerned for his dedication to covering university rugby.

However, I finished the note by explaining that, in point of fact, it was the team's hooker who deserved all the kudos as, at the time of the match in question, I was 500 miles away at a friend's wedding. My performance at that game was something even the great Keith Wood would have been proud of – hitting his man in the lineout from almost 500 miles away.

I got a laugh out of it at the time but, soon enough, I learned the value of keeping my big mouth firmly shut. In the wake of the letter, the reporter, who was obviously rapped on the knuckles by his boss, refused to write anything decent about me for weeks. He even dismissed my efforts in one particular game in which I'd scored three tries – including one which had required me sprinting 50 yards through shark-infested waters – as a case of being in the right place at the right time.

Lesson learned. Don't be a smart arse.

● ● ● ● ●

In my first year there, Otago University defeated old rivals, Southern, to win the Otago Club Championship.

We were captained by Garth Poole who, today, is a well-respected surgeon in Auckland hospital. A charming intellectual with the knack of making everyone feel appreciated, Garth had a sharp wit. He embraced university life, playing hard and partying hard.

A second row, Garth skirted around Otago B level, but on one occasion I was playing with him in a Town v Country game. This was the annual game between the best players in the city against the best from the country, and it acted as an unofficial main trial for the Otago Rep teams. As such, it was always a fierce ding-dong, with the Town team mainly made up of trendy, high flying students against a Country team drawn from the ranks of the hardnosed sheep farmers. Every year, the two sides would reach new highs, and lows, in their efforts to outdo each other.

In our Town side, captained by Garth, there was a player by the name of Steve Hotton. A heavily tattooed, former New Zealand Maori prop and one-time South Island heavyweight boxing champ – although he won't admit that he only had one fight to get the belt, after the title was vacated – Hotty was hugely popular in New Zealand rugby. In the 1980s and '90s every team knew about the Hot.

A stereotypical Kiwi prop in many ways, Hotty was a unique individual. In time, he become a national cult hero for the entire country but, back in my university years, Hotty first found fame amongst the student population of Otago.

They loved his lifestyle as much as his playing style, adopting him as an icon and even holding an annual university ball in his name – The Hotty Ball. Students would advertise the event around campus by wearing T-shirts bearing the legend, "See you at the ball – how low can you go?" At the ball itself, they'd cover themselves in false tattoos, shave their heads and adopt the same monosyllabic lingo that the Hot spoke.

Hotty was great fun and far less harmful than he looked. A former truck driver, bouncer and hospital porter, he loved the adoration of the wider student body but, as far as many of his teammates were concerned, Hotty's main claim to fame was that he was so darned gullible.

On one occasion when we were playing a club game, Hotty started screaming that he had been somehow, tragically blinded during a match.

Panicking, he cried out for Garth, a trainee doctor in those days.

"Garth. What do I do? I'm blind," Hotty screamed in terror as everybody else looked on.

Drawing on his extensive medical experience, Garth reached towards Hotty's face and pulled up Hotty's head-band which, in the last scrum, had somehow slipped down and covered his eyes, causing his 'blindness'.

"There you go, Hotty. You can see again… " said Garth as he trotted away.

As a prop, his face and head came in for a lot of attention during matches with the result that his ears were a major problem. Like many forwards, Hotty found that unless his ears were drained regularly they would fill and harden, leading to that common rugby player's complaint, cauliflower ears. Today, the introduction of headgear has cut down on the issue of cauliflower ears but, back then, they were seen as a badge of honour among some players and there was much debate about what to do with them.

Some culinary comedians advised white sauce as the best solution, but Hotty came up with his own unique answer to the problem: leeches. He kept a jar of leeches and, every Monday, would put a few on his ears and have them suck the blood out. He swore by it and actually persuaded me to try it. The leeches drank their fill and fell off.

In fairness to Hotty, the leeches were less painful than having your ears drained by syringe. That experience was a bit like pulling knotted string through a small hole and you had to keep the pressure on the ear or else it would fill up again, something I often used a clothes peg for, though that was a painful experience in its own right – don't try it.

• • • • •

During those Otago University years, I was introduced to one of the nicest and funniest coaches it's ever been my privilege to know – Duncan Doodle Laing.

Duncan was Laurie Mains' understudy for a while. A talented technical coach, Duncan variously coached the university and Town teams – or the Otago second team. Occasionally, when Laurie was away, Duncan was left in charge of the full Otago side.

Laing is immortalised in Otago sport. An internationally respected swim coach, he helped train Dunedin's double Olympic gold medallist and former World Record holder, Danyon Loader.

Less well-known, is the fact that Duncan once had a play written about him by a former junior All Black, Otago student and would-be playwright. Entitled Foreskin's Lament, the play focussed on Duncan's hilarious experiences as a coach and anyone who has watched the movie 'Mike Basset, Football Manager' will immediately understand the kind of manager he was.

A big man of 20-ish stone, Duncan had a touch of narcolepsy and it wasn't uncommon to spot him, halfway through a game, snoring away on the sideline. I'm not sure it had anything to do with the narcolepsy, but he would take about an hour to name the weekly team, often getting confused about who was playing where. Though the players would already know the team because it had been published by the selectors in the local newspaper, Duncan would insist on running through it again in our presence.

The result was comedy gold.

"Full-back… " begins Duncan, before his voice tails off into silence. Pause for about five minutes…

"… that will be, John Cooper."

Everyone looks at each other. Who the hell is John Cooper?

One of the lads stands up: "I think you mean Greg Cooper, don't you Dunc?"

"… crap, that's right, it's Greg. Ok. Greg and his brother Brian will be the centres…"

Another player stands up: "Sorry, coach. Greg doesn't have a brother here."

"Oh. Right. Well… Who the hell does have a brother then?"

Cue sniggering around the dressing room, followed by another five-minute pause…

This would continue for about an hour, the players already aware of the team but too polite to interrupt Duncan, preferring to sit there shuffling in a bid to avoid getting too cold. Until he finally finished.

Training was worse.

Duncan was very gullible.

He'd send the forwards up to train on the hill telling them to do fifty scrums – or whatever Laurie Mains had instructed him to do – while he oversaw the backline.

Up the rise we would charge, until we were out of sight. Then we'd roll in the mud and scream and do … nothing.

During one particular training session on a dark and stormy night, Duncan sent us off. Within minutes, under cover of darkness, all the big, hard Otago forwards were huddling together in the refuge of a women's hockey shed. Every now and again, one of us would open the door and scream out, for Duncan's benefit, into the storm: "ONE MORE SCRUM LADS! ONE MORE SCRUM!" At one stage, somebody even lit up a cigarette.

Then, a quick roll in the mud and back down the hill we trundled, mucked to the eyeballs and appearing out of breath. Duncan took in the spectacle before turning to the backline and berating them: "While you useless bastards have been dropping the ball and messing up, the forwards have been up there busting a gut."

The closest we ever came to busting a gut in one of Dunc's training sessions was trying to hold in the laughter.

At unveristy he coached David Kirk, the All Blacks' 1987 World Cup winning captain. Shortly into Duncan's training sessions, Kirk would vault the fence behind the training paddock and head for his university flat. Accompanied by a couple of other escapees, David would have a cup of tea, watch an episode of Dallas, jump back over the fence and rejoin Duncan's fitness session which, by then, was half over.

Not only would Duncan fail to notice but he'd often single Kirk out for special praise: "If everybody trained like Kirk we would be fine."

Duncan led one of the most inspirational team talks it's ever been my privilege to hear. It came against Southland in a game in which Laurie had been taken ill and passed the baton of motivational team-talk responsibility to Duncan.

He started well, hitting all the right buttons. Pretty soon the players were climbing up the walls to get at the opposition. Then, just as Duncan reached the zenith of his talk, the dressing room door quietly opened and Duncan's son, Billy, walked in. Billy, who was a smaller version of Duncan, had been called in as a late, late replacement for prop and now, sheepishly, took his seat as his dad reached the climax of his team talk.

Annoyed at his son's late arrival, Duncan turned on him and, in full voice, delivered his damning assessment.

"That's right! Bloody typical, late and unreliable … just like your mother!"

That was it. Dunc's motivational team talk was over as the tensed up players dissolved into a puddle of laughter. It was Duncan's only major team talk that season.

A much-loved character among the players, each of us who were lucky enough to be coached by him has a Duncan story. But none of us knew about the true scale of the amazing kindness of Duncan until after he had died. Then we discovered that Duncan and his lovely wife, Betty, had fostered many young children. He was a big man in more ways than just physical size. Duncan was awarded an OBE, in 1993.

•••••

My motley university crew also included a teammate by the name of Mike Gibson. Mike was a virtual Adonis: big and broad with a long mane of hair, women loved Mike. Different from the mainstream rugby types, Mike didn't drink but liked music and art and so we got on well.

Though a very good centre or wing, Mike always seemed to be injured and regularly had to take painkillers. He was so well-known for getting injured that we'd rib him endlessly. But he'd take it in good spirit and give as good as he got.

After one particular match, for Otago, his calves swoll up. It looked sore but we dismissed it as a muscle tear and, because I had a car, I agreed to drop him at the hospital so he could have his legs checked out by a doctor.

As things turned out, Mike's problem wasn't a simple tear.

He had cancer.

He was dying.

Not long before he passed away, I spent a weekend with him in Wellington. We just walked and talked and spent the time discussing things we loved. At the airport, saying goodbye, it struck me that in my embrace, I could almost crush this once-big, strong man. He died not long after and is commemorated by an annual trophy contested by Wellington and Otago. I think about Mike to this day.

Mike wasn't the only great friend and rugby man we lost, back then. Gordon Hunter, a former Otago and later All Black coach, who trained me in Otago after Laurie retired, also passed away. Another warm and generous man, Gordon would always have a meal or a beer waiting for you at his house.

For reasons known only to him, in the early '90s Gordon selected me for Otago ahead of the soon-to-be All Black great, Josh Kronfeld. Sporting his glass eye, Gordon was famous during training sessions for roaring at players not to "stare at my bung eye", which only caused some poor unsuspecting player to be drawn to it even more. A detective with the Dunedin police, Gordon's notes on our games were hilarious. Each week, we'd listen to a match report that sounded more like the description of a crime scene.

"… at approximately 2.15pm, I witnessed the player, Brent Pope, miss the tackle. I reported the incident… "

It might sound unlikely, but that was how Gordon operated. With a little black book and accompanying pencil, it was a 'total rugby' approach far ahead of its time – real 'Otago CSI' stuff.

Looking back now, those seven seasons in the blue and gold of Otago were the best days of my rugby career, and that includes playing for the All Blacks and spending eight years in Japan as a professional rugby player. Before deciding to come to Dunedin, I recognised that Popey was the current Otago No. 8 and, if I were to be successful as a player, then I would have to knock him off his perch. So, when I formally met this joker, you can imagine how annoyed I was when he invited me out for a couple of beers with him and a couple of the older players. Popey's humour and way was always to position himself as the guy who has all the bad luck – with girls, with injuries, with everything. Poor old Popey – he won the lotto once but lost the ticket. We ended up nick-naming him, 'old fuss fuss'. He generally saw the glass half-empty but knew it and laughed at it, and himself. Laurie Mains, who scared us all, once mistook me for John Leslie and called me 'JL'. Without thinking I immediately said, "JR MATE, not JL". The senior players loved this, especially Popey and from then on I was "JR MATE" but, though he was ribbing me, I also felt I'd earned his respect. You served an apprenticeship in those days – said little, did everything, as you searched for respect on and off the field. You had to have credability with the older players and, to have that, you had to do your time or be endorsed by 'one of the boys'. As a young player I felt that I earned that with my rugby but I also felt the endorsement was also there and that came from my old friend, Popey. A unique bloke, funny, a good friend and a bloody good No. 8 in his time.

Jamie Joseph (JR MATE!)
Otago. All Blacks. Japan. Highlanders Super 15 Head Coach.

7

Otago Days

Laurie Mains was, without doubt, the toughest and probably the most influential coach I ever had. During my long stint with Otago, he taught me a huge amount which I, in turn, attempted to pass on in my later coaching career.

His training sessions were tough and comprised of hours on the scrum-ruck machine – a big wooden sled that, if you got your head in the wrong position on entering the archaic looking machine, would certainly slash your ears or head, or even knock you out.

Mains made us hit the scrum, then sprint to the sled, pile into that, then keep going, time and again.

Scrum.

Ruck.

Scrum.

Ruck.

Scrum.

Ruck.

Over and over again.

He brought us to a ground, Bathgate Park near St Kilda beach, where the little grains of sands swept in by the sea breezes would cling to the ruck pads. After slamming into them for endless hours, the grains would cut our ears and shoulders to ribbons. We hated Laurie's contraption with a passion. Players split their heads and their ears and vomited from using that torture machine.

But it worked.

Slowly but surely, Mains turned us into one of the fittest forward packs in the country. We were tough and hard and fit.

His training sessions would always end with 'down and ups' where we would slide down over a line, get up and slide down again, army-style. We would do as many as Laurie ordered.

He'd shout, "Have you had enough?" but as soon as we answered, "Yes!" he'd force us to do more. If we shouted, "No!" he'd force us to do more. We could never win.

In my time with Mains, I saw many a player throw up, we even had a couple of lads who passed out after the valves to their heart closed due to pure exhaustion. That's how hard Mains pushed us.

Along with manager Gerry Simmons, Laurie changed everything about us. They changed how we trained, how we played, how we thought about the game. Their good cop/bad cop routine was a perfect blend. At times we hated Laurie with his stoney attitude and his ruthless approach, but Gerry's affable nature offered us a different face of management. When Laurie shattered us, Gerry was there to pick up the pieces and put us back together. Looking back, it's clear Laurie wanted it that way. It was his master plan for success.

And it worked.

Each year we got better.

He brought the scarfies on board. From barely being able to disguise his contempt for the students, Laurie now welcomed them into the fold, en masse. As the university, and especially its popular degree in physical education, began to attract the most talented young rugby players in the country, Laurie took advantage of the situation.

He was nothing if not pragmatic. Many of Otago's future All Black stars had, or would, sign up to Otago University during my era: players like Arran Pene, John Timu, Taine Randell, Jamie Joseph, Ant Strachan Josh Kronfeld and a future Scotland captain by the name of John Leslie. And, when Laurie found gaps in the team that couldn't be filled with local or university talent, he signed players like All Blacks Greg Cooper, Arthur Stone, Gordy Macpherson and Stu Forster or Maori All Black, Paul Cooke.

It was a potent mix. Suddenly, Otago started beating the likes of Canterbury and Wellington on a regular basis. Nothing breeds success like success, and crowds started flocking back to our games. The pre-Mains era trickle of supporters suddenly became a flood. From 1988 until 1991 we were a great side, beating many other First Division teams with ease, apart from most teams' nemesis during those years – Auckland. In that same period, the Otago side was built from the ranks of the All Blacks or All Blacks in waiting. At full strength only Auckland had more silver ferns in their team.

Mains' reputation grew quickly. He was soon given responsibility for the South Island teams and All Black trials. It was only a matter of time before he landed the big job.

But for us, his players in those great years, Laurie was Mr Otago Rugby. He wasn't always popular, in fact many players and adminstrators disliked him. He had more than his fair share of run-ins with other people in the Otago set-up. But no one, not even his detractors, could deny his success. He put Otago rugby on a map they had been in danger of sliding off completely. In my own opinion, even when he was in the wrong, he still had Otago's best interests at heart.

Old Funeral Face was a pretty cold customer. The owner of many nicknames, we called him 'Lemons' because of the bitter look on his face. It could take years for him to even talk to you. If you were seen to be messing at any stage, either the night before a game or on the day of a game, Mains would stare at you, and then drop you.

At team talks, he'd look around and if he thought someone was trying to hide he'd single them out and berate them. By the end of the team talk, every single player would understand that, even if they were able to hide from the opposition on the pitch, there could be no hiding from Lemons. He struck fear into our hearts more effectively than any rival side could ever do. Losing a game often meant going into 'lock-down mode'. Mains would lock us into our hotel rooms without beer, food or craic.

Even at the best of times, this severe disciplinarian would insist on players being under lock and key at a respectable hour the night before a game. Any player seen fooling around in the corridors, messing or distracting others would be dropped. It didn't matter who you were, Laurie would give you that harsh glare of his and you wouldn't play the next day.

You wouldn't expect a team full of grown-up rugby men to be so scared of a single individual but no one dared question his methods, not least because his methods were working. But most of all, we just didn't know any other way.

Mains' notorious 'lock-downs' led to one of the greatest motivational speeches I've ever heard. During one National Championship game against Counties, a strong rugby province just outside Auckland, we found ourselves losing by a couple of points, deep in our own 22 and facing the last play of the game. It was what American footballers would call a Hail Mary moment, but Laurie Mains wasn't a man who hung around waiting for divine intervention. Nor was he a man whose religious beliefs stretched to forgiving players who failed on the pitch.

Captain Dick Knight called the team together and laid out the stark reality of the moment.

"Right, guys, here are the choices. We can lose this bloody match and we know what's going to happen… Mains is going to lock us in the hotel. Or we can win, go out on the piss and have a great night."

In my time, I've heard more eloquent and, certainly, more long-winded speeches. But I've never heard anything that hit its target audience more accurately.

Driven by the fear of a hotel lock-down policed by Lemons, sans beer and fun, we played like a team possessed. Up the field we surged, play after play, phase after phase, until we scored and won the match. We collapsed, as they would say in Dublin, in a bleedin' delighted heap.

And Laurie? Well, he was pleased. Not overly-so, but pleased enough to let us out that night.

• • • • •

Around that time, Laurie decided we were being too well fed, especially on tours. Food formed a big part of his lock-down strategy. At meal times, he'd walk behind us, counting up the extra chips we were shovelling onto our plates and making a mental note of it so, if he needed something to hit you with later, he'd have an à la carte menu of things to choose from.

Losing, or sometimes just the prospect of losing, earned an entire team a food ban – not the basics but the extras. A shrewd man, Laurie knew that after living on scraps, as most students do, his Otago University scarfies couldn't wait to order anything and everything when on duty for Otago province. But he wasn't about to let that happen. The wrong, or fatty, foods can take a lot out of players and, in Laurie's mind, you didn't become the best by ordering a side of fries. There was method in his madness: controlling the food intake wasn't just about diet, it was about making us focus and think about what it would take for us to become the best. If we won he, like many coaches, would turn a blind eye but, if we lost, then he'd go back to his army sergeant drills, slinking behind the tables recording who had what.

A couple of times his tactic left us starving, but Laurie wasn't a man who issued an order and then relented. If his order stated, 'no over-eating', then he meant it. Players would find nearby hotel restaurants or cafés closed to them and policed by ever-vigilant members of Mains' gestapo. A few hours of that and rugby players, who were training and playing at full pelt, began to get desperate.

During one ban, things got so bad that when one player scrounged a single packet of sausages, well past its use-by date, a load of lads piled into his hotel room. As word spread of the chance of food, more fellas were on their way.

The lads had a problem, how were they to cook the bangers? Well, where there's a will there's a way and, by the time I arrived, there was half a dozen or more full-grown players – All Black household names among them – sitting in a circle. In the centre was a boiling kettle, lid already prised off, and into the bubbling water was thrust half a dozen wire coat hangers, each with an out-of-date sausage on the end. Following this delicious repaste, the ravenous players had a quick whip-round and, under cover of darkness, sent off one of the younger squad members to the local garage for a few Kit-Kats.

Despite the best efforts of coaches such as Laurie, the importance of diet as a crucial sporting concept was still in its embryonic stage in the 1980s. In fact, we were so ignorant of what was good for us, especially as hard-up university students, that my friend and flat mate, Gerard Prendergast, and I once lived for a whole week on a single bag of potatoes.

We had run out of money and food, save for the big sack of spuds my dad had bought us a fortnight earlier. Too embarrassed to call home for yet more money, and with just a week to go before we headed home for the university holidays, Gerard and I opted for a week of extreme carb loading.

By the Thursday night, it was still possible to see the funny side of life. That evening, in the run-up to a match, I cooked a 'last supper'. It was a veritable smorgasbord of potato delights – mashed potato … boiled potato … chips … all rounded off with some roast potatoes – variety being the spice of life and all that.

But, by Saturday, Gerard, who was a hardy blindside flanker with a normally placid nature though an explosive temper when pushed, was reaching breaking point. Starving, moody and pissed off, he arrived at the match only to be told that he had been relegated to the bench. A team player who would usually have accepted his demotion to the bench graciously, Gerard lost it. He grabbed the university coach by the lapels of his coat, shook him violently and glared into his face.

"Look, mate," Gerard spat at him, "I've been living on nothing but potatoes for a week, like a bloody Irishman. I'm mean and I'm hungry. Let me on."

The shocked coach was too stunned to speak, so it was left to Gerard's replacement in the starting line-up to react first.

"For Chrissakes, let him on," the guy yelled, "he's fuckin' mad!"

Within minutes of kick off, Prendergast was hitting everything that moved and some things that didn't. He snarled, growled, threatened and fought and, by half time, had scored a try and already done enough to win the accolade of Man of the Match. It was his greatest game – all because of the humble potato.

But even as Gerard Prendergast crossed that try line, it was clear the 'Day of the Potato' was passing. The wheels of the food science departments in universities around the globe were turning and, in a few short years, our unenlightened approach to diet would be dead.

Back then, the perpetually hungry player's pre-match breakfast usually consisted of a big fry up, especially when on tour. Like its counterpart in Ireland, England and everywhere else, that meant bacon, eggs, sausages, potatoes, and so on – the works. The advice from our coaches was simply to eat whatever we would usually eat at home, and not break with the normal routine.

Problem was that, in my scarf-dragger years, you were lucky if there was anything left in the bloody fridge after your flat mates had cleaned it out the night before.

One flat mate, a biology major, told me that potatoes and seafood were very nutritious before a game. He was right, of course, but not when you were stuffing your face with deep-fried battered fish and chips and from the local greasy spoon.

Not exactly the breakfast of champions. Imagine the Irish Grand Slam team lining up at Burdocks the morning of a game and Rob Kearney yelling out: "A battered sausage, two spice burgers and chips, please."

By the mid-'80s a new breed of educated coach was arriving on the scene, armed with dossiers of carefully researched information on diet and nutrition.

Colin 'Pinetree' Meads, probably the greatest second row the world has ever known, once spoke about the introduction of the new nutrition regime to the All Black set-up during his time as the national coach.

The NZRFU had just employed some smart young female nutritionists from a university to advise the All Blacks on what they should, and should not, be eating. Each player was individually interviewed about his diet.

During the interrogation by a young food scientist, Colin was asked what he would eat prior to a game, back in the days when he was a player. He was only too delighted to regale the youngster with details of his personal regime. After a morning's work on the farm, he explained, he'd return to the farmhouse and tuck into the big pile of buttery mash and delicious steak his wife had lovingly prepared for him. Recalling those playing days and, in particular, his delectable diet, Colin virtually smacked his lips as he finished his history lesson.

The young girl in front of him shook her head in disgust and disbelief at Colin's nourishment.

"You know what, Mr Meads?" she ruefully told the 133-capped All Black legend, "You don't realise how good you could have actually been... "

Priceless.

During my early provincial days with Otago, preseason army training camps were all the rage. These camps were held over the course of a weekend and players were asked to bring a plate with them for mealtimes.

Grant Dearns, a university teammate of mine, was attending the camp with the rest of us. Dearnsy was a 20-stone, body-building giant who looked like Tarzan but, unfortunately, played like Jane. Still, he knew how to eat.

As the rest of us produced our little breakfast bowls and carefully spooned in a small portion of fruit salad, Dearnsy produced a cauldron that most families could have washed their dishes in.

He shovelled in the fruit salad with a soup ladle, followed by twenty Weetabix – yes, that's right, twenty – and that was his normal, pre-match breakfast.

A tough prison officer and a talented prop, Dearnsy was possibly the strongest player I ever lined up with. Sadly, he only lasted a handful of games for Otago at the highest level.

He was just too emotional. When a coach or a teammate criticised him, he would sometimes well-up and his eyes would glaze over with tears. Even his job as a prison officer, working with New Zealand hard nuts, failed to smother his emotional side and, in those days, there wasn't much call for nice, caring props, no matter how talented they were. He wasn't always alone in that regard, though. I can recall waiting for a lift to training along with Dearnsy and Matt 'Nut' Peters. With nothing to do, we switched on the telly and became engrossed in a particularly dramatic, and sad, episode of Little House on the Prairie. By the time our lift arrived the three of us were leaning back into the furthermost corners of our chairs, hands to our foreheads, talking deeply and acting tough … as we attempted to cover up our sniffs, cracking voices and glazed-over eyes.

I always got the best out of Dearnsy's game, because I treated him with respect, realising he wouldn't respond to shouting. As already explained, some players needed 'tickling' while others needed less direct encouragement. Learning that different players respond differently was an important lesson in life for me and, unfortunately, one I forgot about for much of my later coaching career.

Even though he was 6 foot 3 inches and over 20 stone of chiselled muscle, Dearnsy was just a quiet guy who would only get aggressive a couple of times in a match. Similar to a lot of modern props, including the likes of John Hayes and Tony Buckley, Dearnsy had a difficult job scrummaging, he was simply too big to pack down in a scrum.

Still, he had his moments and one of those came during a Tour in Australia against the Australian Barbarians, when Dearnsy's opposite number made the mistake of having a cut off the gentle giant. After a few heated words, and a few handbags, a maul began to form. In the middle of the maul, I spotted Dearnsy with his opposite number in a headlock but at a loss as to what to do next – kiss him or squeeze him.

Instinctively, I barked out the order, "Squeeze, Dearnsy!"

And he did.

In fact, he executed the kind of perfect 'sleeper hold' that any professional wrestler would be proud of. I could see the Aussie player's head turn bright red and then blue.

"For Chrissakes, Dearnsy..." I barked out again, "Let go, let go!"

And he did.

In one fluid motion the other guy sunk to his knees and keeled over, out cold. Physically, the bloke recovered in a few minutes, but mentally he'd been conquered. When the next scrum formed, he was wise enough to offer Dearnsy a sheepish 'sorry'.

Who could blame him?

•••••

If props like Dearnsy were at one of end of the emotional scale, then it'd be fair to say that Otago wasn't short on lads at the other end.

One guy, who was the walking personification of the stereotypical front row, was NZ folklore legend, Mad Jack McLennan, who occupied the loosehead side of the scrum.

A Willie Duggan-type of player who was as hard off the field as on it, Mad Jack would often vomit at half time and then finish off his cigarette as he jogged back on to the pitch for the second half.

The glint in his eye was only slightly less mad looking than his mop of red, Celtic, hair and, among his many tough jobs, he worked as a butcher in a local abattoir. He had his own training regime, which involved a series of personal challenges he had to complete each week.

One such goal was to drink half a dozen pint bottles of beer after every midweek training session, on Tuesday and Thursday nights, before his lift reached the crossroads at Owaka where his wife would pick him up and take him home.

Not quite the ideal preparation for a big match, in ten years of rugby Jack never failed to rise to this challenge – come rain or shine any player giving him a lift always had a crate of beer in the boot.

But Mad Jack wasn't the exception. Those were the years when everything worked 'the back of the bus way'.

Literally.

There was a hierarchy whereby, the more caps you earned, the more esteem you gained and the further back you moved in the team bus. You kept moving backwards until you were one of the most-capped four players in the backseat. These were the guys who, at any time, could call on all of the other players in front of them to join them in drinking competitions, jokes or singing.

Sound barbaric?

It was.

But it was also great fun.

Theoretically, it was possible for the lads at the front of the bus to challenge their 'betters' at the back. But this was an unwise move. The backseat was usually occupied by props or second rows and the battles – especially at All Black level where the same hierarchy operated – could become fairly serious, as various players tried their luck. Teams frequently suffered more stitches and injuries on their bus than on the pitch.

After ten years, and nearly 100 provincial caps, I finally made the back of the bus and spent my final few years extracting my revenge.

As well as the bus routine, part of the team ritual back then called on senior players to room with younger lads, so they could pass on their experience and expertise. In essence this boiled down to the new bloods being treated as rugby slaves. They had to clean boots, get food, make coffee, always take the single bed and, generally, obey every order from their 'senior roomie' and de facto slave master.

A few years ago, John Leslie from New Zealand became the Scottish captain and, I think, still holds the record for the fastest International try after scoring direct from the kick off for Scotland against Wales in the Five Nations.

But John, despite his many sporting decorations, had once been my slave for a couple of northern Tours, fetching me chocolate from the shop, washing my gear etc. Watching him reach the pinnacle of Scottish rugby, I noted to myself that it was nice I had made such a positive impact on him…

At least John was lucky. I wasn't too tough a taskmaster, not like Mad Jack had been to me.

When I first made the provincial team as a young university player, I was given the dubious honour of being Mad Jack's roommate. Jack was a stickler for tradition and any notion that he might not treat me as his 'slave' was soon dispelled. I was expected to do everything for Jack.

While my other teammates from university would go out for a few drinks to the trendier spots, I had to accompany Jack to some of the rougher bars in town. Places like the Wharf Bar or the Docksiders, hardly the kinds of places where a scarf-dragger could meet girls. I'd sit there, bored out of my tree, while Jack smoked two packets of Rothmans and downed twenty pints before heading back to the hotel.

It was … an experience.

Jack was truly a one-off – exactly the kind of guy about whom coaches commented: "He's a hard bastard … but he's our hard bastard".

The last time I heard of Mad Jack was during a sevens game, versus Australia, in Kuala Lumpur. One of the Aussies was an International who came from Perth and, at one point in the game, told me, "Mad Jack says hello".

Of course, I replied, "How is he?"

"Great," said the player, going on to explain that Jack was by then a coach. According to the tale recounted by this Australian International, it seemed that, even in his golden years, Jack was refusing to dilute his uncompromising approach to the game.

In a particular game involving the team he coached, one of Jack's young charges was given an awful going-over by an older, more experienced rival.

No one abused one of Mad Jack's youngsters, only he was allowed to do that.

So, in a pair of borrowed boots and some multi-coloured Bermuda shorts, the old warhorse trundled on to the field to demonstrate some of the finer points of rugby strategy.

A couple of flare-ups later, Jack dropped the player with a right-cross, muttered something about the bloke picking on someone his own size, then causally jogged back to his coaching position on the side of the pitch, his Rothmans cigarette still burning gently in the corner of his mouth.

Mad Jack the legend.

Our hard bastard.

• • • • •

I had a strong appreciation of the value of players such as Mad Jack, having once spent an extremely uncomfortable twenty minutes at senior provincial level in the cockpit of the scrum against Richard Loe, the eye-gouging All Black prop.

We were playing against Waikato in the mid-'80s, a team which boasted an All Black front row of Graham Purvis, Warren Gatland and Loe. Leading by a single score and with twenty minutes left to play, our hooker was sent off. Everybody refused to play in the front row, especially against Loe who was regarded as a bit of a thug.

I pulled the short straw and was thrust into the tighthead prop position. I had an extremely strong upper body and skinny little legs like a spider, but at least at tighthead I could push upwards rather than have to go down, which is terrifying.

I pleaded to Loe to take it easy on me. It was my first time in the cockpit, and I asked him to give me a break. But with Waikato down by a single score, he was in no mood. I hit the scrum and, as expected, he put the pressure on me: I bent upwards and outwards like a staple. Angered by his reaction we exchanged a few choice words, and a couple of digs, after the scrum broke up. Ever the generous man, Loe finally promised to give me a break – warning me that, at the next scrum, he'd, "break my bloody neck".

There was no such thing as an uncontested scrum in those days and, taking Loe at his word, I took it upon myself to kick the ball out every time there was a break in play. Our All Black scrum-half, Dean Kenny, wanted to run the ball, but I grabbed him and warned him, "If you don't kick the bloody ball out then you can go in the front row." There were no more scrums in the match.

It was my first, and last, time ever to play in the front row, but at least I can say I joined the exclusive front row brigade at provincial level. Are you listening Peter Clohessy?

●●●●●

Every now and again, we came up against an individual who not even a fighting-fit Otago forward could not contain. Steve 'Cumby' Cumberland was faced down by one such character when a group of us went for a couple of beers in a popular rugby bar called The Shoreline.

Cumby was a tough guy who once spent a season with Blackrock in Ireland.

He didn't distinguish himself as much as some of the Blackrock contingent would have liked. But to others, including Rock stalwart Bomber Browne – himself a tough hombre back in the day – and future Ireland coach, Eddie O'Sullivan, Cumby was a vital part of their promotion push to Division 1 of the All Ireland League (AIL), especially in Munster where Cumby relished the scrum. Every team needed a Cumby, a bit like every Munster team needed a Peter Clohessy.

So, while bars like The Shoreline were full of hard men, an Otago contingent that included Cumby, ex-All Black second-row Gordy Macpherson, and myself wasn't unduly nervous about having a couple of beers there. Gordy's girlfriend at the time, Nicky, was with us and, for some reason known only to the anonymous individual involved, Nicky was approached by a huge woman who attempted to burn her with a cigarette.

We quickly intervened and quietly dissuaded this 20-stone 'lady' from burning our friend. Finally, she left and we sat back on our stools to finish our beers.

From out of nowhere the woman suddenly reappeared.

Pow!

The unfortunate Cumby, who was mid-sup of his pint, was the first in her line of fire. This gigantic woman 'king-hit' poor old Cumby to the side of his head with a blow so ferocious that she fractured his jaw.

Then, like a great white shark appearing out of the depths to snaffle some unfortunate surfer and sink back beneath the waves, she was gone.

In her wake, she left chaos. It was bad enough that she left poor old Cumby with a broken jaw, but that was nothing compared to the stick he got from his teammates about being ambushed by a woman. As far as some of the lads were concerned, the whole thing was hilarious. But I was there and I can tell you, being sledgehammered on the blindside by a woman the size of The Bull Hayes was no joke. She was a monster.

We could have done with the help of another Otago prop that night, our Samoan teammate, Siu Fanolua, though it would have been a battle getting Siu into a pub in the first place. Immensely powerful, a lot of the Polynesian players are quite emotional, especially off the field where they can be shy.

Siu was a bit like that. Built like the proverbial brick shit-house, he was endearingly softly spoken and emotional at times, though a dangerous opponent if wound up during a game.

During one match against arch-rivals Canterbury, we faced a very strong front row which included All Blacks and prominent players. He was having a torrid time at the hands of his opposite number and, at the next scrum, he quietly turned to me for advice.

"Popey," intoned Siu in his broken English, "What Siu do?"

I looked this big, softly-spoken Samoan in the eye and gave him the only advice you gave any rugby player in those days.

"Smack the bastard at the next scrum, Siu."

"Ok, Popey."

The next scrum duly came around and, from my vantage point in the back row, I could see Siu's arm drop its bind, cock back like an old-style musket and, suddenly, BANG! Siu launched a punch to the heavens. I heard a thump, and then a groan as the unidentified player felt the wrath of Siu.

The ref blew the scrum up immediately and the two sides retired to their respective corners. Siu turned to me, a broad grin breaking across his now-sunny face.

"Siu do good, Popey?"

"Yes, Siu, you did good," I reassured him, for good measure patting him on his curly head of hair. "But next time, try to hit one of them and not your own bloody player!"

Somehow, in the mayhem of the scrum, when Siu unleashed his Samoan thunderbolt, he had swung right through the scrum and walloped his own hooker. The poor teammate was was left stunned and out for the count, wondering what the hell he'd ever done to Siu to deserve such a bludgeoning.

Playing with the Islanders was like that. They were fabulous people and great players with their own peculiar blend of religious, quiet outlook and murderous strength. Coming from sheltered Island lives, many are very religious and, until they start playing rugby can be quite naïve, especially when travelling overseas. Many of the Islanders don't travel much as they are very family-oriented home birds, who tend to get homesick very quickly. That stills holds true, even today, and many rugby teams understand that to get the best out of new signings from the Islands, they must already have some Island players who can help the newcomers assimilate and fit in. Years ago, gigantic Fijian prop Joeli Veitayaki arrived in Ulster. At an early season training session carried out on an unusually hot day, the Ulster lads turned up in shorts and singlets, but big Joeli arrived in fingerless gloves, leggings and a hat, wondering aloud about how he'd be able to handle the cold.

The Islanders march to a different drum. During one Tour in South America, we had a gun pulled on us after one of our Island teammates failed to realise that the money being thrown on the bar in front of him was for the woman dancing on it and not for him…

But, if many of the South Sea Islanders were on the quiet side, the same could not be said for most of us Kiwis. If my Samoan teammate in South America almost fell foul of gun law down there, at least he knew to stay in his seat at the bar.

It was a different story when I, along with my long-term teammates and future All Blacks, Arran Pene and Ant Strachan, ended up in a bar in Auckland after a game.

We were staying in a hotel in a suburb of Takapuna and, after the match, some Auckland lads brought us out to a local club attached to the hotel for an afterhours tipple.

In search of a beer, we overheard a commotion in the next room. The duty manager explained that US male stripping sensations, The Chippendales, were in there, performing their unique show to the delight of hundreds of screaming women.

Any gathering which involved hundreds of women warranted further investigation. Led by one of the Aucklanders with inside knowledge of the hotel, we followed a route through the kitchens which brought us out into the bar at the back of the room. Sure enough, arrayed before us was row upon row of excited ladies delighting at the sight of the oiled-up American beefcakes strutting their stuff.

Ant, whom I knew from university, was a mad party animal at the quietest of times who couldn't resist the opportunity to have a laugh. Unable to contain his own excitement, Ant hopped onto the bar behind these yelling, whooping females. With a body ripped from hours of training and body building, he liked nothing better than shedding his shirt and flexing his washboard stomach. Faced with a roomful of screaming beauties, and the prospect of taking on the greased-up Yanks at their own game, Ant couldn't resist.

True teammate that he was, Arran Pene was unwilling to allow Ant to go into battle alone and so he, too, scaled the bar counter and discarded his shirt. A huge man of Maori heritage, Arran weighed in at around 18 stone but, like Ant, boasted a ripped torso he was only too happy to show off.

So, there they were, dancing on the bar at the back of this roomful of female striptease-fans. With fewer, recognisable muscle groups, and less booze behind them, I opted to stay on the ground and watch the fun unfurl. Soon enough, bored with just dancing, Ant and Arran started into their own clumsy strip routine and, as they peeled off the layers, they began to catch the eye of some of the women at the back of the room as they returned from the toilets.

Word spread that The Chippendales were not the only act in town and, soon enough, Ant and Arran were the subject of many wolf-whistles and cat-calls – much to the embarrassment and annoyance of the American professionals.

Arran recovered his humility long enough to remember to be shy and climbed down from the bar but Ant, a natural showman, carried on into his full routine, flexing like a body-builder and responding to the increasing excitement. The girls loved him and he loved showing off.

The Chippendales finally had enough and complained to the management about the competition. Ant was 'persuaded' down from the counter by a couple of bouncers who, in deference to the dented pride of the professional strippers, tried to keep a straight face. They failed miserably.

Next morning over breakfast, there was talk among the hotel staff that the Americans had demanded compensation for the night before and were considering suing Ant for wrecking their show.

We made our excuses and left.

• • • • •

Arran Pene was a central figure in another escapade during a tour of South America, when we ran the gauntlet of Laurie Mains' infamous lock-downs. It was during the CANZ Tournament which involved matches against top, Canadian, New Zealand and Argentinian sides.

On this particular Tour, Arran, Stu Forster and Paul Cooke decided the lure of Buenos Aires' nightlife outweighed the risk of Laurie's punishment. They escaped the hotel, had a good night and were attempting an intoxicated re-entry when they were spotted by the ever-vigilant Mains. Lemons called an emergency meeting next morning with Otago captain, Richard Knight. Thinking on his feet, Dick informed Mains that the players were so jetlagged they couldn't sleep so went for a short walk to get some fresh air. To this day, I'm not sure Mains believed the cock-and-bull story, but no further action was taken. The lads were lucky – if Mains had decided they were all telling him lies, he would have sent them all home, without question. He was ruthless that way.

At least, he was usually ruthless.

There was one player who had an even luckier escape from Laurie's wrath – me. I've ridden my luck many times in my career but my most outrageous piece of good fortune came the night before an important National Championship game against Waikato in Hamilton.

I was rooming with Arran Pene, soon to be an All Black No. 8. Next door, sleeping, as he did twenty-three hours a day, was Otago flanker and All Black Paul 'Ginge' Henderson. The two rooms had an adjoining door and we'd be in and out of each other's rooms all the time, having a bit of fun and exchanging banter.

After dinner, the players were sent to their rooms. This was classic Laurie – no one was allowed to mess around. Some played cards while others watched movies, but I always went down to our team masseur, Donny Cameron, to have my hamstrings rubbed. They'd tear if I moved too quickly without warming up, earning me the nickname – one of many – 'Ping Pope'. They were so tight that I struggled to cross the road quickly enough if a truck or a car unexpectedly came around the corner.

After the ritual rub, I headed back to my room where Arran was stretched out on the bed watching the telly. I was covered in massage oil so opted to take a hot bath which would serve the dual purpose of removing the liniment and further relaxing my leg muscles.

Stripped down and wearing only a towel, as I passed the door adjoining our room and Ginge's, I gave it a good old rattle and roared at Ginge to open the door urgently.

No answer.

So I banged it harder and shouted louder.

This time Ginge heard me.

As he swung open the door, I turned my back to the door, dropped my towel, and in a single fluid movement, bent over and slapped my buttocks, demanding loudly: "Well, what do you think of that?"

No reaction.

Silence.

That was unlike Ginge, so I opened my eyes and peered back through my legs. There, staring back at me with a mix of shock and fury was Mains who, unbeknownst to me, had swapped rooms with Ginge earlier that evening after the flanker complained he couldn't sleep with all the noise outside. As lazy as he was, Ginge had neglected to inform us of the move.

Without a word, not even a smirk, Mains slammed the door shut. And I mean slammed.

Arran dissolved into gales of laughter. He was the reserve No. 8 and, after watching one of Otago's starting forwards baring more than his soul to Mains, Arran figured he must be a sure thing to start the next day's game.

Mortified, I went to bed with a pillow over my head. I was convinced Laurie would bench me. I couldn't even offer an apology: I'd deliberately bared my arse to my provincial coach from a distance of about two feet. How exactly do you apologise for that kind of thing?

As things turned out, Laurie didn't drop me and, fearing for my rugby life, I played a stormer, earning the Man of the Match accolade.

Why he didn't drop me was a mystery which went unsolved for many years. The incident was never mentioned. Then, unexpectedly, five years later, Laurie finally came clean about his reaction that night. It seemed that, after slamming the door, Lemons had turned around and cracked up laughing.

*Brent played in my Otago team for six or seven years,
and became one of the very best No. 8s in New Zealand.
He was equally dynamic at open or blindside flank, such
was the arsenal of skills he possessed. A fast, powerful
carrier of the ball made him a prolific try scorer for
Otago. His combination with All Blacks, Mike Brewer
and Paul Henderson, gave Otago the equal of the great
Auckland loose trio of Michael Jones, Zinzan Brooke
and Alan Whetton. But for the presence of Buck Shelford
and Zinzan Brooke, I am sure Brent would have been
a good All Black. In 1987, Brent was a member of the
South Island team I coached as part of the World Cup
All Black trials. Brent was the forward star of that All
Black trial match only to dislocate his elbow in the
final seconds of the game. The then-All Black World
Cup coach, Brian Lochore, was impressed enough to
comment to me on the strength of Brent's game that day.
That was Brent's All Black opportunity lost, as Zinzan
made the team and went on to be Buck Shelford's
understudy. A great team man who always gave
100 per cent. He knew no other way.*

Laurie Mains
Otago Rugby Coach.
South Island and All Black World Cup Coach, 1995.

8

All Black and Blue

"Aaargh! Jesus, doc, that's bloody sore, are you sure it's supposed to hurt that much?"

"Relax, son. You'll be all right. Now, lie down and I'll do that again," said the guy in the green scrubs.

I lay back on the treatment table and waited for the next electrical current to shoot through my leg.

"Aaargh!"

My hamstring felt as though it was being prodded with red-hot pokers. I wanted to be fit again but, at this rate, the cure was going to prove worse than the malady.

The principle was that an electrical current would be passed through your leg which would break down scar tissue that may have been forming. They would put wet pads in four different locations on your leg, wire you up and let rip with a constant electrical current. At one stage, when he upped the voltage, my leg was twitching so much I could hardly lie straight on the bed, and blisters the size of golf balls began to form under the pads.

"Seriously, though? This can't be right."

"You're fine, Mr Pope, you're fine," he replied, checking his handiwork, "that should do it."

Otago had just played a game against one of the lesser-known Third Division provinces in some rural outpost on the North Island. I'd ripped another hamstring and the opposition team manager had sent me to their team doctor in his local one-horse town so that I could receive treatment straight after the match. But the pain of the tear was nothing to the pain after the electrical current treatment: my leg was in bits, red raw and covered in blisters.

I asked one of the opposition players about their team doctor. "Geez, that team doctor of yours is a bit rough," I said, pointing to my red, blistered leg.

"Doctor?" he laughed, "He's not a doctor, he's the local vet."

Now, I'm a big enough guy and, in my rugby days, I was a bit of a beast on the field, but even I felt the agony when this vet treating my hamstring injury forgot to turn down the power level on the electrical current machine which had been left on the 'race-horse' treatment mode.

The resulting experience was, excuse the pun, shocking.

It might seem strange in the more genteel European civilisations that a top sportsman should be treated by a vet, but such was the way of the Kiwi rugby player back in my day. No cold baths or trips to high-tech refrigeration units in Poland, just patch him up and get him back on the park. Pronto.

At best, injuries were thought of as a mild eccentricity. If you were unlucky enough to get one, then you were honour-bound to walk, run or play it off. If it was more serious, then in the early days you were given a bag of frozen peas to hold against the problem, told to rest for a couple of days and then just "guts it out". When you got to the upper level of New Zealand rugby, of course, you had the usual team physios and decent medical care, especially in Dunedin with the Otago medical school based there. But if you played in some remote rural outpost the team manager was also the bus driver, cook and medic all rolled into one. The magic water sponge was as good as anything. I spent half my rugby career in various A&E departments, and the nurses understandably hated us. Who could blame them? Waiting rooms full of smelly rugby players, bleeding, broken up and impatient. The stock answer for any break was to slap you in a cast for six weeks or until you saw a specialist – most times I foolishly took the cast off after about two so that I could play. Once I even got an engineer friend of mine to fabricate a metal plate so that I could cover a bad break on my wrist. It was just what you did, you took crazy risks with your body and, unfortunately, later in life a lot of my generation is paying the price for their ignorance, and that includes me.

There was a lack of knowledge about injuries and that went hand in hand with an uneducated approach to training among players. Like everyone else, I was obsessed with pumping iron. These were the days before anyone realised how much damage an over-emphasis on weights training can cause. We didn't give our long-term health a second thought: more weights meant bigger chests, shoulders and arms and that, in turn, meant we looked better to girls at the beach and on the field. In fact, so focused were we on what kind of a dash we cut in the surf, that they were commonly known as 'beach weights'. Big Chest, big guns, no legs – I was the walking definition of a beach weights trainer. I hated leg weights and could see no point in doing them, especially as I blew a knee out during one of my few experiences of deep squatting.

The daily sessions usually involved rushing to the gym at 6am, or after work. Then, without any adequate stretching or warm-up, we'd get stuck in to the bench press, above the shoulder press, pec-deck and bicep curls. The end result had both short-term and long-term consequences. In the short term, you ended up with a massive chest that Pamela Anderson would have been proud of but, in the long term, you ran the risk of serious injury.

We never knew how to balance our workouts and our bodies by, for example, spending as much time on the back muscles as the front.

And anyway, who cared? Ours was the macho approach to doing weights. It was all about size and intimidation and, even then, there were guys that I am certain took steroids to achieve the look they felt they needed. One player I knew, who always struggled to gain weight, spent an off-season in Italy and gained about 10 kilos of muscle. He said it was due to the pasta, but when he returned home he just started fading away. I didn't do enough upper-back work so, when I retired, my chest was still big but my back muscles were relatively weak. So much weaker in fact that, decades later, I still have painful ligament damage where my pectoral (chest) muscles attach to the shoulder ligaments. There was simply no symmetry to my shape. Today, I can last about three weeks' training before my chest gets so painful at these same attachments that I can hardly hold a pencil for a few days. I've spent twenty years trying to undo the damage of foolish, macho, misinformed training routines.

But I wasn't alone.

Some hookers actually got so muscle-bound they could no longer throw the ball in – they didn't have the flexibility any more. These days, people claim that the modern game is more physical, and that may be true, but many players of my generation paid a higher price with their bodies precisely because they attempted to train like professionals in an amateur environment. I personally know hundreds of retired players who can barely walk without pain, who have deep scar tissue and injuries that will never heal. Players broke teeth because they played without mouth guards and were repeatedly concussed with head injuries because they didn't wear head guards.

Granted, the hits are much harder now, but players today are at least on the same wavelength as each other: They train properly and, most importantly, they have great medical and nutritional advice. The IRFU's player management procedure – something that the English and French do not have – that allows players rest and recuperation time is a great leap forward. It's vital that modern players who put their bodies on the line, week in and week out, get some time out. Still, in a packed season and the modern 'bang-for-bucks' game, affording players' bodies time to recuperate is becoming increasingly difficult to achieve. As a result, a player's lifespan at the elite level is getting shorter and shorter. The new, professional game is a hell of a way for a player to make a decent life for himself and his family, but he should never – and I mean, never – risk himself by repeatedly playing through injuries. Your health is your wealth.

But, back then, we all played through the pain barrier, again and again and again. Even at university level, we were never really told to take time out to recover from injury nor taught how to train correctly. Everybody did their own thing. Some guys didn't prepare at all while others trained on their farms employing methods that would be frowned upon today.

But we all learnt the hard way.

In late 1986, while playing for Otago, I was preparing for my assault on the All Black's World Cup squad. The first-ever World Cup was due to be played on

New Zealand soil in early 1987, and I was determined to leave no stone unturned in my bid to be part of it. I developed my own training regime that would, I was convinced, leave me fitter and in better shape than any other player in Otago or New Zealand. In the end, I achieved the first goal and became fitter than any of my teammates in Otago, or my rivals, for that coveted silver fern. But, as I would soon discover, fitness isn't the only thing of crucial importance when it comes to training.

• • • • •

Each year, the New Zealand Rugby Annual, a book covering all things rugby, was published. A key part of the content was coverage of all the provinces that year, starting with the top Division 1 sides and working downwards from there. The Annual would name the province's Most Promising Player, its Most Improved Player and, finally, the province's Most Outstanding Player.

In my first three years in Otago rugby, I was voted as the province's Most Promising Player, Most Improved Player and, finally, in 1987 and 1988, Otago's Most Outstanding Player alongside powerful winger, Noel Picher.

I had been touted as a potential All Black, and was even talked up as a consideration for the All Black tour to France in 1985, with the media running stories about how impressed the national set-up, and one influential selector in particular, was with my abilities and talent.

To be named Otago's Most Outstanding Player from one of New Zealand's elite rugby provinces steeped in history and tradition was no mean feat for a kid from Ashburton. Moreover, I'd won the honour in the face of stiff competition from future All Black legends like Greg Cooper, Arthur Stone, Dean Kenny, Gordy Macpherson, Paul Henderson and Mike Brewer, to name but a few.

But the World Cup was all I could think about in 1987. Getting to perform the Haka in front of the world was more than a goal, it was the only dream I had. I lived and breathed for a chance to play in, and win, that inaugural tournament with the All Blacks.

Back then, the All Blacks seemed untouchable. Though New Zealand was amateur in principle – some players seemed to be able to go to the likes of Italy in those days and make a pretty good living – it was the most professional set-up in the world, it was by far the most advanced nation in terms of its training methods and fitness levels. When they eventually won that first World Cup, it was by such a large margin over the other countries that, in my opinion, they deserve to be considered the best team ever to compete in the competition.

The '87 All Black team was simply unparalleled.

Most of its World Cup stars hailed from Auckland, and were part of a squad that was possibly the strongest provincial team ever assembled, anywhere in the world. Auckland was so strong that world-ranked players like future Samoa and All Blacks stars, Pat Lam and Frank Bunce, couldn't even make it into the starting side. The Auckland contribution to the All Black team which defeated France in the '87 final was so overwhelming that only a handful of players from other provinces were able to claim a place. Only full-back, John Gallagher, backs Warwick Taylor and Craig Green, and second row, Murray Pierce, weren't Aucklanders, or hadn't played for Auckland. Instead, the national side was dominated by Aucklanders of the stature and talent of John Kirwan, Michael Jones, Grant Fox, David Kirk, Zinzan Brooke, The Whetton twins Gary and Alan, Steve McDowell and Sean Fitzpatrick.

So, in early '87, the mountain I had to climb in order to break into the All Blacks was immense. I'd played at openside flanker for a couple of seasons for Otago, and had established myself as first choice in that position. Then, late in 1986, a rumour began to circulate that All Black U-21 flanker, Paul 'Ginge' Henderson, was looking to make his way up to Otago from his province, Southland. The story went that Ginge was priming himself to make a run at the World Cup squad and needed the exposure that Otago – a top First Division team and one of the top three provinces in the country – could give him.

I didn't know what was in Ginge's mind and I wasn't about to ask him. I had only one goal: I wanted to break into the World Cup squad myself and the first step towards that was nailing down the No. 7 shirt at Otago. Ginge was a great player and a good guy, but he could sod off back to wherever he came from, if he thought he was going to use me as a doormat to greater things.

I decided to make it impossible for him to take my position, so, in the summer of 1986, I trained like a madman, determined to be the fittest I had ever been.

Each day, before I began work as a property valuer, I trained relentlessly like a triathlete, traversing the steep hills around Dunedin, swimming in the Moana

I loved to run with the ball. Here, I'm in action in the 1983 DCL Cup final for Lincoln College in the Canterbury senior club competition.

The original O'Brien clan from County Limerick: my mother's side of her proud Irish ancestry.

Goodfellas: My dad (far left) with some of his friends in Christchurch Square.

My father, Mick, during his days as a flying winger for St Bede's 1st XV. Note the nose guard on the defender!

Left, Dad as a Canterbury 100m sprint champion, and a New Zealand long jump champion. Right, A family photo.

Top and bottom left, 1962 — Bouncing Baby Brent's year in nappies and bath-time for the Pope boys! Meanwhile, bottom right, my gorgeous God-daughter Hannah Cooper, daughter of former All Black full-back, Otago teammate, and long-time friend, Greg Cooper.

And I still believe! With Mark and Father Christmas, Christchurch, New Zealand.

My brother, Mark, on the bay, Tantrum, and me on the grey at the Ashburton horse show. Tantrum was eventually crowned District Champion.

Top, my mother, Helen, winning the local, Ashburton Sportsperson of the Year Award, in 2011, for her years of loyal dedication to New Zealand horse racing, and, bottom, my dad accepting the Queen's Medal for his community work.

Top, a family portrait at our Ashburton home and, bottom left, Mark (24) and I (23) pose together. Meanwhile, bottom right, Dad and Mark visit me in Templeogue, Dublin to mark Christmas, 1992.

Top, first taste of the big time as a Representative or provincial player and a flying centre for Mid Canterbury junior school team, while, bottom, I'm second from right in the front row of the Ashburton Rep Team of 1974.

Top, equestrian rider, rugby player and a promising leg-spin bowler? I'm second from front left in the 1977 County Rep cricket team. Below, I'm in the middle of the second row in the 1979, Mid Canterbury U-18 Rep Team.

The infamous Pig Pen at Otago University, and Dozen Day, when students had to consume a dozen big bottles of beer at twelve different student digs. Ours was the last stop because it was the messiest and, at any given time, had at least eight people living in it.

Surf's up dude! Hitting the waves in Papamoa Beach in the North Island with friends, Richard Taylor and Lou Green.

Top, in Wanaka, Queenstown with another of my beloved Volkswagen Beetles: I would eventually own three of these great little bugs. Whitewater rafting, below right, in Queenstown, where I spent a wonderful summer working as a commercial property valuer and, bottom left, enjoying some summer fun with my good friend, Gerard Prendergast, on our annual beach holidays to the North Island.

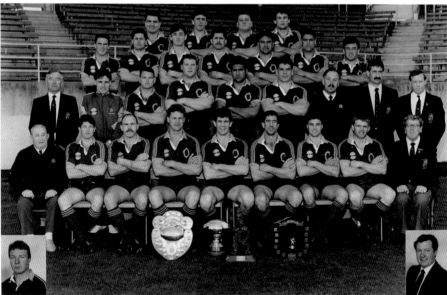

Top, I'm in the middle of the third row of the New Zealand RFU, South Island Team in the build-up to the 1987 World Cup while, below, I'm first on the left in the back row of the Otago team which were crowned Division 1 champions in 1991.

Top, playing for Otago Uni while, bottom and inset, I spent almost a decade playing in mud and bandages for the great Laurie Mains, who we affectionately knew as 'Funeral Face' or 'Lemons'.

The International Warblers Sevens team in Bahrain, for the Dubai Sevens, in 1987. All Blacks and friends Gordy MacPherson, Matt and Greg Cooper, Murray Mexted, and Aussie Internationals Greg Martin (now a commentator with Sky TV) and Dirk Williams (later a physio with Conor O'Shea and London Irish).

At the annual sports awards (1988-'89), where the Otago rugby team was nominated for Sports Team of the Year. Pictured with then New Zealand Prime Minister, the Hon. Jim Bolger. Three of us, Mike Brewer, Dick Knight and I would go on to play in Ireland in later years.

Top, celebrating my 50th Otago cap in Argentina – Egyptian-style – with Otago All Blacks John Timu, Arran Pene, Ginge Henderson, and Munster's Rhys Ellison. Meanwhile, below, a typical after-game kangaroo court session during a tour, this one ending in a massive drunken food fight.

Playing Representative rugby for Mid Canterbury U-18s at the South Island Regional Tournament, aged 16. Inset, old cabbage-head himself: a self-portrait for an award-winning article entitled, 'Pope's Passions', written by journalist, Brent Edwards, about my children's books.

pool, and running up and down the gruelling steps around the university, like a Kiwi Rocky Balboa.

I ran a six-mile course through hills overlooking the St Clair beach and around the golf course. Then, at lunchtime, I headed for the beach to complete a series of 4x4 sprints, sprinting repeated lengths of the field as many times as I could. Each day, I would increase the speed by shortening the distance and cutting out the rest time. After that, I hit the surf at St Clair for a swim. In addition, I would alternate daily workouts between the gym and the swimming pool. That was my routine, seven days a week.

The punishing regime worked. I became fitter than at any time in my career and, as far as I was concerned, I was on track for that shot at the All Blacks.

There were a few setbacks. The Otago team doctor, Wayne Morris, put an unexpected bout of illness down to over-training but I ignored him, viewing my getting sick as nothing more than a speed bump. Wayne wasn't convinced and warned me that the excessive training was running down my body – I wasn't giving it time to recover and, as a result, I was picking up more and more infections.

But I kept training.

My plan was working. I nailed down my Otago position against all challengers and finally, just after Christmas '86, I was included in an enlarged All Black World Cup training squad. The group had been set up by the NZRFU to assess potential All Blacks in different parts of the country, and one of its first jobs was to carry out fitness tests on the candidates. A key part of the test was a mini-circuit of weights where individuals had to do as many repetitions as possible of a particular weight, until exhaustion set in.

My favourite piece of equipment was the pec-deck machine, a supposed measure of upper body strength. The machine is familiar to most gym-users: it's loaded with weights and the user has to bring their two arms together in a motion that increases the chest muscles. I loved the machine and so, when the big day came around, I climbed into it feeling pretty strong. The machine was set at the same weight for everyone, so I just sat down and started pumping. I was enjoying it so much that, when the assessor told me to stop at 100 reps, I was disappointed. I felt strong enough to go another 100. What made me feel even better was the guy behind me – an out-half from another province – couldn't budge a single one.

But, if I was blessed with the chest of a young bull, I was cursed with those damned legs of a chicken. It wasn't as though I didn't exercise them, I loved to run and back then I could think of no better way to spend a lovely Dunedin summer's day than by running through the nearby soft, grassy hills before finally plunging into the ice cold surf at the beach. And I was good at running, I was pretty fast for a big man, I guess I inherited my dad's speed. I ran 1500 metres competitively and competed in the South Island, and later New Zealand schools, cross-country trials.

But, for reasons beyond me at the time, running failed to increase my leg power. In fact, I was hopeless in that department. My fast twitch fibres made me quick enough, but the rest of my legs suffered from underdevelopment and skinniness. I was built like a carrot – if someone had hit me with a mallet, I'd have disappeared a foot into the ground. I was all chest and no legs.

In the midst of a hard-hitting game, opponents would yell out, "get chicken legs," which doesn't do much for a would-be hard man's sense of self, to say nothing of the effect on my ability to intimidate rival players. It wasn't all negative. At university, my teammates told me I was the proud owner of a pair of "lucky legs" – as in, I was lucky they didn't break and go up my arse.

In that All Black World Cup assessment, I was told that I was second in the country, in my weight category, for upper body strength, trailing only to the Herculean All Black prop, Steve McDowell. The same assessor went on to tell me that I was second to last for leg power. Apparently, I had the same leg strength as All Black and Auckland star, Terry Wright. That doesn't sound too bad until you consider that Terry was a winger, built like a greyhound and weighing in at no more than 12 stone, dripping wet. From a back row's point of view, Terry was not good company to be keeping.

Still, even allowing for the scrawny pair of twigs hanging out of my shorts, I was in the best shape of my life. In the Otago preseason fitness tests, which consisted of twelve-minute tests, and bleep tests, I was laps ahead of most of the other players.

At the beginning of that World Cup year, I had set out with a single purpose in mind and, finally, I was ready. I was in the best shape of my life.

In April, Otago played a preseason game in Central Otago against a Barbarian's selection. The opposition included many players who went on to make the World Cup team but, from my point of view, the most interesting inclusion was that of Ginge Henderson, the well-respected schoolboy star who coveted my position. I needed a big performance and I delivered. In a fantastic game I scored two tries and set up a third. I was everywhere on the park, so fit that I was at every breakdown quicker than anybody. I played the game of my life.

A few years later, I found myself reminiscing about that game with Ginge. Life has a funny way of working out and, despite my best efforts that day, Ginge eventually came to Otago anyway. Not only that, but he went on to captain the All Blacks in some of the less crucial games in the 1995 World Cup. But more important – to me, at least – than becoming an All Black legend, Ginge became a great friend. And, as we talked over a pint, he confided that, based on my performance in that Otago v Barbarians game, he seriously considered packing in his attempts to get to Otago, thinking he could never replace me. Moreover, in one of the most generous compliments I've ever received, this All Black great named me in a rugby magazine article as his hardest ever opponent. Coming from one of the most underrated players I ever competed with, that was praise indeed.

But there were other crucial consequences of that match. Among the spectators at the Central Otago ground, not far from Queenstown, were two World Cup selectors: assistant All Black coach, Alex 'Grizz' Wyllie, and All Black coach, Brian Lochore. Within a few hours of the final whistle, my name was being carried in all the tabloids. My match performance was singled out and there was much speculation that I was a 'must' for the upcoming, first All Black trial match.

I was ecstatic.

I was on my way to fulfilling my boyhood dream of becoming an All Black. Better still, I was on the cusp of making a team that was about to play, on home soil, the first ever World Cup. Within a week, the All Black selectors had trimmed the initial fitness training squads to the All Black trial nominations. My name was there, alongside current All Black legends like Murray Mexted, Mark 'Cowboy' Shaw, the late Jock Hobbs, Alan Whetton and Buck Shelford as well as a promising young Auckland boy who had just burst on to the scene, Michael Jones. Every player wanted to be involved and the initial list for flankers seemed to go on and on. I felt I had a chance but, given the calibre of flankers listed – current All

Blacks, ex-All Blacks, All Black U-21s – it was clearly the most competitive area.

A couple of weeks later, the first official All Black trial team was announced. I'd made it, and my first opponent would be Michael Jones. I struggled to take it in. Sure, I'd played for my country at underage level, and was a key player in one of New Zealand's elite rugby provinces, but I couldn't believe that I'd finally won a great chance to be included in New Zealand's first-ever World Cup challenge. To be involved in the World Cup preparations was an honour almost beyond my imagination.

Almost immediately, the hype began to kick in. Along with everyone else, I received all the Steinlager promotional gear. I'd never received this kind of attention before. All I'd ever been given for representing Otago was a kit bag, a pair of runners and, if you were lucky, your sponsored Number 1s – shirt, tie and trousers – though, even then, you might sometimes be asked to pay some sort of contribution.

The 1987 World Cup was scheduled to be played in what was effectively New Zealand's off-season. So, to ensure match fitness, the All Black coaches arranged a series of challenge games. Teams like Ireland, France and the other Five Nations squads were just coming out of their season and would be match-fit and battle-hardened while, Down Under, our guys would be just returning after their summer holidays and bound to be overweight and out of shape.

The All Black coaches brought in Jim Blair, a revolutionary fitness coach from Auckland, in a bid to get the players fit. Jim had developed a concept he termed 'grid training'. Rather than just running laps or bleep tests, players trained in small grids using various skill and ball drills. His training techniques were destined to become famous as teams from around the world adopted them. Sports like GAA and soccer eventually followed suit and, even today, Blair's grid training remains a popular way to build both fitness and skill work.

Other efforts to get the team into peak physical condition included an official All Black trial, followed by a series of games in which teams competed for the George Nepia Trophy. Named after a famous All Black, the contest basically featured the nation's best players squaring off in a triangular tournament. Broken down into, more or less, South Island v North Island matches, these games were All Black trials in all but name. Auckland, Waikato and Wellington, helped out by a few players from lesser-known provinces like Taranaki, made up the bulk of the North Island selections. The South Island team was predominantly from top First Division heavyweights, Canterbury and Otago.

I was named at openside flanker for the first All Black trial and I squared off against the relatively unknown, Michael 'Iceman' Jones. I didn't know much about this rising new star. He'd played a few times for Auckland and had just come back from a world tour with the New Zealand Barbarians where he had impressed none other than All Black selector, John Hart. He gained the nickname 'Iceman' or 'Ice' because he was ice-cool as if ice flowed through his veins. The newspapers duly noted that, "The All Black trial will be made more interesting for the battle to the loose ball by two of New Zealand's outstanding young openside flankers, Otago's Brent Pope and Auckland's Michael Jones, both excellent prospects for the World Cup."

So, I travelled to Auckland under the guidance of Alex Wyllie, who was coaching South Island. It was an awesome experience... I was about to get the chance to play with the All Blacks that I had respected from afar. I was ready for my shot. I was fit and, more importantly, I knew that I was fit which worked wonders for my confidence. Better still, I was playing alongside my Otago teammate, scrum-half Dean Kenny, himself an All Black. That would give me an advantage as Dean understood my main strength as a player was carrying the ball. He was sure to use that knowledge to my, and the South Island's, advantage, which meant I'd get a chance to show how much damage a 'reverse hovercraft' could do to a rival team, and to Michael Jones.

It felt as though the planets were beginning to align for me. After so much time, effort and dedication to my chosen sport, I was about to get the perfect opportunity to grab hold of my dream.

A couple of days before the trial, Alex Wyllie put us through our paces in a final Captain's Run. Wyllie was a tough taskmaster and he called a series of set scrums. I was advised by some of the Canterbury players to put every inch of strength into the scrums, so I did. Not only did I put my back into it but, following one scrum, I burst off to follow the backline in a mock attack.

Whack!

I felt a sudden, sharp pain in the back of my leg.

My hamstring had torn like a broken rubber band.

Dean Kenny had heard it snap.

I collapsed in a heap, unable to run.

I got back up, determined to carry on.

Wyllie was a hard man and my job, first and foremost, was to impress him. Past injuries had never stopped me, I'd always just played through any pain barrier. It simply wasn't in the job description to show weakness. Or fear.

But this was something new, something I'd never encountered before.

Suddenly, I had no power. The pain didn't concern me. After all, I'd played most of my rugby in some sort of pain.

But this … this was different. I felt as if I was literally, well, hamstrung. Whatever that means metaphorically, in reality it meant I was rendered virtually immobile.

After the game, I didn't panic. Instead I tried everything I knew to get it right. I iced the leg every hour for forty-eight hours, trying to get it right for that first All Black trial. But my efforts were futile and, eventually, I grew to realise it.

I was forced to pull out of my very first All Black trial match.

In the beginning, I was too stunned to be heartbroken, but I got over the shock soon enough. Another friend, Paul 'Butch' Renton, was called in from Hawke's Bay as my replacement. He played a stormer. In fact, he was so good he outplayed Jones and received the Man of the Match award, though Iceman's below-par performance would later be attributed to jetlag. Despite his outstanding performance, Butch didn't feature again after that game. Clearly, he wasn't in the selectors' minds which, to be fair to Butch, made a bit of a mockery of the system in the first place.

But, however bad I felt for Renton, I was disconsolate for myself. I was shattered. My grip was beginning to loosen on the All Black dream.

Still, there were more trials in the coming months and my focus switched to getting ready for those. I had two weeks before the first game and I was prepared to do anything, go anywhere and talk to anyone, if I thought it would help me get onto that pitch.

That included seeing a physio who had a unique way of treating new hamstring tears. He told his patients, including me, not to ice the leg: he would repair the tear by massaging the scar tissue out.

What ensued was one of the most painful experiences of my life.

I lay on the carpet in his house and he warmed the area with a fan heater before setting about me. He used his elbows, hands and knees to bleed the tear out. My leg came out in a massive black bruise and, Christ, it was painful. I was virtually in tears crawling along the floor as he sat on my leg trying to push the tear out.

Don't try this at home.

In the run-up to the second trial, my leg was purposely strapped so heavily that it couldn't hyper-extend. The selectors thought enough of me to name me in the South Island team which, once again, was mostly made up of Canterbury players. In the 1980s, the two great provincial teams of New Zealand rugby were Auckland (North Island) and Canterbury (South Island). Under the guidance of Laurie Mains my own province, Otago, was climbing up the pecking order but, back then, we were still lagging behind these two giants. So, to again be named in the trial side was a further honour for me. Moreover, the game was to be played in my hometown of Ashburton, so Mum, Dad, friends and family would be there to watch me.

North Island had a back row of Buck Shelford, Michael Jones and Alan Whetton – a line-up that, in time, would become the All Black's World Cup-winning back row. But in the second trial I was switched to No. 8 and, despite the hamstring injury, played well enough to receive great reviews in the newspapers. Regardless of losing to North Island I had the consolation of being named amongst South Island's best forwards. The selectors intimated to me that they were very happy with my performance and one source close to them confided that they were looking for a player who could cover all three positions in the back row. I was a perfect fit for such a role: quick enough to play at openside, big and strong enough in the upper body to play No. 8, and was an option at blindside flanker, though I was always going to struggle as a lineout jumper against players three or four inches taller than me.

In the third trial, South Zone v Central Zone, one of the last games before the All Black squad was announced, I was switched to No. 6. As a specialist openside flanker, I knew they would only take two players and Michael Jones had one of those spots sewn up. From what I was told, the second No. 7 spot would probably be between myself and Auckland's Mark Brooke-Cowden. But there was a further complication: Michael Jones could not play on a Sunday due to his religious beliefs. He was once asked how he could reconcile his Christian morals with his infamous tough tackling. Speaking biblically, Iceman replied caustically, "It's better to give than to receive."

While I admired Michael's religious principles, I was more concerned with the added advantage it gave me. I now had a chance of being named at No. 7 or, better still, being named as a utility forward, given my ability to move between all three back row positions. I thought I was perfectly placed to make the World Cup squad, and so did the media.

There was one other player out there, but he wasn't in the shake-up at the trial games. Zinzan 'Valentine' Brooke was playing for Auckland in the South Africa Series as the rest of us strove for All Black honours. The All Blacks' other assistant coach, John Hart, was in charge of Auckland and knew enough of the youngster to rate him highly. But Zinzan was far from my thoughts as we went into the final George Nepia game.

I was to mark one of New Zealand's greatest hard men – blindside flanker, Mark Cowboy Shaw. Shaw was a veteran All Black but, despite his brilliance, his way of playing the game may have been considered slightly out of vogue by 1987. The All Black selectors wanted to play a new style of rugby, and players like Shaw found themselves on the outside. Shaw had been a tough enforcer who, in later years, had taken young All Blacks under his wing on various tours. He showed them the ropes and protected them in the far-flung, and unwelcoming, fields of France and Argentina. He was the kind of tough guy whose very presence made teammates better players – a role filled for Ireland by men like Mick Galwey and Paul O'Connell.

It must have been tough for great players like Cowboy to realise that, after years of service to their nation, they weren't going to make it to the World Cup stage.

Still, veteran that he might have been, Shaw was a tough man and he obviously felt threatened by some new upstart from the 'Deep South'. He introduced himself at an early lineout by connecting my chin to a haymaker punch that left me needing stitches. I'd committed the heinous crime of stealing a lineout throw from him. But, while the move represented a rare success for my chicken legs in the lineout, it also embarrassed Shaw. In his eyes, I'd got the better of him and that, simply, could not continue. So, the Cowboy connected me to an almighty punch that sent my head spinning and my legs buckling.

But, despite the groggy head and the battle with Cowboy, I was still having a great game and, as the game headed into its final minutes, I finally began to relax and feel confident about my chances of making that All Black squad.

The effort, hardships and sacrifices of the last year, and all the accumulated effort of previous years were, hopefully, about to pay off. Even the trauma of the hamstring tear in that first trial was wearing off. It had been a long, tough year but I knew that, before you get something out, you have to put something in. In the last twelve months of training, I'd put plenty in … now I was due to win the biggest prize of all.

I refocused, and stopped my mind straying.

We were on the attack but the clock had run down, and now all that remained was for the ball to go out of play.

Then it'd be game over.

All I'd have to do was wait. It'd be a matter of keeping my fingers crossed for maybe only a week, and I'd be named in the World Cup squad.

The pinnacle of my career…

Focus, Popey, focus.

I had the ball in hand. *Go for the line? Score the try?*

Why not?

Ball carrying was the reason I was here. It was what I was best at.

This would be the last play of the day, so I drove for the line, just inches away.

As I did so, the radio announcer in the stand was already preparing to inform his listeners that Brent Pope was the official Man of the Match.

And then…

Silence.

And then…

Searing pain. Actually, for a moment, I couldn't feel anything. For a fraction of a second I could see the pain before I felt it – white and so bright it blinded me.

Then I felt it.

The pain was indescribable, so overwhelming that I didn't hear the referee's whistle immediately stopping the game. Darkness flooded my vision and I began to black out, only for the pain to bring me back round again.

It was so excruciating that I was unaware of the twenty-nine other potential All Blacks trotting off the pitch as I was stretchered from the ground to a waiting ambulance. Every bump and lurch on that hellish drive to the hospital caused me to lose consciousness again, though even the black outs failed to mitigate the searing, screaming pain.

Worse even than the physical hurt, however, was the anguish of seeing my broken, useless arm dangling at my side. In the Accident and Emergency department, a careless hospital porter whacked my stricken arm against the elevator door.

The indescribable hurt only left me when I was given morphine.

As relief flooded over me, the doctors kept talking to me ... at me ... around me... They'd never seen a dislocation like it... They'd have to consult a surgeon in Auckland... The dislocation was so severe that if they couldn't get it back in place, I could lose the use of it altogether.

It was hard to take it all in but, gradually, I began to focus. I was lying in a hospital bed on morphine and my arm... What about my arm?

Slowly, I began to piece together those last few moments of the trial.

In that final play of the day I was driving for the line with my arm stretched straight out. Unfortunately, I was near the goalpost and my straightened arm was caught right in front of it. Unaware of my precarious position, but determined to get me over the line for that precious try, my South Island teammate and All Black, Andy Earl, dived in to add his considerable 17 stone to the cause.

But he dived straight on my arm. The limb was straight out against the goalpost in front of me and had nowhere to go so, as Andy landed on it, the limb gave way at its weakest point. The elbow dislocated, not to the side as it normally would, but with the back coming completely off the ball and socket joint. It fractured and compounded out the back of my arm in a freak injury that my doctors later admitted they'd only ever seen once before, when a hang-glider tried to save himself from hitting a cliff face by reaching his arm out.

My elbow was shattered, my arm broken in a number of places. I've always had a high threshold for pain. I've had a lot of injuries in my career and I've played through most of them. But I've never experienced pain like I did that day. Because of the all nerve endings at that point in your body, the elbow is one of the most sensitive areas of the human body – even getting a tap on your 'funny bone' can hurt. Anyone who has dislocated an elbow or shoulder, which cannot be immediately put back, knows that the pain is excruciating. Due to the severe nature of my elbow's dislocation, medics at the game were unable to manipulate it back into place, so they brought me to hospital and pumped me full of drugs.

And, as I lay there in the arms of sweet, sweet Morpheus, the doctors tugged, operated, cut, tore, broke, pinned, stitched and finally put my arm back in one place. Then they plastered my limb from shoulder to fingers and fitted me with a brace so that I couldn't straighten my arm.

My Otago coach, Laurie Mains, rang the hospital to check on me and I always appreciated that. So, too, did the All Blacks' other selectors. The doctor gave them all the same answer: "Brent's out of the World Cup race and it might be doubtful if he will ever play rugby at the top level again."

Only time, and my arm's ability to straighten, would tell.

Then everyone left me alone. I had my thoughts to keep me company. Thoughts about how my All Black World Cup dream was over.

In quiet moments, alone in the hospital, bitter tears ran down my face. Three decades later, I can still taste those tears. I can still taste my disappointment.

But, at the end of it all, what could be done about it?

Nothing.

My chance was gone and that was that.

My World Cup dream became Zinzan Brooke's World Cup dream. The player who hadn't been involved in the lead-up games was flown in and, without having a trial or a George Nepia tournament match, was selected for the final squad by the All Black coaches who wanted a player who could provide cover for all three back-row positions. Michael Jones's strict observance of the Sabbath meant that Zinzan now stood a chance of playing in some of the World Cup games. In the end, he played against Argentina, scored a try, and went on to become perhaps the greatest No. 8 in international rugby history.

In the aftermath of missing out on the World Cup I was overwhelmed by self-doubt. I wondered whether my missing out was down to lousy luck or something closer to home. At times, I convinced myself that missing out on All Black immortality had little to do with bad luck and everything to do with me: my sanity, my head. Was I responsible for what happened? Did my chronic self-doubt conspire to sabotage me? Did I stack problem upon problem until some molehill became a mountain? Did my own self-doubt somehow cause my injury? I pushed the thoughts from my mind but somewhere, deep in the recesses of my mind, the doubts remained – hidden, buried, but ever-present.

They've always been there.

I left hospital around the same time as Zinzan, Michael Jones and the men who, in my mind, were supposed to be my teammates were moving into the team hotel and preparing for the greatest rugby tournament in the world.

But instead of reclining on a bed in downtown Auckland, I faced a trip home to Dunedin and months of sleeping upright in a chair. Cards and letters poured in from well-wishers all over New Zealand and, at that low ebb, I was truly thankful for them. But kind thoughts couldn't compensate for having to watch the World Cup – my World Cup – whilst propped up in a bed, popping painkillers.

● ● ● ● ●

It's maybe idle speculation on my part, but it's difficult, even thirty years later, not to look back and wonder.

History, of course, records that New Zealand went on to win that inaugural World Cup and the players involved were all, rightly, lionised for their triumphant efforts. It took subsequent All Black sides almost a quarter of a century to win another World Cup, a failure that elevated that original winning team from lions to gods. Their place in New Zealand history – not just rugby – is assured forever.

And it's impossible not to think, *That could have been me.*

It's impossible not to look back and feel regret. To have missed out by a wide margin would have been one thing, but to have come so close and still miss out … well, that's harder to take.

The World Cup. 1987. I had been so fit. So ready.

To have come from such a small, rural town and to have stood on the cusp of World Cup glory and stardom – and all that goes with it – was an achievement in it itself.

Sport is cruel and life is more cruel but, even acknowledging there are greater calamities happening every day in the world, for me the pain of missing out on that World Cup, and knowing that 4 years later I would be too old, is as acute today as it was twenty-five years ago.

I was devastated. Still am. I know it will never leave me.

Like an action replay of some famous try or great tackle, I often rerun it all in my mind. Despite my best efforts to push them from my mind, there are the 'What ifs?'

What if I hadn't been injured? What if I had been the one to run out onto that World Cup field instead of Zinzan? What if I had played against Argentina and what if I had scored that try?

What if?

What it?

What if?

I don't begrudge Zinzan his place in history. He's a friend and a wonderful standard bearer for the All Blacks and the Maoris, and it was obvious to everyone that he was always going to be a magnificent player. His ball skills, aggression and competitive streak were almost incomparable.

Still … sometimes, in the still of the night, I picture myself in Zinny's No. 7 jersey, darkest black, save for the silver fern on the breast. And, in my mind, it's not the great Zinzan Brooke smashing into the opposition. It's a young, unknown, freckle-faced kid with a dodgy mullet and a pair of chicken legs from a bump in a dusty New Zealand road. And I wonder if I could have made it like Zinzan. Could I have been the No. 8 whose name was on everybody's lips?

Who knows?

Straws in the wind.

• • • • •

Months later, my cast was sawn and split from me.

New Zealand was still drunk, literally, on the glory of winning the World Cup. The players had already passed into legend.

Meanwhile, I stood at a crossroads, knowing full well that I was in danger of slipping into obscurity.

I had a decision to make.

Sink or swim.

I'd swim.

If there was one plus to take from the whole sorry fiasco, it was that the last two years had given me a taste of top-flight rugby and I'd proven to everyone I belonged there. Most importantly, I'd proven it to myself. I'd played with the best

147

and bested most of them.

I got the medical all-clear to play and started battling back to full fitness. Admittedly, I was never again able to fully stretch my arm, and the medical prognosis was that, due to the extent and nature of the dislocation and the damage to the ball and socket joint, I'd only get back about 60 to 70 per cent movement. But I diligently followed medical advice to build the muscles gradually and, soon enough, I was able to get most of my arm movement back.

My first training regime was carrying an iron around the house all day. Even that was painful but, slowly, I returned to full training, though neither my hamstring nor my arm were ever 100 per cent again, and became injuries that dogged my future career.

Still, I recovered enough to make it back into the Otago Firsts team. But this time, I'd play at No. 8. The great All Black, Colin Meads, had seen me playing at openside flanker and suggested that Mike Brewer and I swap: Colin told Laurie Mains that I was much better-suited to that position given my power with ball in hand.

It was a master-stroke which exemplified Colin's vision in the game. I remained at No. 8 for the rest of my career and it was the position in which I was best. The switch defined my own play and my view of rugby. The great experience I had at No. 8 is why, today, I push for Leinster's Sean O'Brien to play there. Sean has a similar build to me and, like me, running with the ball is his greatest strength.

Despite my bitter mid-season disappointment, that season ended well for me. I finished as one of the leading try scorers in the First Division and was ranked, by the media, as the third best No. 8 in the country behind Buck Shelford and Zinzan Brooke, two players who, in turn, were probably the best No. 8s in the world.

I was named as Otago's Player of the Season, and attracted a number of nominations for the title of domestic New Zealand Player of the Year among the likes of Jones, Grant Fox and Kirwan.

The All Black World Cup squad was due to travel to Japan for an end-of-season tour, and there was a rumour that a few fringe players would be selected to travel. My name was among those deemed almost certain to be selected.

The notion gained further credence when I received a letter to sign from the NZRFU regarding sponsorship deals with the All Blacks. A quick phone call to the other two players being touted for that position – Wellington's Dirk Williams and Manawatu's Kevin 'Herb' Schuler – encouraged me. Neither Dirk, who went on play for Australia and work as a physio at London Irish RFC, nor Kevin, my old New Zealand Universities teammate and a future All Black, had received a similar letter. They both took it as effective confirmation I was about to be selected and both congratulated me. Further confirmation seemed to come via my mother. She was contacted by a friend on the NZRFU committee, who had just heard I'd made the All Black trip to Japan and wanted to congratulate her. One newspaper ran a story saying, "All Black Certainties: 3 Otago players, Mike Brewer, Dean Kenny and Brent Pope seem certain to be named in the All Black Tour Party to Japan tomorrow."

But fate wasn't quite finished with me.

Despite not exactly being a world force in sport, the Japanese Rugby Union requested the travelling party contain as many of the actual World Cup winning squad as possible. That cut down the available places and, when a proposed game against the Asian Barbarians was cancelled, the NZRFU decided to cut the travelling party by two players to just twenty-four. Considering Clive Woodward's Lions utilised fifty players, the decision seemed a little ridiculous.

But the decision was made. I was out, collateral damage in the drive to cut the squad by two players to the bare minimum.

There was a view in some quarters that the fact I wasn't from Auckland may not have helped. But, no matter. The deed was done and I was out in the cold again. Months of enduring and overcoming physical and mental torture counted for naught. In an instant, my effort was dismissed. I was dismissed.

The All Blacks went on to win their games in Japan by 100 points per match. Their victories were facile really – an end of year jaunt and a reward for winning the World Cup: a John Hart ego trip.

Watching from South Island, I could understand the Japanese fascination with the All Black stars, but I found it hard to fathom what they were learning from the repeated humiliations of that tour.

From a New Zealand rugby point of view, the benefits were virtually nil. The All Blacks learned nothing and the chance to make something of it – using the tour to blood fringe players or encourage guys like me who'd worked desperately hard to fight back from injury – was jettisoned.

I don't think the selectors ever considered how difficult it was for someone in my position to pick himself up mentally and get back to such a high standard of rugby. They couldn't have considered that aspect, otherwise they would, surely, have concluded that a second, last-minute, rejection based on something so arbitrary as rugby politics could destroy a young player's confidence – my confidence.

I'd lost out first time around to injury and could blame no one for it, save myself. But losing out this second time, because of politics, was a bitter pill to swallow. I felt that I had done enough in a whole season of consistency, to merit a place. I'd never been fitter and I'd fought back from an injury many people thought would stop me playing competitively ever again. I could have done no more and now here I was, just inches from where I wanted to be.

I felt that I deserved a shot at my dream. Dammit, I did deserve that shot.

But it was not to be.

If the disappointment of coming so close to getting to the World Cup was heart-breaking, then missing the cut for Japan was an altogether more bitter experience and had greater repercussions for me personally.

Following the World Cup disappointment, my self-doubts had resurfaced but, after a struggle, I pushed them from my mind and concentrated on the task ahead and winning that coveted black shirt with the silver fern.

But, after Japan, I found it almost impossible to pick myself back up again. The doubts began to gather again in the darker corners of my mind. I began to despair. Fate … the gods … whatever … they would always be the final arbiter in my life and they were destined to be cruel to me. I could not influence my own destiny – unless it was to sabotage myself.

These emotions, perceptions, thoughts were a disastrous combination. Slowly, but surely, I began to drown in my own doubts.

Within a week of missing out on Japan, I made the decision to get the hell out of New Zealand. I accepted an invitation to play for a London side, Askeans RFC, alongside a trio of All Blacks; Greg Cooper, his brother Matthew and one of my best mates, Gordy Macpherson.

I couldn't hide completely, though, and soon after I arrived a leading English rugby magazine ran a headline story in which my Otago coach, Laurie Mains, launched a scathing attack on the All Black selectors. Laurie fumed that, despite

Otago's second place ranking in the national First Division, only one of the province's players, Mike Brewer, had been selected for the All Black tour to Japan. Mains pinpointed me as the obvious candidate to have gone and many in the country agreed with him.

But it was too late. I was, by then, on the other side of the world, living with three Kiwis above a gaming arcade on the main street of Bromley in Kent.

It was the right decision. Askeans RFC was the perfect tonic and the lads were magnificent, we had a ball. I'd been brought in by Graham Briggs and Alan Hunt who treated me, and the other lads, like part of their own family. There was an Irish connection – the team was later coached by Irish ex-International, Stewart McKinney who, despite his tough reputation, I found to be a real gentleman.

That year in London was fantastic. It was good to be in such an exciting city. I loved spending Sundays in Covent Garden, Leicester Square or Camden Market. I loved the vibe, the music: I even dressed like Rick Astley for a while, sporting a pair of fawn chinos, a black zip-up polo top and a pair of trendy boat shoes. Bands like Wet, Wet, Wet, Johnny Hates Jazz, The Smiths and The Housemartins were riding high in the charts and we went to concerts, tours, films and generally enjoyed life.

By the end of the year, I'd given myself the break I thought I'd needed. I was ready to go home and resume my duties with Otago. But, though I didn't realise it, the previous year and the disappointments of missing out twice on the All Blacks had taken its toll. I'd been able to run away to London, but I hadn't been able to escape myself. Though I couldn't see it at the time, I was already on a countdown to personal disaster.

Popey was always a man with brilliant contacts and who built relationships with anyone. It was a supreme irony that he could not manage to do the same with women. Popey was always seen as the 'safe' option by women – a huge man, lots of noise and fun, but never threatening to them, always a gentleman. They flocked to him and adored him, but he found it hard to have long-term relationships with them. It frightened him – he'd often sabotage his own chances of long-term alliances. But he would never break friendships and is one of the most reliable friends you could ever encounter. Morally he is very, very strong and even when he was seriously screwed over by a friend years ago, to this date he has continued to be supportive when this mate went through some hard times. The key point is this – Popey is a mate you can always rely on!

Kevin Putt
All Black Sevens. St Mary's. Natal. Springboks.
Natal Coach. Waikato Coach. NZTV Rugby Pundit.

9

Half-Empty Heart

"For there is nothing either good or bad, but thinking makes it so."
Hamlet, Act II, Scene ii
William Shakespeare

In 2009, I was diagnosed as being dysthymic or, rather, having a dysthymic personality.

I hadn't a clue what that meant. To me, it seemed like a new-fangled American term and, in some regards, that's what it is. It's best described as a state of chronic discontentment. It was previously described as a personality disorder but seems to have been reclassified over the past few years as a mood disorder. It's not that uncommon and, to some degree, exists in a lot of people's lives.

At the time, I was in a relationship that I desperately wanted to work. But I was having problems; self-doubts and insecurities started to emerge, old patterns of negative thinking began to resurface. This wasn't uncommon for me.

In most relationships I've had with wonderful, loving women who I've cared about deeply, I've found things incredibly difficult. However hard I've tried, I just cannot seem to go with the flow. I overthink things too much, bombard my mind with negativity and then, in spite of myself, I start to withdraw emotionally, afraid of getting hurt.

I desperately wanted to avoid repeating the same mistake and, consequently, sought expert help and was diagnosed as being dysthymic. The condition's causes are unclear although genetics and the body's inability to produce normal levels of serotonin – a type of chemical that can influence brain cells related to mood, appetite and sleep – appear to play a key role.

I don't know. I've searched through my own genetics and family history for clues. My father has always been a wonderful, thoughtful man, but I think he would admit that he is also an anxious person. That's no criticism of my dad, it's just his nature, as it is mine. My brother, Mark, a well-respected counsellor and psychotherapist in Wellington, has suffered from some form of depression throughout most of his life. He's taken medication for many years and, most likely, will continue to take it for the foreseeable future.

When I told Mark I'd been to see a psychologist he asked if the expert had mentioned dysthymia. I replied yes, and asked him how he knew, but Mark simply replied, "I always knew, Brent, I always knew."

I've never discussed my dysthymia as publically as this, though I've touched on it in some ways. But, in the last couple of years, I've come to understand it as being part of my life. Likewise, I've come to understand the importance of my own resilience which has helped me to live and function well in most aspects of my life.

I'm no poster child for mental health, nor do I want to be. I don't have the right to assume such a role. Even writing about it now is raw for me. But I hope that, by discussing my own dysthymia, other people might understand how chronic anxiety and low self-esteem can affect people's lives. I'd also hope anyone suffering from the effects of chronic anxiety might be encouraged, like me, to seek help and start healing.

Whatever name it goes by, the only thing I now know is that I have had it for as long as I can remember. Perhaps the best description I've come across that sums me up was by an American clinical psychologist, Dr Alan Downs, an outwardly successful man who penned an excellent book entitled, 'The Half-Empty Heart'. Downs' book went a long way to explaining to me why I had been so negative or pessimistic as a rugby player and sometimes as a person, why I had low self-worth, and maybe why I found things like love and relationships harder than most people. This would often not be other people's perception of me, as they would often credit me with being a very loving, lovable person, but my own lack of self-confidence led me to believe I could not sustain a loving relationship because of feelings of low self-esteem. The effect of dysthymia has been very difficult for me, and still can be today. In his book, citing first-hand experiences, Downs explained how 'chronic discontent' like mine can affect relationships with partners, friends and family. He pointed out that the condition if not recognised and worked on can develop into something deeper and darker. But he also identified indicators that could identify when such a mood was taking hold and he offered solutions and exercises to help people conquer their symptoms, solutions which I now utilise daily.

I now know this half-empty heart has always been with me. The signs and symptoms were always there. I just didn't recognise them for what they were.

I've always been a high achiever in what I've done, whether that be in sport, in education or employment. Whatever I've started – with the exception of small areas of my personal life – I've succeeded in, and when I've set out to do something in my life, by and large, I've achieved it.

But, accomplishing my targets has never fully satisfied me and, almost as quickly as I'd complete something, I'd moved on to the next goal, convinced that, once I'd achieved it, I'd find that elusive feeling of satisfaction. I've spent all my life in search of that feeling of euphoria which others speak of. But I've never found it: real happiness has always been transitory and the ability to anchor it in my everyday life has always eluded me, and continues to do so.

As a young sportsman I suffered from low self-esteem. Despite being told by various coaches that I was good, I never wanted my mum and dad to come and see me play. While all other parents crowded the sidelines on match day, I was happy to give my parents the wrong address for a ground or an inaccurate kick off time, so that they couldn't find and watch me. Funnily enough to other parents, their sons and my teammates, and my coaches, I was often the star of the team.

But not in my eyes.

The same lack of self-worth afflicted my relationship with girls even at a young age. Despite having a string of popular girls often vying for an invitation to get to know me, I was painfully self-conscious of how I looked and never confident anyone would want to go out with me. But I masked my insecurities well preferring, like Pagliacci, to keep my sadness hidden. So, I became the class joker, the messer. The inward tears of a clown couldn't make my friends and classmates uncomfortable.

It was the perfect cover.

I often became very anxious at school, especially around exam time, almost to the point where I lost control of the worry and self-doubt. In my reports teachers often commented how intelligent I was, but I found it impossible to be convinced. In my own opinion (the only one that counted) I was always on the point of failure and letting people down. My glass always seemed half-empty.

My habit of cramming for exams just exacerbated my anxieties: I'd often leave my preparation so late that I was convinced of failure. Not the usual kind of worry that many school kids suffer before tests – I would literally make myself physically sick with worry. Exams usually started on a Monday so, by Sunday evening, I'd be in the grip of severe panic attacks. These onslaughts were irrational and groundless – despite winning a full university scholarship by finishing in the top percentile of my school, I still spent the days leading up those exams alternately frozen by worry or shaking with fear. At home, I'd try to relax by taking a hot bath the night before exams but I'd sit there, bolt upright in the tub, my hands around my knees, paralysed and shaking with dread, until the water went cold and I went blue.

In my mind I would flunk my exams and flunk in life. I was destined for some low-paying, menial job. I would never be happy.

I would tell myself that I would fail and be miserable.

Fail and be miserable.

Fail and be miserable.

Over and over I would tell myself this. I would bombard the positives with my negativity. It wasn't intentional, but it was as though my mind was a seesaw and the guy on the negative end was much heavier than his opposite number. I just couldn't stop it, and no matter how much I tried to counter-balance the good with the bad, the pull towards being a failure would inevitably win out.

I told no one.

I felt I was weak. What had I to complain about compared to others? I felt selfish even thinking this way. Instead, I told myself that I needed to get on with things, get back on the horse and stop indulging myself. Family and friends reading this will wonder how they never knew, but hiding my weakness was vitally important to me. No one could know, the shame and humiliation would be too much.

To this day, having a bath on a Sunday night can be a traumatic experience for me, but one which continues to hold a fatalistic attraction. I know I shouldn't do it but, in a strange way, I feel compelled to. Then, of course, as soon as I hit the bath water, I am back in those school days and the feelings of doubt, low self-acceptance and fear of failure flood over me again. I can't explain then why I have to have a Sunday night bath. It feels like I'm addicted to self-torture, as though I'm continuously testing myself to see if everything is sorted.

Even as recently as a few months ago, I once again stepped outside my comfort zone to try and learn the clarinet for an RTÉ show called Instrumental. Following the first public performance, I'd somehow convinced myself that I had failed while others on the show thought I was taking things too personally. But, the following Sunday night, a bath suddenly transported me back to those teenage fears and insecurities, and I experienced another panic attack.

To most people, my difficulty playing the clarinet was insignificant. So what if I couldn't play a very difficult instrument after just a week or so? But, to me, my perceived failure overflowed into all aspects of my life, and I began to spiral, once more, into negative thinking. I worried I was going to continue to fail at everything, that my life up until now had been a waste. This all-encompassing negative thinking was not born out in reality – I knew that at a deeper level – but it was a very personal reminder of the grip, good or bad, that the mind has over me.

This wasn't just something that affected me at school. Even rugby, at which I excelled, was affected. During my early rugby career I was respected and admired, winning a prestigious Sports Blue for university rugby and captaining many university and provincial teams. It was a carefully cultivated façade. Secretly, I was still prey to my panic attacks.

In the mid-1980s my name was suddenly linked to that year's All Blacks tour of France. Newspapers started running stories reporting that, "Brent Pope, the promising young Otago flanker, was going to be the surprise 'bolter' in the All Blacks and that the national selectors, Colin Meads in particular, 'liked him.'"

My dream had always been to be an All Black and, to everyone else, it seemed a huge honour that my name should even be linked to the All Blacks. A few years later, I would be devastated at missing out but, in 1985, I was hoping the stories of my making the squad were only half-true. I wanted to go and yet didn't want to go. I was panicking inside. Strange as it might sound to any young Irish or New Zealand rugby player, as the team was announced over the radio, I was secretly praying that I wouldn't be selected. How could I possibly measure up to my rugby idols, Murray Mexted and Cowboy Shaw? I felt I couldn't.

My prayers were heard and I wasn't selected. My sense of relief was mirrored by the disappointment of other people on my behalf. I received letters and phone calls from well-wishers, telling me how upset they were I hadn't made the cut. I'd deserved my chance, they said. But, in my mind, I didn't deserve such an honour. No matter what everyone else thought, I wasn't up to the task and, most likely, never would be.

I've long suffered from 'down days' where panic attacks or irrational worries would leave me thinking about nothing else, where I wished I had a tap on the side of my head that I could release to stop the racing thoughts which can be exhausting.

I've had success in my battles though I understand that, most likely, my dysthymia will always be with me in some form. But at least now I understand what I am facing and I won't let it beat me.

Back in the late 1980s, I was ignorant of what was wrong with me and living in some form of denial. Though I couldn't admit it to myself, or my friends, I was forever loading my subconscious with negative thoughts. My "can't do it, won't do it" mantra meant I would never be disappointed if the eventual outcome was negative. That was my way.

On the outside I was this popular, confident person who had done so much with his life. In other parts of my life I'd even helped other people to believe in themselves, to take chances, and the reason I do that, the real reason, is because I wanted people to be positive in a way that I couldn't.

Mark, who has always been a rock for me at my worst times, is right – what good are negative thoughts, really? So, and this will sound contradictory, I have used my negativity in a positive way, and yes at times it has been hard, but I was still resilient, I was determined to prove myself wrong.

Missing out on the All Blacks in 1987 had been a hammer-blow to me. My negativity and lack of confidence had resurfaced and, while my time-out in London had allowed me to paper over the cracks, in reality it had only delayed the inevitable for a couple of years anyway. My return to Otago in 1988 set in motion a chain of events that saw great highs transformed into deep troughs. My years of insecurities and painful self-doubt, combined with medical problems and events in my personal life, would eventually fuse into an explosive mental cocktail. I can only describe what happened to me in that period as a meltdown or an anxiety overload. I struggled, out of control, with various mental health issues which included nightly panic attacks, feelings of depression, and feelings of being unloved or incapable of love – utter hopelessness.

In hindsight, I should have seen it coming. Mark's bouts of depression should have alerted me to my own mental health issues. But I was young and headstrong – I was nothing like Mark, or so I thought. As things turned out, I was about as wrong as it's possible to be. The problem of irrational anxiety or depression – whether mild, chronic or major – lurked at the farthermost edges of my own mind. Once it overwhelmed me, I was catapulted into the kind of tailspin many people do not come out of. Those who have experienced something similar will know that, when a tool as powerful as your mind starts pulling against you, it can be very difficult to pull back.

Once you disappear into the abyss of your own mind, all you can do is hang on with every fibre of your being to any ounces of normality you retain. You forget what it's like to think rationally about anything. You alienate yourself. You are suddenly a burden to all those around you. Your friends, your family, your partner leaves you or, more likely, you drive them away. In the end, you achieve your self-fulfilling prophecy – the exact thing that you simultaneously most wanted but most feared – you are left alone to battle yourself.

• • • • •

Unfortunately that experience was still ahead of me. I'd returned to Otago from playing with Askeans in London, and the team was on the point of entering the

CANZ series, a new rugby tournament involving Argentina, Canada, Waikato and Otago.

The series was a riposte aimed at the NZRFU, which had set up a South Pacific tournament a few years earlier involving the top three provinces in New Zealand, Samoa, and South African side, Natal. At the time, the top three provinces were defined as Auckland, Canterbury and Wellington, but much had changed in the interim. Otago was now ranked above Canterbury and Wellington while the likes of Warren Gatland and Garryowen's future Kiwi imports, John Mitchell and Brent Anderson, had steered Waikato close to the top.

I'd been with Otago right from the start of their charge, under the guiding hand of Laurie Mains, from the lower depths of National Division 1 to, by 1990, becoming the second best team in the country. A year later, in 1991, Otago surpassed this to finally claim the National Championship.

Suddenly, Otago was a big noise in domestic NZ rugby and further afield, after wins over the touring Lions and Springboks. But, denied a place in the prestigious South Pacific Tournament, Otago turned its attention to the CANZ series. The competition was the envy of the rugby world, with trips away each year to places like Buenos Aires, Mendoza and Rosario, Vancouver, Ontario and Los Angeles. And CANZ was followed by tours to Australia and the Samoan Islands.

By that point, I'd left university rugby and crossed the city to play for Green Island, aka The Panel Beaters, so-called on account of their working class origins. Along with All Blacks Greg Cooper and Gordy Macpherson and Hawke's Bay winger, Paul Cooke, I was lured to the club by the offer of a seriously attractive professional deal – free accommodation above the Royal Tavern on the main street of Green Island, and a side of beef from Moyle's supermarket!

The area could be rough at times. There was a murder committed just outside my bedroom window in which a woman was bludgeoned to death though, fortunately, the murderer was caught by the police.

But playing for The Panel Beaters had other, unforeseen, advantages. Every Sunday, the owner of the Royal would leave us the keys to the bar, effectively giving us our own private bar. It was like leaving the inmates in charge of the prison and we hosted some massive parties.

Despite the generous terms of my professional deal with Green Island, it was clear the side of beef wouldn't feed me forever, and I might need to work for a living. I was lucky in that I had my own valuation arm of a big real estate chain, Robertson's, and I'd just published another one of my children's books. Life was okay. I had a good job, a decent car and nice clothes.

On an evening to the cinema to see Nicole Kidman in that Irish epic, 'Far and Away', Gordy Macpherson and I received an intriguing call from an Otago teammate, Dave Callon. A sister of Dave's girlfriend, Clare, had spotted Gordy and I and thought one of us was rather attractive. The sister, Sue, had just returned from London and was very striking so, naturally, I thought she had eyes for Gordy. But word came back that, "No, it's you she fancies, Popey."

So, with a push from Clare, now married to Dave, I plucked up the courage and asked her out on a date. We hit it off immediately and Sue fitted easily into the rugby world. She was eventually bridesmaid for my teammate, Mike Brewer and his Irish wife, Beverly Keegan, who had travelled all the way from Dublin to be with him.

In so many ways, we seemed the perfect couple. We had heaps in common. She loved rugby and other sports, was a qualified aerobics instructor and, as well as working in TV production, she was also involved in acting. She was an attractive, hard-working, intelligent, go-getter, at one point even running an electoral campaign for a would-be city councillor.

Just after we started going out she rang me up in floods of tears. Her older sister was getting married in less than a week and, following some sort of hairdressing disaster, her beautiful long, blonde hair had started falling out in clumps. She had no option but to have it cut razor-tight to her head, à la Sinead O'Connor. It was not quite what she had intended but, no matter, she could carry it off – it suited her.

So, life was good. My rugby was good enough to keep the likes of Arran Pene and Jamie Joseph on the bench and, a few years later, players like young Otago Reps Taine Randell and Josh Kronfeld. All four were destined for fame as future All Blacks but, from around 1986 to '87, Otago's first choice back-row when fit was myself, my old adversary, Ginge Henderson and Mike Brewer. Only Auckland's great trio of Michael Jones, Alan Whetton and Zinzan Brooke could match us. Ginge wasn't as dynamic or game-breaking as Jones, but Ginge was better on the ground, especially in the wet. Mike provided the lineout option and the brains while I contributed the power. Our trio provided the perfect blend of ball-winning and ball-carrying ability and remains the back-row blueprint every coach searches for.

Up until then, I had been a No. 7, then a No. 6 to accommodate Ginge, but Laurie Mains had taken on board a suggestion from the great Colin Meads that my power might be better employed from the back of the Otago scrum. After that I never played anywhere other than No. 8.

There were some injury problems. Every week seemed to bring a new hurt, particularly to my hamstrings which couldn't last a full game. I'd get one back, then tear the other. Years of not stretching and imbalance were finally beginning to take their toll.

The injuries cost me a place in key games, including one against a touring Australian side, though I did make a game against the touring Welsh who accused me of unnecessarily roughing up their winger, Glen Webbe.

But Laurie continued to pick me whenever I was fit. He was loyal like that, and while Arran and Jamie and the others continued to press their claims, I knew Laurie nearly always selected me if I was healthy.

Otago was a good place to play rugby. It was like a family, albeit a family with some odd characters. One such was Judson Arthur, a tough farrier from the country. Jud had a deep operatic voice and loved to sing, many times he'd entertain us during our kangaroo court sessions with an emotional rendition of 'Old Man River'. But after a second knee reconstruction Jud, who also represented New Zealand in show-jumping, decided to change direction and try something entirely different. He took a few singing lessons, his talent was spotted and he's currently performing in leading roles with operatic societies in Australia and New Zealand. He must be the only player to ever represent his nation as a player and then go on to become the professional asked to sing the national anthem before games, which he did for New Zealand when they played Ireland.

Otago was scorching up the First Division and, alongside winger John Timu, I was credited with being one of the country's scoring machines. I spent an idyllic summer working in Queenstown, and enjoying days off by rafting, swimming, running or just taking in some of the most majestic scenery in the world.

I felt, in so many ways, on top of the world. I'd come through a year of intense disappointment after twice missing out on becoming an All Black. But I'd fought back from injury and, more importantly, had overcome the mental doubts which had begun to crowd in on my mind. My resilience was shining through.

I'd met someone I really cared about who seemed to feel the same way about me. She shared my interests and led an interesting life of her own. Best of all, slowly but surely, we were becoming very close.

Maybe it was precisely because things were looking up so much that I decided on a bold new strategy. I don't know. I still wonder about it. But, whatever the reason, I was about to make a series of decisions which, although I didn't realise it at the time, would change my life forever.

It began when Sue auditioned for, and then won, a part in a new TV sitcom. Around the same time, my old team in London, Askeans had been back in contact, asking me to come back and play another season in England. Looking back on it, it was a convenient time for her to follow her dreams and me mine, so I decided to end it.

But even then, I should have seen the warning signs. There was a storm brewing, which had nothing to do with Sue and everything to do with me. Even though she was upset I felt she was prepared to continue the relationship, albeit a long-distance one, for a while.

But deep down, though I tried to mask it, my own insecurities were returning. I was beginning to doubt why someone like her would actually want to be with me. My self-doubts were exacerbated by a previous relationship in which I had not been treated particularly well. Though Sue was fiercely loyal to me, I was convinced that she'd find someone else while I was in England. I didn't tell her of my concerns and, instead, opted to do what I'd always done – run away before I could be hurt. The fact that the relationship was strong, except for the concerns I'd created in my head, made little difference to me. Instead of believing Sue when she said she wanted to be with me, I preferred to wonder what this attractive, talented, intelligent woman was doing with me.

Worse, this time I'd be in London on my own. Neither Gordy nor Greg were with me, and although the local lads laid on great hospitality for me, I felt very much alone. I did develop one great friendship, with my Kiwi housemate Colin Botica, who was a tower of strength for me. But, despite Colin's best efforts, I missed home desperately. I missed my friends and I missed Sue, as we began to drift apart. London became cold and grey and I became very homesick.

I began to suffer the odd panic attack again and then I was struck down by a debilitating illness. The illness hit me like a train, its draining effects made even worse by the fact that no one seemed able to diagnose what was wrong me. It would take eight months of constant trips to see consultants and specialists, tests and biopsies before one of them finally identified it as a virus.

But, at the outset of this illness, I had no idea what was going on. Out of the blue I began to get very ill, and suddenly lacked the energy or physical and mental strength to play rugby. I had no power or commitment. I just wanted to sleep and felt tired all the time. It was affecting every part of me and, while nothing was showing up in the blood tests, I knew something was wrong.

I was tired and lonely and homesick and, instead of relaxing and trying to recuperate, I sank deeper into an abyss of worry. I began to convince myself that the problem was more serious than it was.

I began to believe I was about to die. That might sound stupid in retrospect, but I persuaded myself that something sinister was happening to me and no one could tell me different.

I couldn't play rugby any more so I decided to withdraw all the money I had and fly home. I made a stopover in Miami, hoping that some sun would give me a boost and arranged to meet Colin Botica there. But even that turned to dust – on my first day there, I was robbed of every cent I had. The hotel put me up free of charge and the police recovered my passport in a gutter.

Dad had said he could wire me money to stay but I was sick, alone, broke and just wanted to see my family. I used the money Dad sent for a flight home but the last-minute booking meant I ended up transferring around half the world before I got home. By the time I reached New Zealand I had flown something like sixty hours non-stop, and was sleep deprived and jetlagged.

Everything … the illness, the robbery, the misery, the stress, the lack of sleep … everything was piling up, brewing up a storm in my mind that I was, as yet, unaware of.

I wanted to see my parents but I wanted to see Sue again. She understood me, cared about me and could help me. She had always been able to put a halt to my worries and calm me down. Deep down, I also hoped that going home would give me the chance to rekindle our relationship.

So when Dad met me at the airport I told him of my plan to travel on to Dunedin to see Sue. He told me, as gently as he could, that Sue was engaged and due to be married within weeks.

My hoped-for reunion was over before it ever began.

I rang her to give her my regards and wish her good luck, but struggled to know what to say. I felt that I'd just lost my best friend.

It was the final straw. I was shattered physically, mentally and now emotionally, it was too much all at once – so I simply broke down.

Once more, I'd pressed the self-destruct button in my life. As they say in the movies, I'd "run off anybody that ever loved me".

And thus began eight months of hell.

●●●●●

Shattered and disconsolate, I returned to Dunedin to my job and, I hoped, to rugby. With the help of a friend, I found and secured a beautiful one-bed apartment overlooking Dunedin Harbour and Bay. It was one of the most stunning penthouse apartments in the entire city but, over the next few months, it wouldn't matter.

I was distraught and angry. Not at Sue – she had every right to move on – but at myself. Once again, I had conspired to destroy the very thing that meant so much to me, and I'd succeeded. I tried to be happy for her and, eventually, I managed that but, at the time, I could only despair for myself.

I was still weak, both physically and mentally, and Dad took me to an immunologist and various specialists and consultants. Some of them took painful biopsies from my lymph glands and sent them off for tests, tests and more tests. The consultants told me what I didn't have but seemed incapable of finding out what I did have.

And so, reinforced by my anxious personality, the irrational worry that first surfaced in London took hold again. I quickly descended into the realms of hypochondria, newly convinced I was actually going to die of something that no one could identify or treat. Every mole was cancerous, every cough a sign of leukaemia. I lost weight. Oblivious to the senselessness and selfishness of it all, I spent hours in the public library, reading up on every symptom of every illness.

I woke up at night, shaking, sweating, panic-stricken. I was convinced my end was nigh.

None of it made sense to me.

I tried to be rational with myself. I argued with myself. I told myself I'd always been a tough guy, who even enjoyed pain at times. I had never lain down on a rugby pitch and I hardly went to the doctor, outside of when I'd been ill as a child.

But I was fighting a tough battle.

I withdrew mentally and physically. I rarely went out any more. I felt that I had become a burden to everybody, and I didn't blame them for getting frustrated with me. People were great with me, they loved me and didn't want to see me like this, my family worried, my friends worried but not as much as I did, I worried that they must be fed up – that I was a burden, a burden, and a burden.

So I withdrew even more.

I closed the doors of my apartment and isolated myself from almost everyone and everything during that period.

● ● ● ● ●

The only time I would open my door was for rugby. Rugby kept me going. Despite the weight loss and the anxiety, and in between the days spent in isolation in my apartment, I pulled myself together long enough to train and play. Maybe that seems strange, but in my mind it was a straightforward decision – rugby was the only thing that was keeping me moving in a positive direction.

And my parents and Mark were there for me. They were wonderful, calling constantly, taking me to the doctor. But it was hard for them. They didn't really understand the gravity of the situation and it was impossible to explain it to them. The intensity of my feelings scared me then, and still scares me now when I look back on it. It felt like my mind had taken over and was starting to more or less eat me up from the inside out.

I prayed to God that if he could just help me through this, then I would get better.

At rugby I'd put on a brave face for my teammates and friends but, later, I would go home alone and wonder what the night would hold... Not that my mask fooled anyone – pretty soon my feelings were clear for most people to see. At times, they were simply put down to 'Popey's negativity', or Popey's self-defeating, but hilarious, hard luck stories. But, eventually, the lads on the rugby team got sick of me. They couldn't understand what I was going through, the loneliness, the fear, the anxiety, the pain that crippled me and the feeling that at times I wanted to give up.

I wanted to be alone.

I don't blame my friends for distancing themselves from me. In reality, it was I who alienated them. Still, there were a few who, despite not understanding what was happening with me, stayed strong and supportive friends; players like Steve Cumberland, Arran Pene and Gordy Macpherson and my Irish friend, Beverley Keegan, to whom I owe a lot.

After a while, even my interest in rugby was slipping away, and with it, my best chance at getting through everything. I tore a hamstring again, and missed the provincial game against Australia and other touring teams. Now, I couldn't play rugby, was living alone, wasn't able to talk to Sue and, all the while, my mental health issues gripped me tighter.

I was in deep.

Otago coach, Laurie Mains, couldn't understand what was wrong but remained patient and continued to select me.

Few people understood what was happening to me or how deeply I'd sunk in my struggle to retain my mental health. Only myself, my parents and a few friends knew the extent of my problems. Despite the enormity of what was happening to me, I couldn't talk to most of my friends.

I couldn't because I was ashamed. How could I tell them that the big, strong, Kiwi rugger bugger they so admired was often, in the privacy of his bedroom, reduced to a shivering, negative-thinking, anxiety-ridden mess?

No. That was something I could not share with anyone, and so I chose to battle on, chin out, head up, convincing the world there was nothing to worry about.

But my reality was different.

All the while, the mist, which other people saw as 'negativity', and which had always hovered at the far reaches of my consciousness had descended.

I reached a new low-point when I walked out on the Otago team in Hawke's Bay. Dad drove me to Mark's place in Wellington. I was at my lowest ebb that day, and I still remember it well. Mentally and physically, I was exhausted. I tried to keep a brave face but, underneath, I felt desperately alone. I'd never walked out on any team before, in fact, I was a team-man first and foremost. Rugby was the one thing my life I could rely on, my crutch. Now, every time I tried to get back up, another problem would come along and pull me back down again.

For the first time in my life I didn't care about rugby. About anything.

I lived like that for nearly eight months. The days just blurred into one another. I felt my friends and family were sick of my whining about stuff that made no sense to them, sick of trying to cheer me up, sick of me.

I'd become a burden to just about everyone I cared about, worse, I'd become a burden to myself.

I was better off alone, better off alienated from everyone.

Nobody suggested I seek professional help because I was managing to just about keep going. The mask was doing its job.

But, once alone with my worry and shame and in the privacy of my apartment, I had the foresight, maybe desperation, to call some helplines, talking to as many people as I could. I still recall how one man spoke to me when I phoned his helpline.

He simply greeted me saying: "Hello, friend."

What a wonderful thing to say. I suddenly felt someone did care. This wasn't the first person to say such a thing to me – my family and friends had constantly reassured me in those months of meltdown. But, somehow, hearing it from a stranger made it easier to accept – perhaps just harder to dismiss.

And I felt something else, that the warmth of the people at the other end of the line rewarded the bravery it took for me to call in the first place.

And, slowly, painfully things began to change for the better.

Calling the helplines, opening up about my feelings and just talking helped me immensely.

My bravery and resilience – and that is what I believe it was – in talking to those people sparked a realisation in me that I had to fight my way out of my mental state. Gradually, my health started to pick up, I started to feel stronger physically and mentally each day.

I ate better, stopped drinking for a while and met with good, positive people who buoyed up my spirits. I am not ashamed to say I sought professional help by myself: I accepted that Sue had gone and found something positive to get up for in the morning.

My recovery reached a watershed moment the day I actually tidied my own apartment and went for a run again, something I hadn't done in all those months when it felt hard just to get out of bed.

Each day got better.

The mist started to clear.

I began to play rugby again.

The team was going well and I was getting back to the old Popey – class clown, team funnyman, big, hard, robust. There were yet more good days, great days ahead with Otago but, even as I began to put my life back together, I realised that things had changed inexorably for me.

I had to make changes in my life, positive changes and, to my surprise, those changes brought me to Ireland. In the time I've been here, I've forged what I believe to be a successful career in both sport and life. I believe I am a good, kind person with a big heart and I try to give something back to society.

It took a long time for me to heal. In many ways, I am still healing. My problems have not gone away completely, they are always there, lurking. They've continued to frustrate aspects of my personal life, which I still have problems trying to explain to even my closest friends and family, but my vulnerability to my issues just makes me stronger, more determined to milk life for all its worth.

I still struggle at times to overcome my problems. I am a voracious reader of self-help books and books on the power of the mind, I've sought professional help off and on for many years for my dysthymia, panic attacks and anxiety-based issues. At my age, I'm not embarrassed to say it, nor ashamed. I don't view it as my weakness, but rather my strength. Through my troubles, I believe that I have become a more sensitive and more understanding man.

• • • • •

I don't expect everyone to understand this part of my life.

They're not me. They haven't lived my life.

But I hope that by reading about this aspect of my life, people will come to understand anxiety and negativity as it has affected my life. Through trying to stand in another's shoes for even a short while, I hope people can empathise with people like me, who have experienced some mental health issues.

I don't expect that to happen quickly. In fact, I only really learned recently that it's okay to struggle with feelings like mine. During an RTÉ interview with Ryan Tubridy, in early 2012, I discussed the subject. It wasn't the first time I'd talked about it, I'd already decided to write about it in my autobiography. But it was the first time I'd talked about it in public and it was a liberating experience.

I admitted that, two years previously, I'd spent three months in New York. I'd always wanted to live there, as a New Yorker, seeing that great city through the eyes of a local, not a tourist. Through friends of friends I rented a Manhattan apartment from a NY fireman, Peter Rodriguez, who became a good friend. But, though I badly wanted to enjoy the experience, I became lonely. People thought I'd be able to breeze into a bar and make friends easily. It wasn't an enjoyable trip.

When I came back to Ireland, I was invited on to Ryan's radio show to talk about rugby and my love of Outsider Art. He caught me at a vulnerable moment and asked: "Did you go to find yourself, Brent?" I found myself saying, yes. We discussed some of the things I've written about in this chapter, more so about my anxiety around aspects of love and relationships.

By the end of it, the phone lines were hopping. Some people rang in to offer kindness and support, others rang in to say they suffered the same kind of anxieties I did.

I suddenly realised that I was old enough, and had been through enough, to say, "Okay, this is who I am. This is Popey."

I realised it was okay to feel the way I do. It's not a sign of weakness, but one of strength. The listeners' support had lifted a huge burden of shame and expectation off me. As I walked out of RTÉ, I felt, for maybe the first time in my life, that I was fine. It was a release.

Many will wonder if I simply hurt more easily than others, if I'm too soft. That's certainly not true physically – physical pain is something I've faced all my life, and I don't really mind it. But I think I probably feel mental pain more than many men. I am sensitive and emotional. When someone criticises me, or slates me, I try to understand their point of view. I understand that, once I put myself into the public eye by developing my profile on television, I was 'fair game' for comment. People will say, "If you can't stand the heat, stay out of the kitchen."

I agree, but I'm not made of steel: the personal criticism often hurts. Still, while my public profile opens me up to a wider commentary, it's also true that

I love what I do. Ireland has been good to me, good for me. I've grown to love it and its people. Of course, I'm still proud to be a Kiwi as well. But, most of all, I'm proud that – as the bumper sticker says – I've managed to keep on trucking.

Yes, I have had many dreams crushed and, no, I am not where I thought I would be in my personal life. But many of us aren't. And that's okay, too. We just need to let each other know it's okay.

One of the most important lessons I've learnt in all of these years is that you cannot presume to know what someone is going through. People take their own lives or self-harm over something which appears insignificant to others – we need to stop, look and listen. Offer understanding before judgement and try walking a mile in the other guy's shoes.

During my time in Ireland I spent a day, in the run-up to one particular Christmas, meeting staff from the ISPCC. The wonderful counsellors there told me they receive nearly 70,000 calls to their lifeline per year, hundreds on Christmas Day alone. All from kids who just want someone to say, "It's okay". Some of those youngsters were waking up in the middle of the night shaking with fear. Maybe they can identify the cause of their fears, maybe they can't. But regardless of the whys or the wherefores of it all, they know they are gripped by a deep-seated fear that may cause some of them to self-harm and some of them to tragically take their own lives.

In that descent into the mist, they are already suffering from mental health issues and countries like Ireland sometimes don't recognise the enormity of these young people's suffering or the extent of the problem facing them and us. There are children as young as six years old approaching suicide help groups confessing to wanting to end their lives. In recent times, we've seen the effects of cyber-bullying on children and the despair that makes them take their own lives. How many more are out there, too terrified to reach out and ask for help? And not just little children, but teenagers and adults.

Each year suicide alone claims more lives than our roads. We all know of someone who has taken his or her life. Suicide and mental illness do not discriminate; they affect all areas of society – young or old, skinny or fat, rich or poor. Yet government funding often overlooks bullying, self-esteem issues and the stigma surrounding some mental health issues.

Over my life, I have lost far too many friends to suicide. Two teammates, wonderful people from the same rugby club I played with in the United States, have taken their own lives, despite appearing to have everything to live for. In 2009, a total of 552 people took their own lives in Ireland, and suicide prevention groups say the problem is growing out of control, especially in young males. How many of us in the last few years in particular have stood at the funeral of a victim of suicide who we knew and loved, and cried, "Why?" Many of them seemed to be in control – a few problems here and there – but seemingly nothing serious, nothing worth ending their lives for.

It's a horrific thought that the beautiful Cliffs of Moher in County Clare has now become one of the world's locations of choice for people wishing to end their lives. Every single day, volunteers walk the banks of the Shannon in search of floating bodies.

When will we wake up to what's going on? This is not a trickle, it's a flood. We are not experiencing a few accidental deaths – it's an epidemic and the true tragedy of what's going on is that many of these suicides could have been prevented with early diagnosis and a more accepting society. Many of these lost citizens took their own lives because they felt engulfed by hopelessness.

But they are not victims by choice.

They have not chosen to give up on life.

The reasons for suicide are legion and can stretch from affairs of the heart, to illness, to bankruptcy. But in all cases, there is a recurring theme – people have been overwhelmed by their despair. That despair, that depression, is a mental health problem which, if discovered, can be treated successfully by professionals.

There is no reason for anyone to commit suicide. That it happens is an indictment of all of us. It's a disgrace that some ignorant people see mental health problems, or an admission of it, as a weakness.

I see things differently.

I view it as the ultimate strength for a person to acknowledge when something is wrong and seek medical or professional help. Why do we interpret the ability to open up and talk as a weakness? Why do we idolise the strong, silent types? They are exactly the wrong role models for our young people, as their lack of communication is much more likely to be masking underlying problems.

No matter what lengths we may go to to disguise it, all of us have experienced days of black, dark despair. I don't just mean because of missing out on a promotion at work or not being picked for a sports team. I mean real pain, the kind that lasts and lasts and makes you despair of ever getting better. In those black moments, it can take gargantuan efforts – every last ounce of strength – just simply to carry on.

For some unfortunate people that journey is too hard and they take a different route, one that ends with them taking their own lives. Such an outcome is dismissed by the well-functioning, so-called 'normal', people in society as 'irrational'.

But that's missing the point. When people are moved to take their own lives, they are already far beyond the point of a rational, internal debate. They are already so racked with feelings of despair and burden that they just simply want those dark feelings to end.

Through my work with the Outsider Art Gallery, I am aware of what Irish people with mental health issues are doing to make themselves better.

The people I deal with are wonderful, warm and beautiful everyday folk who have veered a little off-track on life's journey. But they are trying to find their way back again, and if they can do that through expression in art or drama, or sport, then more power to them.

Depression and mental illness is a complex area which, on occasion, has been glorified by actors, musicians and celebrities claiming to be 'depressed' after missing out on an Oscar or some award, or maybe because their latest album hasn't gone to Number 1 in the charts. I don't want to downplay their emotions and maybe, for a while, they were downcast. After all, it's not down to me to judge the severity of what that loss meant to them. But I feel those feelings are attributable to something tangible in that particular moment and, with time or work, they can be addressed.

The people I sympathise with are those who, for no apparent reason, experience the lowering of the mist. There doesn't have to be a rational explanation for this. They may feel as though they have everything they want in their lives, before being struck down by a sudden, inexplicable anxiety which forces them to hide themselves away, shut off from the people who love them most, and perhaps cause themselves damage or pain.

People in this position, and there are many walking the streets today, need to reach out and ask for help. The dark emotions which afflict us are not a weakness but strength. Remember we are not alone; there are millions of people like you, like me, who are suffering this every day. Only a minority finds the power to ask for help, but it's crucial they do.

• • • • •

In the meantime, I continue to strive to control my negativity, decrease my anxiety and increase the positive through my work, my interests and with the help of my family and friends.

And, while things can be hard and the journey at times exhausting I am, as I said, still trucking.

I recently started keeping a gratitude journal. I begin each day by thinking about what I am grateful for. My five-a-day. I write down five things, or five people or five events I'm grateful for and I smile, knowing that I have these things. I know that they could all be taken away – I know that more than anyone – but, for that moment at least, I am happy.

Like Gloria Gaynor sang, I will survive. I will duck and weave and always find another way. It's what I've always done and, it's worked well for me. But I try to live every day as it comes. For someone with a dysthymic nature that's incredibly hard as we are always peering into the horizon. So, of course there will be down days, or days where I doubt myself – I know that. But I've worked so darn hard to change things in that part of my life, that I feel I deserve a break. I know it will come.

And I have much to be grateful for. I pinch myself that I work on RTÉ television in a sport that I love, that I write children's books, am involved in various charities and have opened an art gallery for mental health patients. Those things made me feel good; they make me want to give something back to society.

I look at my gratitude journal. I look at what I have – my friends and family I love and who, I hope, love me, flaws and all. I try to take the positive out of everything, even if I have to force myself to do so. I can even acknowledge that, while my journey in and out of the mist has been long and hard – inside and out – it has also been the catalyst to making me the man I am today. And I like that guy: I think he's, basically, a good person. I know I'm in a great place. I'm positive and upbeat and looking forward to whatever life brings.

Still, I take nothing for granted.

But, at least now I understand the challenge that is facing me. It's been given a name.

And, sure, I am facing a climb to get over this particular hurdle. Maybe I never will. Maybe this struggle with a half-empty heart is a lifelong battle.

But that's okay, too.

I'll just take small steps, and one day despite taking the road less travelled I will get there, my day in the sun awaits.

Everest was conquered by a Kiwi of Irish heritage, who did it by taking small steps.

Good enough for me.

Desperately unlucky not to represent his country at the highest level, Popey was an integral member of the Otago loose forward trio of Paul Henderson and Mike Brewer, who both went on to play for the All Blacks. If not for the last thirty seconds of the All Black 1987 RWC final trial, when he dislocated his elbow, he would have been the second of the Otago trio to play for his country. After that, Popey continued to be the main part of a back row that contained the likes of myself, Jamie and later Taine Randell and Josh Kronfeld, all All Blacks. In fact, over about seven decades of Otago, Popey was the only Otago No 8 who didn't make it to test level. Now that is terrible luck. "Just as well I still have my day job as a bum model for Brad Pitt," was his view of his non-selection. He often referred to himself as having a, "rugged beauty with a great face for radio," but, to us, he had a face like a busted onion and the Otago front row was known to call him, "old earthquake face". That's ironic coming from Otago's front row of Hotton, Latta and Cumberland which was voted the ugliest front row in NZ. As David Latta's wife often told him, "I didn't marry you for your looks".

Arran Pene
All Black. Captain of New Zealand Maori. Otago.

10

Coming to Ireland

I awoke to a telephone call at about three in the morning.

Either someone was in trouble or someone didn't have a clue what time it was in Dunedin.

Luckily, it was the latter. I could hardly understand the accent on the other end of the line. Some bloke called Paul Chew was calling from a club in Ireland called St Mary's RFC.

Was I interested in playing a season of rugby in Dublin?

Bizarre. This was my second invitation to play in Europe, as I'd just been asked to play at the University of Rome.

I knew I wanted out of Dunedin, out of New Zealand. After the year I'd been through, I wanted to escape to pastures new for a while. It occurred to me that time was creeping up on me, at my age I might not get another offer to play overseas.

Certainly, it was an intriguing choice.

Rome v Dublin.

Italy v Ireland.

Pasta v Spuds!

I'd been in Ireland once before. During my time in London with Askeans, I'd spent a brilliant weekend in Connemara. That was the clincher really – I was Ireland-bound.

When I arrived in Dublin it was nothing like I expected.

I'd played with the Celtic team back home, a Marist club with Irish, and religious roots and I had a vague idea about my Irish heritage. But, in reality, I felt no more affinity for Dublin than I'd felt for London or the US when I'd played there.

I was just glad to be getting away from New Zealand.

I didn't intend to sever my links with home in any dramatic fashion. In fact, I only intended to spend about three months in Ireland, help out this St Mary's team that had signed me and then look to go back to Otago for their new season.

I didn't know what the future held for me but I did know what I was leaving behind. It wasn't all bad – I'd helped Otago win their first ever Division 1 title and I'd put my own rugby career back on track.

I'd learned to live with the disappointment of not making the All Blacks but I hadn't given up hope of one day claiming that silver fern. My old Otago coach, Laurie Mains, had always said that, if he ever made All Blacks coach, then he would select me. Over the years, but especially in 1987 and 1988, he'd made his dissatisfaction over my non-selection for the All Blacks well known in the media. As coach of one of the best sides in the country, Laurie regularly disagreed with the bias, then predominant in NZ rugby, that as soon as you wore an Auckland jersey you were an All Black. Mains felt I had been hard done by on many occasions and told me: "One day I will be coach and I'd love you to be an All Black." It meant a lot then and it still does now.

So, a three-month stay in Ireland was, in many ways, exactly what the doctor ordered.

Certainly, my first night in Dublin in October, 1991, was one to remember. I was met at the airport by a St Mary's meet 'n' greet committee and then it was straight into a bar in town and on to Leggs nightclub in Leeson Street – with my entire luggage in tow. Leggs was run by popular Wanderers stalwart, Aiden

'Deego' Deegan. Deego and I would become great friends in the years ahead. The same was true of Leggs' bouncer at the time, Al Gannon, with whom I manned a few doors in my time and who, nowadays, provides security to the stars.

But that first night in Dublin I knew no one. Successive waves of St Mary's players came along to the nightclub, bought me a few drinks, said "Hi" and then handed on the 'welcome baton' to a fresh recruit. I just presumed that someone would eventually take me to my digs which I vaguely knew was in a place called Knocklyon.

In the end, I stood alone, twisted, on Leeson Street, my baggage at my feet. I had no idea where I was supposed to be staying and the last St Mary's player had long since bid adieu to their new Kiwi teammate and gone home.

I hailed a taxi but, once inside, realised I had no destination for the driver. The only address I knew was St Mary's Rugby Club so I gave him that. He duly deposited me in Templeogue and I did the only thing I could – I took some clothes out of my bag, wrapped them around myself and bedded down like a homeless person in the doorway of the club.

I think it was St Mary's stalwart, Patsy Fogarty, ironically a man once employed with RTÉ's George Hook in the catering trade, who found me the next morning and, eventually, I was delivered to my new digs, a four-bedroom house in Darglewood Close, which I was to share with my old Otago University mate, Kevin Putt and Stu Gemmell from Waikato. We were all new to Ireland – part of a fresh breed of Kiwi rugby players who were making their way over from New Zealand. Along with us three, there was John Mitchell, Brent Anderson, Warren Gatland, Steve McDowell and Bruce Deans all playing for clubs as far apart as St Mary's, Garryowen and Galwegians.

In the years to come, Ireland would be full of ex-Kiwis, Aussies and South Africans, but we were the first of a batch of proud pioneers. In the last couple of decades the lads have all come and gone. I remain the only one to have pitched his tent in Ireland and stayed, though Warren Gatland, once elevated to the top coaching position in Ireland, today continues trying to manufacture our annual downfall with Wales.

Much to the horror of my new club, I'd arrived in Ireland with a badly torn calf muscle. But the calf healed and, in any event, when I arrived I was very fit. I was just off the back of a triumphant season with Otago and I was often a good distance ahead of the others in training. Not everyone was happy about that. One night a senior player called me aside and told me in no uncertain terms to stop showing the rest of the squad up. How dare a Kiwi bollocks come over here and show them how I thought things should be done? He clung firmly to the belief that there was nothing wrong with the attitude of having a pint in one hand and a cigarette in the other.

I wanted St Mary's to have more ambition. The club had a fabulous group of players with real talent, we just had to think differently. My intention was not to be arrogant but I was coming from a background where rugby had already taken its first real steps towards professionalism. Attitudes to training and playing had changed and, while not everyone was happy about it, there could be no turning the clock back.

At that time, rugby was like a religion in New Zealand. From the cradle to the grave everybody, and I mean everybody, wanted to play for their province and their nation. People who didn't know the Prime Minister's name certainly knew the name of the All Blacks coach, especially when they didn't perform. Little kids and old ladies stopped players in the street to berate them or tell them where they'd gone wrong in their last game. When I arrived in Ireland in 1991, top-level rugby in Ireland was serious, but not as far advanced as back home. The playing ability here was good but the game wasn't as professionally developed. There was little emphasis being placed on the level of mental and physical demands required to play at the very highest level.

Still, though the playing culture was different, my first months in St Mary's were wonderful. The club welcomed me with open arms and I made friends that I still treasure to this day: people like Mullers, Paul Glynn, Paul Chew, Robbie Lyons, Rego, Victor O'Connor, Eugene and the guy who would turn out to be my best friend in Ireland, Noel 'Henno' Hendrick.

I also got on great with my teammates, especially players like Aidan White, Tony and Derek Gillen, Babs Dowling, Pottsy, Hally, Gary Lavin, Dave Wall, Mick Corcoran and, later, the Limerick Prince, Nicky Barry. Still regarded as one of the best Irish schoolboy players ever, Nicky got one Irish cap against Namibia and, while I ribbed Nicky about Namibia being the name of a women's face cream, it was clear to everyone that he was a huge talent. If he'd been played in the correct position, as a running out-half and not a winger, he'd have collected a lot more caps in the service of his country.

There were other big characters. On my first visit to the St Mary's clubrooms I spotted a photo of a guy that I knew straight away – a bloke called Shay Deering. A few years previously, I'd taken part in the Dubai Sevens as part of an international composite team, the Warblers, whose players were drawn from the ranks of the All Blacks, Australia and France. Playing in Dubai was an unusual set-up: the grounds were made of crushed coral, kept alive with sewage water and, as a result, any cut would refuse to heal, weeping and festering for months.

Even more bizarre were some of the off-field duties expected of the Warblers. One of these was to do a bit of schoolboy coaching for lads from Bahrain, Dubai and Abu Dhabi. Some of the young players were the sons of rich oil Sheikhs, educated at posh English schools like Harrow or Eton and brought in across the Saudi Arabian border to be trained by us. We were warned that we'd be in serious trouble if these boys, who brought their bodyguards with them, got injured. But, like any kid, these boys wanted to play tackle, so I found myself in the bizarre situation of coaching these rich kids in how to run and pass, and at the same time trying to ensure they didn't get tackled and hurt while two sweaty 19-stone bodyguards dressed in black suits ran behind them on protection duty.

Fortunately, I found it easier to keep the rich kids safe than myself. In the Sevens, the Warblers were pitted to play the Sharlequins – an Irish team made up of English and Irish players, including current and ex-Internationals. In Sevens I played hooker and, as soon as the ball went into the scrum during the Sharlequins game, a vicious punch-up ensued. I found myself engaged with some Irish bloke and we were going so hard at each other that neither of us realised, nor cared, that someone had scored at the other end of the field. It was a serious punch-up, him hitting me and me belting him back. I didn't know this Irishman from Adam but we spent the match going at it hammer and tong, niggling each other all game long.

After the game we got on great, supping a beer and forgetting the onfield shenanigans. It turned out the guy was called Shay Deering from a Dublin club called St Mary's. Deering was a man's man, cut from a different kind of cloth. Years later, I learned of his bravery in fighting the disease that cut short his life, about how he walked from the Bective end of Donnybrook to the Wesley dressing room to see his rugby friends. Ravaged with cancer and crippled with pain, Shay refused to take the arm of another man. What was 100 yards to everyone else must have seemed like 100 miles for him but, head into the wind, he walked the distance unaided. He was a proud, proud rugby man who, despite his best efforts to rearrange my nose in Dubai, I respected immensely.

• • • • •

Part of the attraction of spending three months in Dublin was the fact that my time there would co-incide with the 1991 World Cup. The Kiwi team was based in Dublin so it was a great chance to catch up with some of my Otago and All Black friends.

And that's exactly how things worked out. Along with some of the other ex-pats, I spent my days going to the matches or watching the various training sessions around Dublin. Kevin 'Putty' Putts, Dick Knight and I headed up to the Westbury Hotel to catch up with pals like Ginge and Johnny Timu of Otago and Andy 'Worzal' Earl of Canterbury.

But as a Kiwi who was pretty much convinced that we'd win the World Cup, what I saw shocked me. We witnessed a team that was hugely divided. On one side of the chasm sat once-Auckland coach, John Hart, with his Aucklanders, while facing them were the Canterbury and Otago players with co-coach, Grizz Wyllie. We'd known that Hart and Wyllie – Brian Lochore's assistant coaches during the 1987 World Cup win – saw things differently. It was no secret in New Zealand rugby that on occasions their personalities had clashed. The two were poles apart; for one thing, Hart had never worn the All Black jersey, while Wyllie had been a prominent All Black in his time. In the end, the duo were made co-coaches in what still seems a ludicrous decision but, now in Dublin, we were beginning to see first-hand just how bad things were. Surprisngly, it also seemed that Hart was getting his way with selections, a number of Auckland players appearing to get starts over more experienced players.

Meanwhile, in that same World Cup, Australia got their preparation spot on. They too were based in Ireland and spent their time winning over massive Irish support. The team visited hospitals and schools and the great Aussie winger, David Campese, led their popularity assault, kissing babies and shaking hands better than any politician. The difference in approach was obvious. New Zealand's

Playing for Otago and, bottom, attacking the gain line despite playing with a badly broken wrist, with future Springbok and Terenure scrum-half, Kevin Putt.

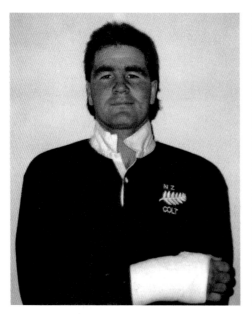

Top left, nursing another broken wrist and, top right, 'Ping Pope' gets his hamstrings rubbed by masseur, Donny 'Hands' Cameron. Bottom, making the hard yards for Otago.

Otago days: Mike Brewer and I, top, taking on Wales scrum-half, Robert Jones, in 1998 and, middle, the announcement of the All Black trials for the 1987 World Cup finals. Middle right, I was nicknamed the 'Bulldozer' but that nickname belied my infamous chicken legs. Bottom, I'm pictured with Otago University teammate and the man who could eat two boxes of Weetabix for breakfast, Grant Dearns.

— souvenir Programme — $2.00

ALL BLACK TRIAL

RUGBY PARK, HAMILTON
TUESDAY, APRIL 7th, 1987
KICK OFF 3.00 PM

ALL BLACKS
Steinlager
World Cup Challenge

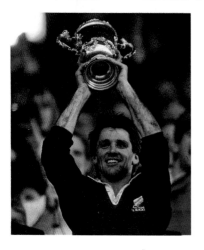

I thought 1987 would be a year of World Cup triumph for myself and the All Blacks. It didn't quite work out how I planned it, but perhaps the greatest All Black team ever managed to win the Webb Ellis trophy. Right, All Black selector Grizz Wyllie, who was in charge of my first All Black trial team when I had to pull out the night before with a hamstring tear.

Top, on tour with Otago. This time to Canada and Argentina for the CANZ series with the ugliest air stewardesses you ever saw – Rhys Ellison and Steve (Hotty) Hotton. Middle, touring Argentina and a typical Mendoza BBQ with All Blacks, Arran Pene, Arthur Stone, and masseur, Hands Cameron. Bottom, Despite being national USA rugby champions, we did not always enjoy the best facilities. These are the OMBAC players in San Diego showering up after a game – professional rugby at its peak.

Out from Down Under. The Penguins, an international selection that I captained on many occasions and toured with in wonderful countries like Brazil, Chile, Uruguay, Malaysia, Hungary and the Czech Republic, over many years.

I was a member of a New Zealand XV that thrashed English Premiership side, Northampton, by over 60 points in 1993. I'm with All Black, Brent Anderson (Garryowen); Otago captain, Dick Knight (Wesley College); and All Black captain, Buck Shelford (Northampton).

My walk of shame. Sent off by referee Dave McHugh after I punched Young Munster's Francis Brosnahan during the 1993, AIL title decider between St Mary's and the Limerick men.

Top left, the Darglewood Gang of 1992. The Irish knew what to do with Kiwi rugby players when they came to the Emerald Isle – throw them in a house together and let them fight it out! My housemates, Kevin Putt and Stu Gemmell (Terenure) Dick Knight (Wesley) and me (St Mary's). Top right, my first Dublin car. A dirt brown mini, that an old lady in Templeogue gave me for mowing her lawns each week. It had no brakes and the Lord's Prayer where the tax disc should have been. Sorry, Garda! Bottom, me against Leinster captain Chris Pim of Wesley in the Leinster Senior Cup semi-final, I would later leave Lansdowne Road with a serious spinal concussion that left me terrifyingly paralysed for a number of hours, St Mary's would, however, go on to win the Leinster Senior Cup that year.

The other side of the line: my coaching days in Ireland. Top, I'm with Irish International, Vinnie Cunningham, and St Mary's while, bottom, as head coach of Clontarf RFC.

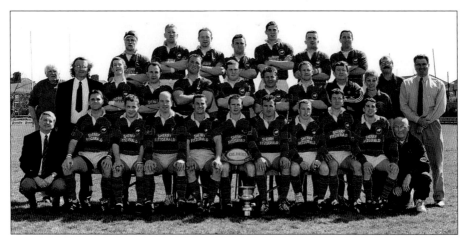

Top, the magnificent Clontarf team while, middle, captain Trevor Brennan is raised aloft after St Mary's win the 2000 AIL First Division title. Bottom, one of the Shamrocks touring sides. I was proud to coach them all.

Charity work for: top, Concern; middle left, my Outsider Art Gallery; middle right, fundraising as a children's author; bottom, with Habitat for Humanity's Karen Kennedy, and Irish rugby players Paddy Johns, Liam Toland and Angus McKeen.

Top, with the lads, Zinzan, Mike Brewer, Rhys Ellison and Mark 'Huddo' Hudson, celebrating another birthday. Left, with my idol Sean Penn and, right, with The Pogues legend, Shane McGowan. Meanwhile, bottom, I'm doing the Haka, with the Maori boys at my 40th birthday party, not a washboard in sight!

Top, my original 1995 World Cup TV debut, dark hair and all. Bottom, the original RTÉ panel before the emergence of Tom and George: Old pro, Bill O'Herlihy, the late, great Mick Doyle, Wardy, me and the best tan in refereeing – Alan Lewis.

George, Tom and myself clowning around as part of the current panel, though George, top, looks as though he's ready to call for some player or coach's head.

Top, I lead George, Tom, Ryle Nugent and Michael Corcoran in a Northern Hemisphere Haka while, below I treasure my career with RTÉ which included singing in Charity Eurostar and my 2012 challenge to learn the clarinet in two months.

Top, headlocked with
Trevor Brennan and
bottom, well ...
that's all folks!

over-the-top arrogance and refusal to mix was in marked contrast to Australia's mission to win Irish hearts and minds.

In what is, in my opinion, still the greatest World Cup game ever, Ireland lost to Australia in the dying minutes of the quarter-final. Gordon Hamilton had just scored a sensational 50-metre try and punched the air in celebration to send the Dublin crowd wild. He did the same for me: with the Aussies downed in Dublin, it was shaping up to be some night to be a Kiwi. But the Irish just didn't have the necessary self-belief to last another five minutes. They thought they'd done enough... But they hadn't. Still, it was a great occasion. Later that same night, stumbling home from Leggs nightclub past Lansdowne Road, I found a signed Australian jersey and a signed ball lying in the gutter. I still have them today, fond memories of a great game.

Outside of defeating Ireland in the quarter-final, perhaps Australia's greatest victory came off the pitch. Despite beating their hosts in the toughest of circumstances, the Wallabies had done such a great job winning over the Irish that, when they met the All Blacks in the semi-final, they had massive local support at their backs. Having seen the division in the All Black camp for myself, I commented that I didn't think the Kiwis would go all the way in the competition. The view was rubbished: despite a communication breakdown, these were still the mighty All Blacks who could surely still win the Cup, blindfolded.

But I knew Australia would beat us and, in due course, I watched the All Blacks, including some of my friends, lose in Dublin, just as I would watch them lose against France a few years later in Cardiff. In 1987, the hurt of missing out on the World Cup squad was softened a bit by the fact that, like a lot of other Kiwis, I presumed that it would only be another four years before they'd win it again. The All Blacks have, I think it's fair to say, been the best rugby team on the planet in most years leading up to the World Cups, but have only won it twice, with a twenty-five-year drought in between. As much as it is a word that New Zealanders hate, the tag of 'chokers' was starting to stick in the throat of Kiwis everywhere. The All Blacks 2011 win was extremely emotional for me: I realised what it meant to the people of New Zealand, and Christchurch in particular after their earthquake tragedy. I think for the first time ever following a rugby game, I actually cried.

But, in 1991, I wasn't about to let the All Blacks' premature exit worry me. I was in a new country, with a new club and a chance at a fresh start. Soon after that World Cup I got the opportunity to play my first game for St Mary's. The occasion came on a tour to Scotland but the trip sticks less in my mind for the quality of rugby than it does for my introduction to Irish stout – Guinness.

Declan Fanning and Noel McCarthy of St Mary's introduced me to my first pint of the black stuff and, as they saw my face flinch at the first sup, they reassured me that I'd get used to the stuff. I was no greenhorn and, during my time in New Zealand, England and the United States, had played and partied hard with the toughest of opponents and teammates. So, I was determined that I'd play these Irishmen at their own drinking game, and match them pint for pint. The honour of Otago and New Zealand was at stake...

I downed pint after pint of this thick, black stuff and, as the night wore on, I began to feel the effects. But, as I swayed gently at the bar, Fanning and McCarthy stood bolt upright like a pair of drill instructors. I began to wonder how the hell these Irishmen could drink so much without being affected.

In short order, I was locked, incapable of making it out of the hotel under my own steam. Fortunately, help was at hand: while carrying some Irish lassie around the bar on my shoulders, I fell over and was promptly 'helped' off the premises by the bouncers.

I avoided Guinness for the next six months. I was petrified of this mighty, potent, stuff and what it might do to me. I only tried it again after I found out that, on that first night in Scotland, my so-called teammates had been lacing all of my pints of stout with double Drambuie 'depth charges'.

At least I fared better on the pitch than off it.

My first big game for St Mary's came against Garryowen in the AIL, and I managed to pull off a match-saving tackle against a young, fresh-faced Richie Wallace. The tackle saved St Mary's from the threat of relegation and so I suddenly found myself the new 'hero in blue'.

It was beginning to seem as though St Mary's and I were, from my point of view at least, a match made in heaven. Everything just seemed to click for me.

Dick and Putty started sleeping in later and later, getting up just in time for their daily dose of Home and Away, a programme from which Dick soon knew all the characters by name. But I preferred to keep myself occupied and my mind active by doing something. My parents had instilled a serious work ethic in me and I lived my life by the maxim, "The devil makes work for idle hands". In those days rugby wasn't a professional game: clubs would arrange a flight over, find you accommodation and feed and water you, but that was it. Really, it was a chance to see the world for next to nothing and experience life in another culture, just as I had in London and the US. But, sitting around twiddling my thumbs alongside other Kiwis in Knocklyon was not seeing Ireland and, besides, I liked working.

So the club asked a St Mary's man, Geoff Coman, if I could help out with his drinks company in Tallaght. At that stage, Tallaght was a bit of a wasteland. Even the new shopping centre looked as though it had just been planted in the middle of a paddock. It was a hard place to get to and I found myself getting up at 5.30am just so I could catch the two buses that would get me to work on time.

My job was to sweep the yard early in the morning and then help out loading the trucks. Due to my size and height I could load fairly quickly and the quicker they were loaded the faster the drivers could get on the road, so I was soon in demand and fairly quickly found myself as a delivery assistant. I loved working with Geoff: he was a great guy and the truck drivers I worked with were all 'salt of the earth' Dubs. As they drove me around the city, I got an intimate introduction to many of the tough, working class bars and warm, generous people that, sadly, have disappeared in large part during the Celtic Tiger years. It was a wonderful introduction to the 'real Dublin'.

I also got an introduction to the North.

The North of Ireland and its Troubles always held a fascination for me. As a young New Zealander interested in world history our black and white TV beamed us horrific scenes of a country at war with itself.

It always seemed odd to most Kiwis that people on the island could be so different and impassioned about their views. But I was young and naïve, as even in New Zealand we had a somewhat bloody history of a country at war. At school we paid allegiance to the Queen, as of course New Zealand was, and still is, part of the Commonwealth. But, even then, it seemed strange to us to be singing 'God Save the Queen' when she was English. She spoke differently and came from a different country. For young New Zealanders it was often hard to understand the connection, but for the Maori it must have made even less sense. Despite Captain Cook claiming discovery of New Zealand, like the Aboriginals in Australia, the Maori were my country's original inhabitants. The images we would get of

Northern Ireland were the same ones being shown all across the world: streets full of rubble; over-turned, burning cars; bombings; the scarf-covered faces of angry youths throwing flaming Molotov cocktails at British troops dressed in riot gear.

It looked a pretty depressing place to be and I'm sure it was but, strangely, it was The Troubles that gave me my first break in front of a camera and allowed me to captain an Ireland rugby side. In the mid-1980s, a movie was being shot in New Zealand called 'The Grasscutter'. It was the tale of a UVF informer who was tracked down by a hit squad to New Zealand.

What happened in the movie is lost in the mists of time, but I remember my own role clearly – I was the captain of a touring Irish rugby team. My casting had nothing to do with acting ability and all to do with the fact that my team, Green Island, wore green blazers like the Irish and could muster thirty lads at short notice. We spent the day filming at Dunedin Airport and were paid a small sum for our efforts. And that was it: no Oscar and not even a credit for my starring role as a young Willie John McBride.

But going to Northern Ireland with St Mary's to play teams like Ballymena or Dungannon, or some of the Belfast clubs, was a different prospect to play-acting in New Zealand.

I was edgy on my first trip across the border to play a match in Belfast. I'd read stories about the murders of the Miami Showband and, though things were quieter in the 1990s, there were still some pockets of trouble. For a young New Zealander from rural Ashburton, the sight of the border checkpoint, with barbed wire and armed soldiers who boarded our bus, was unnerving. Of course, the rest of the lads delighted in preying on my nerves. They told me there would be snipers on the roofs of the dressing rooms during the game and, while I was terrified, I couldn't wait to see Belfast.

After one game in the North our bus broke down not far from Belfast and, as we waited for help, many of the St Mary's players seemed a little nervous to be stranded in the middle of the city. By that stage, I was a bit longer in the tooth having been to the North before and, while the driver went for assistance for the bus, Johnny Kennedy, Babs Dowling, myself and a couple of others went to a local bar for a pint, unfazed. Fortunately, at times like that I was never asked to explain my surname…

I did have a bit of explaining to do during one particular trip to Derry. I'd gone there to do a favour for a Dublin friend, Paul McGuire, and had agreed to pick something up for the packaging business that he ran in Bray. Derry was at the other end of the country and, as I had been lent a car for the day, I thought it'd be a nice chance to drive up to the northwest and see some of the country first hand, rather than from a rugby team's bus window.

I crossed the border with the usual questions and drove to the factory address where I was due to pick up the packaging. Unfortunately, I arrived at lunchtime and, as everyone had gone for their break, I decided to do the same. I parked up the car and headed to the nearby pub for a bite. Soon afterwards, I heard a commotion outside and could see a crowd beginning to gather. I finished my lunch and wandered out to see what was going on.

Bloody hell!

There were armoured cars and soldiers with guns all over the place and everybody was looking worried. When I asked someone at the back of the crowd what was going on, they told me the army was sandbagging a suspicious vehicle. The helpful onlooker explained that the next step would be sending in the robot to examine the car and then, most likely, a controlled explosion would be carried out on it.

Wow. This was like The Troubles I'd seen all those years previously on the old black and white TV.

"And how," I wondered aloud to the local, "does the army decide what constitutes a suspicious vehicle?"

"Oh, that's easy," came the answer, "the car has Dublin plates and is parked in the same spot everybody knows a previous bomb was left in."

Crap!

It was my car. I bolted for the soldier in charge and, in my best Kiwi accent, explained they were sandbagging my car. It was a terrible mistake, I was very sorry. Could they, please, not blow up my car?

The guy was furious. Pointing to a nearby sign that warned parking was prohibited in that area of the city centre, he started yelling and threatening to take me in. I just apologised and played the naïve Kiwi tourist card. Eventually, they escorted me out of the city. I never collected the goods for my friend but at least I avoided having to explain to him how I nearly got a brand new car blown up.

My other favourite Northern story starred a Kiwi and a South African. My old sparring partner and great mate from Canterbury, Andy 'Worzal' Earl spent time in Ireland coaching both Garryowen and Dungannon and. During his time in Tyrone, Andy complained to me about how sensitive Alan Solomons, the Ulster's Springbok coach, was.

"How's that, Andy?" I innocently asked.

"Well, he [Solomons] rang me to see if he could take one of my Dungannon lads for an Ulster game. I just told him he could 'Fuck off!' That's all, Popey. Then the fucker hung up the phone on me. Talk about being an over-sensitive fucker..."

Maybe Alan should have driven down to Dungannon RFC to haggle with Worzal face to face, that was what I loved about the big, former All Black. He was one of the most honest men you could ever meet, straight down the line, from good, old-fashioned Kiwi farming stock. He was right at home in a club which prized friendship and doing things 'just right'. My overwhelming memory of Dungannon RFC was their lovely ritual, led by the likes of Paddy Johns, in which your opposite number in a Dungannon shirt, would come over to you after a game and buy you a pint. It thought that was a lovely, civilised, way to celebrate the game and the sport.

Despite almost getting one blown up, I got lucky with cars in Ireland and, if VW 'bugs' had been my car of choice in NZ, then I developed a similar relationship with Minis in Ireland.

In my early days helping out at Geoff's company in Tallaght I often passed a little old lady as I walked home. She'd regularly be out in her garden, mowing her lawn, as her son looked on, sucking on a cigarette. Over time, I stopped to chat to the old lady and, after a while, I offered to do the mowing for her when I could. It was no big deal, the garden was small and I was happy enough to chat to her as I did the work.

But one day when she came out she handed over a set of car keys to me. She told me she'd seen me catching the early morning buses to work and wanted me to have her old Mini so I could get there more easily. Talk about Karma.

The Mini was the colour of a turd, had brakes you needed to pump twenty times for any result and a copy of the Lord's Prayer jammed into the tax disc holder where the certificate should have been displayed. But, suddenly, I was mobile.

When I arrived at St Mary's for a training session, the lads accused me of wearing a car, and I had to take the front passenger seat out to fit in the 6 foot 5 inch frame of Dick Knight. One evening as we 'wore' the Mini on the road, some young hoods aggressively and dangerously cut us off, giving us the finger in the process. In the darkness, they couldn't see Dick or me in the car and obviously thought only a little old lady or man would drive such a tiny vehicle. I gave chase and the hoods, anticipating a confrontation with someone's grandad, pulled over to sort me out. But instead of some OAP getting out, they saw Dick and I unfolding ourselves from the Mini – in a screech of tyres they were gone and, in the five minutes it took Dick and I to get back into the car, the chance to resume the chase had evaporated.

The little Mini became a home from home. On one occasion, after a night on the town, my mate Noel Hendrick and I headed back to his house in Kimmage where I was bunking. We were both hammered and, as Noel walked into the house, he suddenly shut the door in my face. Through the window, I could see him staggering up the stairs to bed, completely oblivious to my banging on the door. I was stuck on the porch with nowhere to go and, worst luck, it started to lash down.

My only refuge was my little Mini but the keys were upstairs in the house, so I was forced to smash the windows of the car to get in. Dressed in a suit, but lacking sleeping room, I had to put my head out one window and I rolled up my trousers, socks still on, and stuck my legs out the other. But soon after, alerted by a helpful neighbour who'd heard breaking glass, the local Gardaí arrived. Pointing their torch in my face they enquired, not unreasonably, who the Mini belonged to.

All I could manage was a very weak, "It's mine, officer. I just had nowhere to sleep…"

In fairness to them, they laughed and left me to it.

It wasn't my last dealing with the Gardaí.

Later in my time at St Mary's, I became involved with an Irishwoman, with whom I'd spend many happy years. She loved rugby, and her family was always very good to me over the years. But my relationship with this lady got off to an inauspicious start. Early enough in our romance, I decided, after a few beers, to visit her one evening. Even though I had been there before, it wasn't easy finding her house – in New Zealand, all the houses look different but, in Dublin, they all look the same. So, having finally found her home, I proceeded to bang on the front door. She stubbornly, though understandably given the late hour and my general state, refused to open up.

I banged harder and called her name. Finally, I saw an older lady at one of the windows and, suddenly embarrassed at waking up my girlfriend's mother, I called up, "I'm so sorry."

"Leave, or I'm calling the Guards," came back the reply.

I knew that I'd probably upset her and her daughter but, still, I thought the threat of involving the police was a tad OTT. But I pondered a little too long as, suddenly, I heard sirens and was bathed in flashing blue light. From somewhere in the darkened street, a voice instructed me to move away from the door.

I refused. This was my girlfriend's door and I was staying put.

But there was no talking to the long arm of the law and, in short order, I was frog-marched from the front of the house, arm behind my back, with the officers telling me I had no business trespassing at the house.

"Lads, come on," I pleaded. "I've been here loads of times. My girlfriend really does live here. In the last house on this street. Simple."

"Oh, like that one over there?" replied one garda, pointing at a different house, which just happened to be my girlfriend's actual home. I'd been banging at the wrong door.

What could I say? I was mortified. I bowed and scraped and apologised to the Gardaí and to the lady I had thought was my girlfriend's mother. Then, suitably chastised by the police, I did as they suggested and slung my hook. As I sheepishly walked off home another Garda car arrived to see what the commotion was about. As it drew level with me, down rolled the window and I found myself looking at the same garda who'd spotted me sleeping rough in the Mini with the smashed windows. As my heart sank into my boots all over again, all I could hear was him saying, "You again?"

Despite being geographically challenged, Ireland was great for me – socially at least. At St Mary's we had our training week well organised and highly professional in its approach. Thursday nights after training meant a few pints in Ashton's Pub in Clonskeagh and maybe on to Faces nightclub. Friday nights were quiet due to the inconvenience of regularly having to play rugby the next day. Saturday meant a match, a few pints in the clubhouse and then up to Leggs or Buck Whaleys nightclub, while on Sunday we went back up to the club for a few pints and a dissection of the previous day's game in front of a roaring fire. Then it was cheer on the Seconds, into Blackrock to the Mad Hatter with the likes of Gary Lavin and Dave Wall and, finally, Club 92. Those places were crazy on a Sunday night: we'd actually dive off the end of the bar, rock-star style, for the others to catch us.

But they were fun times and I met my first real celebrities in Ireland. I partied with the Beastie Boys in the Westbury Hotel, in Dublin. They thought it was hilarious when I called them the Beagle Boys, from the comics, and asked me back to the hotel to have a few beers. In Lillie's Bordello on Grafton Street, I met a distinctly unimpressed Van Morrison and asked if he had any of my albums. Clearly he had not heard my clarinet playing.

In the same venue, I met one of Europe's sporting idols. It happened one night when I'd been in the club and dying to go to the toilet. I was politely waiting in line outside the loo when a small guy pushed past me in a bid to jump the queue. I grabbed him by the scruff of the collar and pulled him back, depositing him behind me and telling him to wait in line like everyone else. The guy grumbled a bit but, reluctantly, stayed where I'd put him.

A couple of minutes later, an attractive woman marched up to this guy, thrust a beer mat in front of him and demanded an autograph. Having secured the signature, she then asked me for the same.

The bloke looked up at me and I looked down at him, the two of us obviously stumped as to who the other one was.

"Who the hell are you?" the guy asked.

"Who the feck are you?" I replied.

"Dwight Yorke," said the Manchester United and England star. In return, I conceded I was just some old, ex-Kiwi rugby player. Then we laughed about it all, got the toilet trip out of the way, and I shared a few beers with Yorkie and his Man United mates.

That ability to meet and have some fun with even the most famous of people was one of the great things about Ireland. It still is. Apart from a few actors, movie director Peter Jackson, All Blacks Sonny Bill Williams, Dan Carter and iconic, Kiwi rock band Crowded House, New Zealand doesn't really have too many big stars or a culture that really puts them on a world stage. Thanks to 'The

Lord of the Rings' one or two famous actors or bands will drop in from time to time, to make a film or record a concert, but it's nothing like Ireland where Hollywood legends or music stars are regularly spotted wining and dining. In fact, the culture in New Zealand is completely different: I cannot think of any magazines or too many newspapers that dedicate column inches to celebrities, it's just not the way in New Zealand.

It was a thrill for me – still is – to go out in Dublin at night and see, perhaps even meet, global stars in music, sport and film. I still pinch myself at how lucky I've been during my time in Ireland. What a privilege it's been to have talked rugby with the likes of Gabriel Byrne and Liam Neeson, given advice in RTÉ's green room to the likes of Chris Evans and the stars of Dallas about the best place to go for a late night drink, and had my makeup put on next to 007, Roger Moore. Thanks to the fact that I'm often covering rugby on a Friday or Saturday night, I've been in RTÉ at the same time as many big-name guests and been introduced to them.

After I was knocked out of Charity Eurostar a few years ago, the backing band generously took me into town where George Michael was hosting his end-of-Irish-tour bash. I could not believe it when another member of a well-known English band quickly introduced me to Michael, saying that I'd just been voted off the singing show.

Michael shook my hand and asked me what I had sung.

"Frankie Valli's 'You're Just to be Good to be True'," I answered.

"I love that song mate, great song," he graciously replied. I'd come a long way from singing in a bar with Herman's Hermits.

But perhaps one of the best nights of my life in Ireland was getting to meet two of my greatest idols, and even party with one of them.

Around 2008, I was invited with my then-girlfriend, Ruth, to an event in the Burlington featuring the legendary boxer Muhammad Ali. All the greats of Irish sport were there, so, by the time we sat down, I was already feeling very honoured to be in the same room as many of these people. It was a great night and at the end I got a chance to say a brief but fleeting hello to the great Ali himself. It was a wonderful night for me just to be in the same room as my all-time sporting idol. After the event, a PR guy dealing with Ali asked if we would like a photo with him. Delighted to be asked, Ruth and I politely declined the offer out of pure respect – I'd idolised Ali the boxer all my life. I wanted to be left with the pictures in my mind, the images of the superb athlete I grew up watching on Richard Taylor's dad's new black and white TV.

Then, around 2010, I got a call from a friend – Dave Walsh, the head of security at Samsara in Dublin's Dawson Street. Dave is a great guy who has battled bravely against Parkinson's Disease. He was helping organise a fundraiser and asked if I could help out with giving out the raffle prizes.

I willingly accepted but, on the night of the event I arrived early and was sent to wait in a roped-off area of the La Stampa bar as a lot of the guests had still to arrive. As I sat there having a beer with Henno my all-time favorite actor, Sean Penn, and his entourage including young movie director, Brinton Bryan, sat down beside us. I was star-struck, but copped-on enough to know the rules about this kind of encounter in Ireland. So I just sat there, staring straight ahead, not wanting to disturb Mr Penn.

At one point, I found myself at the bar waiting to order alongside Penn's manager. As we stood there, a couple of rugby people asked me for a photo. I happily obliged and, drink in hand, headed back to my seat and Noel. Beside us I could see Penn's manager whispering something to Sean who then turned to me and said: "I'm sorry, but should I know you?"

"No," I replied embarrassed, "you shouldn't. But I know you."

After that, I spent one of the best evenings of my life with one of the most charming men I've ever met. We discussed what kind of movie roles Noel and I could play: I reckoned I would have been a great hard man, like him, in 'Mystic River', but Penn argued it should be something a little softer. We drank beers and shots, then he disappeared back to his room and, when he came back, he'd smuggled in some poitín. Suitably lubricated, we chatted about sports, movies and life. In the end, Noel and I lost track of time: it was late and most of Sean's entourage had already left to go to another highbrow function, but Sean and Brinton wanted to stay. Dave Walsh arrived to take me to the fundraiser. As I unsteadily rose to my feet, Sean asked me where I was going and, on hearing that it was a fundraiser in aid of the battle against Parkinson's Disease, he immediately volunteered to help. Dave was delighted, suddenly he had an old, half-baked RTÉ rugby pundit and a two-times Oscar winning, superstar to help.

Really, I found Penn a normal guy who wasn't into all the fanfare and hoopla that goes with celebrity status. He was just happy to have a drink with a couple of normal plebs. He was funny, smart and down-to-earth. The fundraiser broke up and Sean indicated that he wanted to go to an early-house but, on second thoughts, we all decided enough was enough. We hugged each other goodnight. The next day as Noel came out of a shop in town, the window of a big black car came sliding down and there was a slightly-shook Penn waving out and saying, "How are ya, Noel?"

They say it's never a good idea to meet your idols, but they're wrong.

• • • • •

By the end of 1991, I was in a quandary about my future.

St Mary's had just about stayed up in Division 1 during the 1991-2 season, my last-minute tackle on young Wallace helping the club to retain its vital AIL First Division status.

As was normal with all overseas players, I intended to go home to New Zealand but the club begged me to come back for another season. I was faced with making a huge decision, one that in many ways would affect my entire life. During my short time in Dublin. I'd grown to love the club and the players and my loyalty to St Mary's was unquestionable.

I'd long since proven my willingness to lay my body on the line for the club. During that season's semi-final of the Leinster Senior Cup against Old Wesley at Lansdowne Road, I suffered one of the scariest moments of my rugby life. At one point in the game I took ball up hard against Old Wesley but, as I ran straight into a tackle, I knew something was wrong. My neck was in an awkward position and, as I hit the tackle, I felt a shot of pain and then… nothing.

The next thing I knew, the medics were hovering over me but, still, I could not feel anything. I felt like I was floating on air, yet I could see the ground. The medical staff were asking me to wiggle any of my limbs, but I couldn't feel them, let alone wiggle them.

This was it, I thought. I had broken my neck. I was paralyzed.

I was stretchered off the pitch and rushed to hospital for an MRI scan. For about an hour I had no feeling, and could only think that I'd never walk again. It was the most frightening time of my life – there was no pain, just a knowledge that I might never be the same.

But someone was looking out for me, praying for me. Gradually, some feeling came back into my hands and my neck began to ache. I was delighted to be in pain, it meant I'd be okay. The doctors explained to me I'd experienced 'spinal concussion' in which the mind presumes the body to be paralyzed and, more or less, shuts down the nervous system. Apparently, this state can last minutes or much longer.

I was one of the lucky ones and, though I had to wear a neck brace for a while and missed out on playing for St Mary's as they won the Leinster Senior Cup final, I only had to spend a few days in hospital. I didn't mind too much, I was just relieved to be okay.

But while putting my body on the line was part of the job, perhaps my biggest sacrifice in the cause of St Mary's was turning down a potential chance to win the cherished All Blacks jersey though I didn't realise it at that time.

In the wake of the All Black's 1991 World Cup disappointment, Grizz Wyllie had resigned, leaving his rival, John Hart, in prime position to take the coach's post. Only Laurie Mains stood in Hart's way and, in a straight choice between the two, few people gave Mains a chance.

Before the final decision was made, I received notice enquiring if I might return early to New Zealand in 1992 and put my name forward for the All Black trials. I didn't think Laurie, despite deserving the opportunity, had any hope of being appointed over Hart, and I knew from experience that Hart would go for his own man, Zinny Brooke, anyway.

So, I declined the request and put it out of my head. St Mary's were still struggling, they needed me and I could not let them down. They had invested time and faith in me and they had brought me over to help them stay up so, by God, that was what I was going to do. At the very time the South Island and All Blacks trial teams were being selected I was turning out for the Mary's win against Garryowen.

As things turned out back home, Laurie was made the new All Blacks coach. Mains' day had eventually and deservedly come. Mine had not.

It was a double blow for me – not only had I missed out on the trials, I'd missed out on playing for Laurie. To make matters worse, Laurie stayed true to his word about picking players from Otago – he selected two of my Otago teammates,

Arran Pene and Jamie Joseph. During my Otago years, I'd nailed down the No. 8 jersey and Mains' loose trio was Pope, Brewer and Henderson while Arran and Jamie had spent a lot of their time on the reserves bench, or featured in various other positions.

With Laurie's ascenion to All Blacks coach, the great Zinzan Brooke found himself replaced at No. 8 by Arran. Such was Zinny's determination that he soon won his place back but, at the time, it was a tough pill to swallow. I'd been the first choice No. 8 in Otago for so many years, and now the greatest jersey in the rugby world was being worn by my rival. In my mind, I had sacrificed the black jersey with the silver fern for the blue shirt with the white star.

But I remained, and still remain, philosophical about once again missing out on the All Blacks. I'm fairly certain that, if I hadn't gone through my year of hell in 1991, I would have made Laurie's All Blacks. He'd coached me for years and knew what I was capable of. If I'd just been 'normal' that year, I'm sure I would have been rewarded. But sometimes things, good or bad, happen for a reason. I can't take back what happened to me that year, I can only learn from it and accept that if things had gone differently, I would never have made my life in this wonderful country.

Ireland and St Mary's had been good for me. In the time I'd been on the Emerald Isle, I'd managed to clear my head of all the rubbish and baggage, and had started to enjoy life again. And that, in the end, helped me to be delighted for Arran and Jamie. And for Laurie. They were great, great friends who had been such an important part of my life. When I'd been at my lowest ebb, Arran was one of the few players who never judged me. Others, and I can't blame them for it, turned their backs on me, not understanding what was going on with me. But Arran, though he couldn't understand either, stuck with me, helping me through my roughest of times. I'll never forget him for that.

● ● ● ● ●

As things turned out, at the end of that first 1991-1992 season with St Mary's, I returned to Otago for another season of Kiwi rugby. The old era I grew up in had ended. The Henderson, Brewer and Pope triumverate that had ruled for so long had been disbanded with Mike moving to arch rivals Canterbury and Ginge also leaving Otago. Hard though it was, I had to accept their places had been taken by the new generation of young All Blacks like Arran and Jamie. I was still put straight back into the team after getting off the plane, though this time at No. 7. The player who made way for me was no less a man than the great Josh Kronfeld, who went on to make a pretty good name for himself in rugby circles as the best flanker in the 1995 World Cup, in South Africa.

I loved being back in Otago. I played quite a few games for the province that season and even got to see my St Mary's teammate, Vinny Cunningham, and an Irish touring team almost beat Arran and the All Blacks in the home ground which Stu Forster and myself had nick-named the 'House of Pain' after one of Laurie's old training sessions.

But times had changed: I had changed. I had moved on just like my old Otago team had moved on. For the first time in such a long time, I knew where I wanted to be – back in Ireland. Despite resuming my life and career in Dunedin, I missed my friends, I missed my girlfriend. I had no job in Ireland, no immediate prospects and no idea if I had a long-term future, but I did know I was happy there.

I knew that my days in the House of Pain were numbered. At the end of that season, I flew back to Dublin and St Mary's and so began a pattern that I'd repeat again and again, as I juggled rugby in Ireland with work and life in New Zealand. Jetting back and forth grew tiresome but I comforted myself with the thought I was building for the future.

Funnily enough, as I plotted and planned, I had no idea that, within a year, my name and my face would be on the front pages of the newspapers, and not for the right reasons. On that memorable night in Dublin, Sean Penn had argued with my ambition to be a silver screen hoodlum, seeing me as a softer character.

On the last day of the 1993 season, I became public enemy No.1 in the eyes of most of Munster. I stood accused of acting like a gangster in what's regarded as perhaps the greatest game of club rugby Ireland has ever seen – the AIL title decider between St Mary's and the Cookie Monsters.

I'm not sure I would disagree on either count.

*The match had started with a punch-up after just ten seconds,
and both teams were taking no prisoners. We were up for it
– all of Limerick and Munster were up for it – and so were St
Mary's. There was nothing malicious in the punch: I was hit
worse before, and I was hit worse after. I don't remember a huge
amount about it. Someone tackled Popey low and I intended to
tackle him higher – to hit where the ball was – to prevent the ball
being recycled back to St Mary's. So, in I went and … then I woke
two hours later in St Vincent's. I'd been out cold from Popey's
blow. They took X-rays and there was a slight fracture to the jaw
but the nurse on duty showed me no sympathy, giving out to me
about how rough rugby was. The biggest annoyance was that I
couldn't even celebrate Young Munster's win for about five weeks
afterwards with a pint as I wasn't allowed to drink. My wife,
Antoinette, who was eight months pregnant at the time with our
second child, Lauren, nearly went into labour after hearing it
on the radio. But it all turned out okay. We'd never won the AIL
before, and we've never won it since. It was, maybe, the biggest
day in Young Munster's history since the 1928 Bateman Cup win.
That win meant everything to us and I don't hold any grudges
about what happened. That was how you played in those days,
it was tough, hard, passionate rugby and you hit and you got hit.
Whatever happened, it stayed on the pitch. None of us were
going to take a step back. Popey felt the same way for St Mary's.
It's what made the game great and a great friendship afterwards.*

Francis 'Brosie' Brosnahan
Young Munster.

11

Young Munster

Young Munster rugby holds a special place in my heart for a number of different reasons, not all of which reflect well on myself but which certainly helped shape my reputation in Ireland.

To be honest, it might have been better for all concerned if I had landed in Shannon rather than Dublin, when I first came to Ireland from New Zealand, in 1991. Back then Munster, not Leinster, had most in common with the New Zealand provinces back home, especially those in the South Island like Otago and Canterbury. That's one of the reasons the recently appointed Munster coach, Rob Penney, will feel right at home: the ethos is similar – no egos, just passionate rugby men.

Young Munster was a down-to-earth club where both professional, and working-class heroes combined on a Saturday afternoon to pull on the treasured club colours and give their all. The dressing room's mix of blazers and overalls was never self-conscious or awkward but, instead, seemed to provide exactly the right blend of ingredients needed to create a great buzz. And along with that great buzz and energy, Young Munster, who were known as The Cookies, grew in popularity and power.

To my thinking back then, there was probably a perceived pecking order and hierarchy in Limerick rugby. Garryowen were probably regarded as the elite club in Limerick, followed by Shannon and then Young Munster. The local derbies were ferocious and, each week, tens of thousands of vocal supporters, dressed in the famous light blue, dark blue or yellow and black colours, would pack the local grounds.

Physically, only a few miles separated the three clubs but in other regards they were light years apart. Today, as emphasis has shifted from club to province, it's possible for players to switch teams easily. But, back then, the rivalry was bitterly fierce and only a player with real strength of character would have ever considered swapping clubs. Players and administrators frowned on it and supporters never forgave it.

When he arrived to play in Munster, any impressions held by Kiwi Brent Anderson about quiet, friendly Ireland, were quickly dispelled. Anderson, a fantastic Kiwi acquisition by Garryowen, told me he was in a local pub when some Young Munster fans sent over a few beer coasters to his table. The writing on the coasters laid out, in some detail, what Young Munster had in store for him in that weekend's derby game.

Anderson was shocked at the time, but quickly came to understand that was how things were in Limerick. Players had to expect to have their mettle tested continuously, on and off the pitch.

Very much like New Zealand, Munster has always lived by the maxim, stand up and fight. That attitude was nurtured and developed by clubs like Young Munster. It was a club with great panâche, numbering legendary stars like Richard Harris amongst its fans. Even the fact that its most famous fan was a hard-drinking, hard-living, working-class hero benefitted Young Munster and helped it develop its image as a tough, uncompromising and brilliant club. Harris was a Hollywood movie star back at a time when the word 'star' meant something. He had been rugby player of some note in his youth and his lifelong dedication to Munster rugby was incredible: no matter what location he was filming in around the world, Harris made sure to stay informed of what was happening back home with his beloved club and province. After developing a belief in later life that he was a jinx to the Munster team in the early days of the Heineken Cup, he denied himself the pleasure of attending games. He was once quoted as saying: "I cry when I think of Young Munster, for whom I will never play." He was even buried in a Munster jersey.

Incredible.

Harris was there for that infamous game between Young Munster and St Mary's in which I gained my own notoriety. And he wasn't alone. He had, reportedly, brought Paul Newman with him. Two of the greatest stars of all time, cheering on a local rugby club. What other club could boast such a thing?

Young Munster's spirit and desire was also encapsulated by one of their favourite sons, Peter 'The Claw' Clohessy. When a player earned his first cap he was often granted the luxury of not risking injury by playing the week before. Nearly every player availed of it – after all, the chance to win your first cap for your country was on the line. Not Clohessy. He declined the offer to rest up, knowing that Young Munster had got him where he was and that was what mattered to him. At the time, it was a huge gesture – the decision showed his dedication to the club and his respect for those around him.

But that was the allure of Young Munster and I understood it. I grew up in a country where rugby was a religion and where players were expected to put their bodies, their minds, their everything on the line for the cause. And that's what it was – a sacred cause.

The Leinster ex-captain, and longtime Munster resident, Liam Toland, once tried to explain to me what it was like to play for Old Crescent in those halcyon days of Young Munster rugby. A side that traditionally was fed from schools teams, Old Crescent was full of young 18-year-olds who were keen, but barely out of school uniform. Putting manners on these youngsters was a favourite pastime of the Young Munsters.

Liam remembers the Young Munster team of that period as ferocious throughout, but the 'Three Gers' back row, containing Clohessy, Copley and Earls, was particularly committed. Ger Clohessy was their captain, Ger Copley their No. 8, but without a doubt the best, toughest and, most importantly, cleverest openside Liam ever played against was Ger Earls. Not that there were many chinks in the Limerick armour. On one occasion, having enquired of Ray

Ryan if it was Ryan who'd just hit him, Liam got the curt reply: "If that was me, Toland, I'd have bust your head."

Fair enough! These bon mots didn't shock this future Leinster captain and Irish International but it was too much for some: Liam laughs when he recalls how Dublin's perceived dandies disliked the Limerick ground, known colloquially as The Killing Fields, was reflected in the many 'unavailables' that pockmarked the team sheet. In the face of such opposition, there was only way to play the Munster men.

Get stuck in. Hit anything that moved.

Then, if you survived, enjoy every minute of their amazing club and hospitality, though it might be hard to take yet another victorious rendition of 'Beautiful, Beautiful Munsters'.

The Munster way was something I recognised as close to my own upbringing. When I was growing up and playing in New Zealand, the all-Maori clubs liked nothing better than to scare the young 'honkys' who came to visit them – especially if they were only a few points behind on the scoreboard. And if the NZ grounds weren't intimidating enough, then there were the Islands where the Tongans, the Samoans and Fijians lay in wait. I once played in Tucumán in Argentina where the groundsmen controlled the passion of the home fans by hemming them in with chicken wire.

Young Munster was like that. The drive into Tom Clifford Park was intimidating. Full of roaring, screaming fans whose pride for their team was unflinching.

The Young Munster supporters would hug the pitch, making it all the more unnerving, supporting their team with everything they had. Meanwhile, the 'elite' sat in the makeshift grandstand – an old double-decker bus bedecked with their sponsors' names. Moments before kick off, the Young Munster fans would bolt out of the bar to the pitchside, ready to go. They were like a wave breaking across the sideline, and it was an intimidating sight.

That was how Young Munster wanted it. Scaring the hell out of the opposition as they drove in was shrewd psychology and it worked. It still does, up to a point, but not to the same extent as in the early 1990s. Back then, Young Munster was a cauldron where the passions and temperature of the fans rose to fever pitch.

My first visit to Tom Clifford Park was in 1991 with St Mary's. I'd arrived just as the new All Ireland League (AIL) was getting going, but was injured so I couldn't play. Maybe it was lucky I didn't. As a spectator that day, I got to watch as a set of powerful, no-nonsense forwards led by the likes of the Clohessy brothers (Ger and Peter), Packo Fitzgerald and Ger Earls displayed their uncanny ability to bully and intimidate Leinster teams. The Limerick club was clearly beating a path to the summit of club rugby and had developed a team that was almost unassailable on its home ground.

In the wake of another mauling, successive waves of Leinstermen would meet on the dancefloors of Dublin nightclubs and swap their sad tales. Trousers would be pulled down and shirts hoisted as the battered bodies of players from the likes of Blackrock, Old Wesley, Terenure, Lansdowne and Wanderers were put on display. Winning in Limerick in those days was a rarity, so these war wounds were the closest many city slickers would come to claiming a badge of honour.

My main memory of that first Young Munster game was the sight of the giant second row, Peter Meehan, jumping over the ground's back fence, his gear bag slung over his shoulder, and a look of grim, utter determination on his chiselled face. Meehan a teak-hard, manual worker who loved the chance to pit himself against the Leinster Ladyboys and, in my opinion, there was no one more physical or intimidating than Peter.

In that 1991 game, Young Munster destroyed – literally – a good St Mary's team. They ruthlessly targeted Noel McCarthy, the tough Connacht captain, and No. 8 Declan Fanning, the experienced Ireland B captain. McCarthy and Fanning were rough men in their own right, battle-hardened at both club and country level. But Young Munster hunted them down. Everywhere McCarthy went, the Young Munster men gobbled him up, double-teaming him in the tackle and driving into him with every inch of Young Munster muscle they had. To his credit, McCarthy never took a step back, bloodied and battered he kept coming back for more. But, with a couple of exceptions, he simply didn't get the support he needed from the rest of his team. That day McCarthy gained much respect, even amongst the Cookie legions. But he was a beaten man and his St Mary's team was out-thought, out-fought and, ultimately, beaten into submission.

Watching Young Munster was like watching a predator in the wild: a lion that sought out its prey, isolated it and then struck at just the right moment. They tested the St Mary's players, prodded the Dubliners' line, checking to see where the weaknesses were. If a St Mary's player stood up to be counted, then Young

Munster simply moved on to the next player, feeling out the defences for the weakest link.

They didn't confine their aggression and hyper-competitiveness to the pitch. One year, a fire hose was inserted into our dressing room just minutes before the game. Everything, and everyone, was hosed down and, along with my teammates, I squelched out onto the pitch soaked to the skin. In the psychological war it was, Young Munster 1: Leinster Ladyboys 0.

But I admired it. Deep down, I admired them.

They reminded me very much of how the great Canterbury or Otago teams, under Grizz Wyllie or Laurie Mains, went about their business. Their blueprint for success included intimidating the opposition.

But, like Al Pacino said in that great American Football movie, 'Any Given Sunday', winning is all about inches. Against teams like St Mary's, even outfits like Young Munster had to claw their way to victory.

By 1993, St Mary's had built a team of genuine champion potential. We were winning as many games as Young Munster, running up huge scores with a terrific backline that sparkled with talent and was led from the centre by the enigmatic, but hugely talented, Irish Lion, Vinny Cunningham. Alongside Cunningham were men with Ireland and Leinster pedigrees, players like Gary 'Horse' Lavin, David Wall, Aidan White, Tony Gillen, Mark 'Fingers' Thorn and the 'Prince', Limerick's own Nicky Barry. Regarded by many as one of the nation's best-ever schoolboys, Barry went on to represent Ireland. White warmed the national bench against Scotland and was desperately unlucky to never be capped, while Lavin was a schoolboy star and Wall and Gillen, great interpros. Coached by Rory O'Connor, St Mary's played an open, quick rucking game that had proven effective against some of the best teams in the country.

In Limerick, meanwhile, Young Munster opted to overpower and overwhelm their opponents with a savagely ferocious pack. They had some great backs of their own: there was the metronomic boot of Adrian O'Halloran, and a huge lump of a GAA player called Francis Brosnahan, a tough, talented player whom I was destined to get to know better. But, in reality, Young Munster's 1993 triumphs belonged to a pack that scared the life out of everybody else.

During the 1992-3 season I was no longer on the sideline, spectating as I had been when I first arrived. I was at the heart of a St Mary's team that, as the season climaxed, were summiting the League. Young Munster and Cork Constitution were still very much in the mix, but we had a cushion of a couple of points and, in the final game of the season, faced Young Munster in what we presumed was a home tie. If we won we'd capture the title for St Mary's for the first time ever.

Young Munster was a tough side and we were concerned about them but we felt that, at home, we may just have the measure of them. Playing at our Templeville Road venue made us slight favourites for the final round, but that tag didn't unsettle us. In any event, fate took a hand in the run-up to the game as the circumstances surrounding the match changed dramatically and a key decision was taken by St Mary's which played into the hands of the Munstermen.

St Mary's pitch in Templeville Road is one of the best in the country but, back in 1993, it probably had a maximum capacity of about 5000 people, if even that. That size of a ground was more than enough for a normal game but the '93 League decider against Young Munster was far from a normal game.

A week before the final, the St Mary's President received a call warning him that as many as 20,000 Young Munster fans were preparing for a pilgrimage to Dublin. As uncompromising as their team, the fans were unlikely to accept being turned back at the gates of St Mary's. So, fearing an onslaught, St Mary's officials and local Gardaí were left with no choice but to switch the game to Lansdowne Road. For various reasons, the most important of which was crowd safety, it was the right decision and it had the advantage of ensuring the game would go down as the greatest club game ever seen in Ireland. In those days, an attendance of 20,000 was unheard of between the provinces, never mind a club game.

But the decision to move the game had a major impact on the result. The day should have been a home match for St Mary's, with us playing in front of a vocal, passionate home support. Suddenly, the match was switched to a neutral ground – albeit a Leinster ground – where our fans would be outnumbered almost four-to-one by the travelling Young Munster supporters whose ranks were swollen by 'volunteers' from the likes of Shannon and Garryowen.

Young Munster's coach, Tony Grant, used the venue switch to his team's advantage effectively. He tapped into that rich vein of 'all of Munster versus the Dublin elite' and stirred both team and fans into a potent, and combustible, cocktail.

Over at St Mary's, an appreciation of the importance of the change of venue took a few days to sink in amongst some. Some players remained oblivious to the head of steam building far to the west. And when realisation of the intensity of the Young Munster build-up dawned on them, it was already too late. Training became different. Some players began to doubt. Not everyone was used to high-intensity games like this.

Still, there were plenty of tough hombres in that St Mary's dressing room. Men like Mick Corcoran, Steve Jameson, Kevin Potts and Kevin Devlin. In the week leading up to the match, I spoke of the need for us to 'stand up and fight'. I'd played in big games like this back in New Zealand and knew what was expected. Young Munster would never hand us their respect – we would have to wrench it from their cold grip. We could not, would not, step back.

Mick Corcoran and I agreed during the week that, no matter what happened, from the very first kick off we would, more or less, grab the first Young Munster man who came our way and show that we were up for it... I warned the other St Mary's players that, like Willie John McBride's brilliant Lions Tour of South Africa, in 1974, we were facing a '99 moment'. Well aware of the Springboks' capacity to dominate opponents with a mix of brilliant rugby and physical aggression, during that famous Tour, McBride instigated a policy of 'one in, all in'. If the Springboks started something, then the first retaliation by a Lion would trigger a general mêlée. Every Lion would clobber or try to clobber the nearest Springbok and the signal for unambiguous violence would be the call, '99'– a shortened version of the emergency number, 999. In due course, the Springboks started, the '99' call went up, and the Tour went down in history. McBride was a brilliant leader of men. Not the biggest, not the fastest, not the most skillful. But he refused to be intimidated and he refused to let the men around him be intimidated. His team-building exercises were legendary – after one hotel was trashed, he responded to the threat of police intervention with the query: "Will there be many of them?" And when his fellow Lion and second rower, the late Gordon Brown, hit the Orange Free State's Johan de Bruyn so hard during one Tour game that the giant lock's glass eye popped out, McBride's only reaction was to instruct Brown to, "hit him in his good eye".

The lead-up to the game against St Mary's was like that.

I warned the St Mary's dressing room that we were all in it together. If we left one St Mary's player to go it alone against Young Munster, then he'd be murdered.

One in, all in.

The build-up was incredible on both sides. Schools in the St Mary's area dressed in the blue with the famous white star, produced banners and the newspapers were full of the big game.

I loved it. I felt I was paying St Mary's back for the confidence they had shown in me. They had brought me to Ireland and, in the time I had spent there, I'd grown to love the club. The camaraderie was great and the club was a home from home for me. We had a damn good team that played together and drank together and had become the best of mates. After Thursday night training, Mick Corcoran and I, with a few other lads, would stop off in Ashton's Bar in Clonskeagh for a few scoops. That was the norm back then: a few drinks on a Thursday night, rest on Friday, play on Saturday and drink for the rest of the weekend. Great craic.

It was a recipe that built team spirit and club loyalty. Like most teams I've played for, I was prepared to lay down my body for St Mary's and those players. I owed them and they owed me.

So, in the run-up to the Young Munster game, we trained, we met, we made ourselves ready. Munster was tooling up as well. Their supporters booked out every form of transport. The Cookies flooded the trains with their bumblebee coloured flags and even brought their famous mascot – a goat – with them. The goat's trip to Dublin is worthy of a movie in itself as the four-legged mascot made its way to the Irish capital via a series of planes, trains and automobiles.

At the ground there was a small island of blue in a sea of yellow and black, the Munstermen – women, children, and goat – vastly outnumbering their Leinster counterparts. The atmosphere was electric and, even for me, fantastic. The Young Munster fans shadowed us up and down the pitch as we warmed up, letting us know where their allegiance lay and singling out ex-Garryowen player, Nicky Barry, for special attention. Ignoring the fact that he'd come to Dublin to work, Nicky was, for these fans, the ultimate traitor. Worse than just playing for a Leinster team, Nicky, who would eventually play a huge role in the result, was a former Munster Representative player who was now lining out against the old enemy.

The stage was set for a game that had everything: St Mary's versus Young Munster; Dublin versus Limerick; Leinster versus Munster; posh versus working class; cucumber sandwiches versus the breakfast roll.

It would be a game that ebbed and flowed throughout and remained in doubt until the very final whistle. It would go down in Irish rugby folklore as the greatest club game ever played here.

But as kick off approached, all that was in the future. We were focused and determined. St Mary's would go home as champions and Young Munster would face a long, lonely trip home. On the pitch we weighed up the Munster men and paid little attention to the young referee, Dave McHugh, resplendent in his shorter-than-short shorts and gripping, what later turned out to be, his eager whistle.

St Mary's kicked off.

As previously agreed, the kick off signaled less the start of the game than the start of the boxing match. Within seconds, both sets of forwards were laying into each other with a flurry of punches of varying quality. Like Nicky Barry, I knew I'd be targeted. I was a foreigner, a mercenary, but worse I was one of St Mary's main weapons of attack. The Young Munster lads were clearly left with no choice in the matter and, suddenly, I was set upon by a couple of their forwards. As usual in most games, it was all huff and puff – a few handbags were thrown, a couple of miscued haymakers and plenty of verbals.

Nothing sinister, but it set the tone for the afternoon.

At the next lineout, the lump of granite that was Peter Meehan trundled up to me. Looking down at the top of my head as I took in his giant, old-fashioned boots, Peter told me in no uncertain terms what he'd like to do to me. I'd heard a lot of that kind of thing over the years from a lot of tough men and, as a rule, threats washed over me. But I made an exception for Meehan – I believed him. He was a tough, tough man a dockside worker who could, and would, mix it.

"Feck this," I told myself. "If you want it, I'm up for it." I knew I was a better player when riled and I knew I could take a punch and give a good account of myself. I made a mental note to be quick enough to steer clear of Meehan but also resolved that, if push came to shove, he'd know he'd been to Dublin.

The game was tough, more like a provincial or International game than a club one, with Young Munster using their set piece game and excellent loose forwards and halves to play territory. We tried to impose on the game the tactics which had brought us there, a loose, more open style that utilised our backline. But every time I touched the ball I was set upon, a bit like Noel McCarthy in that very first game I'd witnessed. The Munster back row would gang-tackle me and, for good measure, give me a good, old-fashioned shoeing. But that was fine, it just made me more determined.

The match was turning into an old-style, highly aggressive arm wrestle. No quarter asked for, none given. Verbal warfare was brought out at every scrum as both teams strove to win the mental game.

Approaching half time, the two sides were more or less on even terms, both having had chances they'd squandered. Then, with only a few minutes until the break, something happened that would change the course of the game and the course of my life in Ireland.

With just a few metres between me and the sideline, I took the ball up on the blindside. As expected, I was tackled by two or three Young Munster players. But, out of the corner of my eye, I could see the huge 6 foot 4 inch frame of Frankie Brosnahan making its way, at speed, in my direction with a tackle poised to poleaxe me. I was out of bounds and not about to be tackled into the metal hoarding.

So I just … reacted.

I dropped the ball, spun around and whacked Brosnahan square on the jaw.

From my fighting days back in New Zealand I knew how to throw a punch. But it wasn't the quality of the blow that sank Francis: rather it was his own momentum – a combination of his speed and size. Unfortunately for both of us, my fist caught him square on the chin and the big Munster man went straight down.

It wasn't malicious. It was reaction made from a sense of self-preservation more than anything else. But it was stupid, both for me and for my team.

I back-pedalled as the Young Munster team arrived to protect their teammate, just as I'd have done if it had been a St Mary's man.

Brosnahan was not getting up. I was saying, "Get up, get up," and thinking, "if he doesn't get up, I'm in the cart." But he was just lying there, prostrate, his jaw supposedly fractured, and definitely groggy.

After the game, I was told that Brosie was play-acting, taking one for the team in the knowledge that if he stayed down, I'd be sent off for sure and, at fifteen versus fourteen, my sending off would be a game changer.

I've met Brosie many times since and I don't believe that for a second. He was too good a player to want to miss forty minutes of one of the greatest games of all time. The reality was that he ran into an unlucky punch from me which, nine times out of ten, wouldn't have floored him.

Anyway, the details of the situation didn't really matter.

The Young Munster fans standing close to the sidelines erupted. Pointing their fingers, soccer-style, in my direction they were rightfully incensed. The Young Munster players pursued me, and I tried to hide, Pottsy pushing me back.

But McHugh, the referee, had my number. He called me over. I knew that if Brosie had gotten up I'd probably have been okay. I'd have been given a penalty, sure, but that most likely would have been it. But once he stayed down, I was off. I pleaded self-defence for the punch, which was described by the commentator as a 'friendly right uppercut' which was thrown in retaliation. But I knew it was a joke defence that would cut no ice. I'd punched him for the entire world to see. Simple as that.

Yes, I thought he was going to do me first and that would not, could not, wash. I just hoped the ref might have seen things as I did but, alas, it was not to be.

McHugh simply said: "You see that gate Mr Pope? Well, walk through it."

And I was out of the game, sent off in one of rugby's greatest games and in my club's hour of greatest need.

My head dropped and I began my walk of shame. The Young Munster fans, rightly, showered me with abuse. Calls of "dirty Kiwi bastard" and "you got what was coming" rained down.

I expected it. I deserved it. I hurt like hell.

But it wasn't the Young Munster insults that hurt me. That was part of the game, part of the fun of it all and any player that couldn't take the abuse had no right to be on the pitch. Instead, it was the knowledge that I'd cost my team. I'd lost my discipline and I was ashamed.

In the dressing room, I sat with my head buried in my hands, distraught that I'd been sent off for something so unnecessary and stupid. I'd cost my team a valuable player in a game in which we needed every shoulder to the wheel. I'd let my teammates, my supporters and myself down.

I pulled myself together, showered, changed and prepared to go back out to cheer on my teammates, but my way was blocked by a couple of Gardaí. It may not, they explained, be safe to show my face just yet. I figured they may be right, so I watched the rest of the game from under the stand, listening to the crowd and trying to decipher what their cheers meant.

Behind me on the field, Pottsy roared that they would win it for me. I appreciated that, I still do. And the players with the white star were magnificent in their response to his rallying cry.

At one point in the second half, Young Munster went 14-6 up, courtesy of a great try from Ger Earls which will live long in rugby history and keep alive a memory of a great player who should have played many times for Ireland. Earls latched on to a loose pass at the halfway line and famously outsprinted Nicky Barry to score the try that would, ultimately, give Young Munster their finest hour to date.

In the years since, St Mary's fans often wonder aloud why Barry didn't tackle Earls earlier. Why he didn't launch when he had him in his sights inside the 22. I can't answer them. From my position under the stand, I didn't see the try being scored. But I can say this: Nicky Barry was an ultra-talented player, a smart but underrated International who knew what he was about. Soon after the Earls try, Barry made a great break which almost led to one try and he was involved in the wonderful, flowing move that led to Dave Wall going over for the try which brought us level, at 14 points apiece with just seven minutes left.

It was an incredible feat – pegging back a Young Munster team which had a seemingly unassailable lead, built on the back of the advantage of having an extra player.

Adrian O'Halloran kicked Young Munster into a three-point lead, the ball clipping the crossbar as it made it over.

Unbowed, St Mary's fought to the final whistle. With just two minutes to go, a great, long-range penalty by Aidan White rebounded off the post, the thud resounding around Lansdowne like a death knell for St Mary's. The Dublin fans roared for a, potential, match-winning penalty in the last seconds when they felt that Vinnie Cunningham had not been allowed to play the ball from White's rebound, but referee McHugh would have none of it and blew for the end of the match.

It was the final drama in what had been a fantastic match – even if I'd only been half-involved in it.

But, at the end, we had lost.

The history books record a win and the title for Young Munster, not St Mary's. We had no complaints, even with only fourteen men, my teammates had given as good as they got. Many teams are galvanised when one of their players are sent off and, personally, I really don't think I'd have made a difference if I'd stayed on. After the Earls try, Young Munster had the self-belief.

I was proud of how St Mary's had played, proud of how they had proven they could stand up and fight and did it in the toughest of games. I was also touched by the fact that they had wanted to win this match for me, a Kiwi they had come to respect. I had come to respect them, too, and after the game I couldn't hold my head up high.

No St Mary's player, nor supporter, ever criticised me. They knew I'd messed up but they knew I realised it. Noel Keegan, a St Mary's stalwart, recognised my desolation. Noel is a true gentleman and clubman: blue blood courses through the veins of a man who has worked tirelessly in club jobs that others would decline. Even now, years later, I recall Noel's words to me with great emotion: "My darling boy. Be proud. We would never have made it this far without you."

Noel's words lifted my spirits.

Enough was enough. After all was said and done, it was just a few strokes of whitewash on the post that had denied St Mary's a famous comeback with just fourteen men.

• • • • •

Almost two decades later, there's only one ghost that still needs to be laid to rest. Every year, when St Mary's meet Young Munster, I'm asked the same thing: Do I regret throwing that punch?

Brosie and I are good friends now and I enjoy his company immensely when we meet over a pint. We both love the story of that match and we both dine out on it. Thousands of Young Munster fans love to relive the outrage of it all and, a bit like how Irish people 'misremember' who was actually in the GPO during the Easter 1916 Rising, the numbers on the sideline where the punch was thrown, continue to swell every year.

And, I must say, I respect and admire the Young Munster fans. Their brand of rugby, their passion and, back then, their blend of working-class and professional backgrounds was exactly the type of environment I grew up in at home in New Zealand. On the pitch they were fierce foes, but off the pitch they were fierce friends.

The year after I floored Brosie, I was in a pub in Limerick in the company of some Young Munster players. A drunk at the bar was determined to extract some justice from me for my transgression a year earlier and made some aggressive moves towards me. But as the bloke approached, the Young Munster players drinking with me immediately surrounded him and 'explained' to him the flaws in his plan – the major one being that I was with them. I've never forgotten that incident, and that gesture of solidarity amongst rival clubs and players. It was the epitome of what rugby is all about.

So, do I regret throwing the punch?

… No.

I'd do it again.

Back then, with me in a blue jersey with a white star and Brosie in the Cookies' famous bumblebee top, playing rugby was about pride in your shirt. I bled blue and he bled, well, black and yellow, and on that day in that match we were all prepared to put our bodies on the line for our club, our fans and our teammates.

In that particular moment, with just 42 minutes on the clock, an entire season of effort, passion and determination boiled down to just one thing… It was him or me.

And, deep down, I think the Young Munster centre knows it could just as easily have been me on the ground. He was a big, hard man who was well able to look after himself.

We both exited the game in circumstances we'd have preferred to be different, Brosie on a stretcher and me with a red card.

But, regrets?

How could you ever regret playing in a match like that? The only difference was Brosie had a winner's medal to celebrate while I left empty-handed. It was Young Munster's greatest day: it still is and, maybe, always will be.

Today's games don't attract the spectators or the top players, but on that day well over 20,000 paid to enjoy the game that had everything. Young Munster celebrated with an open-top bus tour around their city. They deserved it for, in beating us that day, they had done much more than win a trophy, no matter how wonderful that was. They had also erased that pecking order of League and Cup success in Limerick. Shannon would go on to dominate the AIL in later years and Garryowen would have their share of success along the way as well but, in 1993, the spoils firmly belonged to the team from Young Munster.

There was something magical about rugby in those years. It's difficult to describe to young players what was so special about playing club rugby at a time when the game was still shaped by its amateur heritage, and not its professional future.

Perhaps, it's best left to that Leinster man in Munster, Liam Toland, to sum up what we've lost in this professional era:

"Suffice to say that professionalism has robbed us of much but, for the elite of today, not to have experienced Tom Clifford Park as a rite of passage, before Thomond Park or the Aviva Stadium, is a crime. Professional rugby has much to be proud of but to witness opposition players, myself included, lathering Vaseline from head to toe to camouflage the rake marks, was a timely reminder of the battle.

"We loved it!

"You never know how strong you are until strength is all you have. The true measure of a man is how he reacts to adversity, especially when out of his comfort zone. That's where men of the calibre of Brent Pope were never found wanting. That he and many of the protagonists of that momentous AIL 'final' in Lansdowne Road remain friends, long after the amateur game was laid to rest and the old stadium was torn down, stands testament to all that was good about rugby.

"I've played against Brent on many occasions and have even shared an inflatable roll-out bed in Zambia with Habitat for Humanity. But, as that famous punch was landed on Francis Brosnahan, I was sitting in the Cadet School, Military College shouting at the screen with a sense of outrage that quickly turned to joy, as Earls outstripped Limerick's finest protégée, Nicky Barry, to score the winner. I was jumping out of my seat... Beautiful, Beautiful, Munsters..."

I couldn't have said it better myself.

I've always been a believer that character is what defines people during moments of adversity and, if I was ever going to war, Popey would be the man I'd have by my side. What he lacked in finesse he made up for in ruthlessness and dedication. We both had unique running styles: he called me the 'lizard' for my exaggerated wide legs and I labelled him the 'reverse hovercraft' as he would go from high to low and end up nearly scraping his butt along the ground the further he went. He cost a fortune to bandage, often walking out onto the field looking like an Egyptian mummy, and had so many bad injuries, ailments and various blood infections, that we called him 'Puss Pope' for a while. He was always having to scrape the wounds until they bled after matches so they would not become infected again.

Kevin Putt.
All Black Sevens. St Mary's. Natal. Springboks.
Natal Coach. Waikato Coach. NZTV Rugby Pundit.

12

Coaching on the Northside

By the end of the 1994 season, my body was in bits and age was catching up with the many injuries I'd endured over my career. At times, it felt as though I was being held together with duct-tape and, after back-to-back rugby seasons in New Zealand, England, the US and now Ireland for the last decade and a half, I felt that, realistically, I couldn't give St Mary's my best any more.

It's hard for players to recognise when the end has come. But parts of my body that I never knew existed were starting to ache. Injuries were taking weeks instead of days to heal and it was becoming a struggle just to wake up pain-free in the mornings. Mentally, the cracks were also showing. I loved the game, but my motivation was lacking. As a younger man, I loved it when a rival player had a go at me, it spurred me on. Now, I just found it a nuisance.

Ever since the Young Munster sending off, I'd become a target and I was tired of it. I'd always been determined that, when the time came to retire, I'd be honest with myself and the club. I felt that time was now.

There was a lot to consider. St Mary's and its members had been wonderful to me. At a critical point in my life, they'd given me a chance for a new direction and I was, and always will be, grateful for that.

But I had to think about the future, any future.

And while I had loved spending off seasons in Ireland and then heading home, my playing days were over. I loved rugby, and I knew that working in a 9 to 5 valuation job wasn't for me either.

Over the years I'd built up huge experience, and with my body and mind bruised and beaten, the natural transition was to try my hand at some coaching. I'd been lucky enough to be mentored by some of the best in the business. I'd also had success in New Zealand as a forwards coach with Green Island, and had some good feedback with school teams in Otago and St Mary's College when I took some sessions. I felt I may have something valuable to impart.

St Mary's wanted me for another season and I was even selected to play for a Leinster side at that stage. I had to turn that offer down, however, after St Mary's failed to give me their whole-hearted support. They didn't refuse me permission to play for the province but, in those days, Irish rugby was all about the club game, and St Mary's were understandably reticent. If I were injured playing for Leinster, then I'd be of no use to the club.

I was disappointed but, in the end, St Mary's – not Leinster – were the people who'd originally given me the chance to experience Ireland, and I was always loyal. To be fair, if I'd been in St Mary's place, I'd have dealt the same way with an overseas player I'd helped to come to Ireland in the first place.

It wasn't as though I missed out on all opportunities beyond St Mary's. In that same period, I couldn't resist being part of an amazing composite New Zealand XV assembled by future Waikato and Connacht coach, Glen Ross, who was then in charge of Northampton Saints and wanted to pit his team against a side filled with NZ talent. He got his wish – a total of thirteen current or former All Blacks and four 1987 World Cup winners signed up, including All Black legends Craig Green, John Kirwan, Zinzan Brooke and Buck Shelford.

Northampton had huge aspirations under Ross and their side included English Internationals such as Tim Rodber, Martin Bayfield, John Oliver, Matt Dawson, Gary Pearce and Nick Beal. The game drew a huge crowd and Northampton clearly thought they would win, especially as the Kiwis, like the Barbarians, were enjoying the fruits of touring. In the end, we beat them by about 60 points. Craig Green, the ex-Canterbury and All Black winger, playing out of position at full-back was brilliant, scoring almost every time he touched the ball. It was one of the best displays of rugby I have ever been a part of and showed the huge gulf that still existed between the two rugby hemispheres.

Back in Ireland, it was clear I had a decision to make about St Mary's. I gave serious thought to the club's request that I stay with them another year. But there was a rumour circulating in early 1995 that Victor Costello, a Blackrock College player and possibly the best schoolboy forward that had ever played the game in this country, wanted to join St Mary's. Victor, an International star in the making, was an amazing wrecking-ball type of player who happened to play in the same position as me, No. 8.

Taking everything into consideration, I made the decision about my future based on what I thought was best for the club. I felt I still owed St Mary's something after being sent off against Young Munster, but at 34 years old my body clock was in overtime. Victor Costello was the future. In a gesture of goodwill, I approached the powers-that-be at St Mary's and suggested that, for the good of the club, they'd be mad not to take Victor over me. I turned down the opportunity of another season in the famous blue shirt with the white star.

I looked at my options: I wanted to join a club that was further down the ranks a bit, a club I could turn around with a bit of hard work and an ounce of luck. I was offered a coaching role in Galway with Corinthians and, much as I loved Galway and appreciated the offer, I was in a steady relationship by then and didn't want to leave her, nor the good friends that I'd made in Dublin.

So, when a club on the Northside of Dublin came knocking I sat up and took notice. Clontarf was close to St Mary's in that the two sets of supporters always got on very well. I met ex-Clontarf prop, Trevor Merry, in a pub in Rathmines. He laid out what Clontarf was all about and asked if I'd be interested in joining as a player coach rather than just a coach. It was the playing question again and, again, I had to think long and hard about it. I doubted I had a full season of top-flight rugby in me, but figured that I might survive a season of Third Division rugby. Moreover, any overseas player switching clubs in those days faced a lengthy 'sit out' period so, for the first time since I began playing senior rugby, I'd have a decent layoff.

I didn't know much about Clontarf rugby. There were a few Kiwis there and the club came with a great social reputation. Also, Clontarf offered me a chance to gradually ease myself into the coaching role, as I was being offered the forwards coaching role under the watchful eye of coach, and Garda Inspector, Mick Davern.

In the end, I accepted and began my adventure with Clontarf. The difference in attitude between the First and Third divisions became apparent at my first training session. Clontarf had a fine history and had some success in winning the All-Ireland Floodlit Cup. At various points, they'd recruited some fine players like Matt Smith, Jimmy Meates, future Springbok captain, Gary Teichmann, Scottish Kiwi, Martin Leslie, and Damien O'Brien – another Kiwi who was good enough to get capped for Ireland on a Tour to New Zealand, although injury meant the big winger only lasted two games. When I joined, the club also had local talent like Rob and Pat Foley or their enigmatic out-half, Micky Fitzsimons, a player that – when he was switched on – was as good as any I've ever played with or coached.

As I joined, the club was losing some of the older, more influential players like Meates, Merry, Jim Stanley and Gerry Carr and others, to injury or retirement. But, underneath, I could see the makings of a good team – if only they'd bother to see it themselves: Clontarf's ambitions didn't really translate to their attitude on and off the park. It was a great club for enjoying post-game socialising, but my first few months standing on the Clontarf sideline with Mick Davern started disastrously. We lost to teams that we should really have thumped and the hammer blow came just a month before Christmas, when we lost in Galway to Corinthians. Many supporters were disgusted, so disgusted in fact that some, including the club president, declined to board the bus back home.

They were right. If the club had any aspirations to be noticed, then that would not happen in the bottom of the Third Division. In fact, by that Christmas, we were in danger of dropping out of even that league and into rugby obscurity. For a proud club, one of the oldest in the land, that was not an option. The Monday following the Galway defeat, I was called into a meeting with Trevor Merry. The jovial bloke I'd met a few months before to discuss my move to Clontarf failed to turn up. Now that the club was in freefall, I met a different Trevor, one who gave me an ultimatum – take over as coach with immediate effect.

I'd not even played a game as I was sitting out my qualification period, but Trevor's ultimatum showed how angry the club authorities were. I accepted the job but wanted to make sure Mick Davern – 'Dav' – was okay with me. I was never the sort of man to put the knife into another coach or player – I'd had it done to me too many times over the years to want to do it to anyone else. Dav was a good guy who had some great ideas for the side, but, like we all do at some stage in our coaching careers, he just found himself behind a losing team and, as coach, paid the price. Dav knew the change had nothing to do with me.

So, at age 34, I found myself head coach. There were two priorities facing me: First, I had to win over the players, some of whom were understandably unhappy about the turbulent period Clontarf was going through; Secondly, I had to begin alienating myself from the same players, many of whom were already friends, as I tried to create the space to make the unavoidable, hard changes that lay ahead.

My first meeting after I was appointed coach was with Matt Smith. He'd been with Clontarf for a number of seasons and was the sort of loyal, club man that would play on one leg if he had to. I had a lot of respect for Matt and felt that respect was a two-way street. I hoped that, if I could get Matt on board, then he would bring along the others. I was right about Matt. He agreed that we had to make the most of the two-month Christmas layoff before the next round of AIL games. We agreed, whatever it took to turn Clontarf around, we would do.

So, Smith was pivotal to the changing fortunes of Clontarf. If asked today, most Clontarf members would probably cite the decade up to 2012 as the club's best, certainly its most profitable. But, in my opinion, a club's success should be measured from the point where it started climbing the ladder of progress. Despite making countless AIB finals, Clontarf still hasn't won a national title in those years and, in the excitement of that decade, many club members have overlooked the foundations laid almost twenty years ago. Those foundations were laid by people like Trevor Merry, Colm Menton and numerous others, including players like Matt Smith.

Matt was a huge character. I once lent him a pair of expensive shoulder pads I'd brought from New Zealand. About a month later, I asked for them back and was handed a bunch of shredded pads which were missing some vital parts but covered in dog hair. Matt's explanation was that the pads just disintegrated on the first big tackle and suggested the real problem must have been a manufacturing fault.

The mystery was cleared up soon afterwards when, during a visit to Matt's place, I spotted the missing bits of my costly pads lying in his dog's sleeping basket, chewed to pieces. Matt's dog had eaten the darn things. His dog wasn't the only member of the family to eat strange things. Matt's party trick was to drink his drink and then eat the glass he was drinking out of. I'm still not sure how he did it but I wouldn't advise anyone to try it at home.

He employed some of the Clontarf players in the business he referred to as his 'lucrative interior design firm', but others knew this to be a white van with Kiwi painters and decorators in it.

"What's the bloody difference?" Matt would ask, "Only a few years at college."

Aided by Matt and others, I set about rebuilding Clontarf. I took a leaf out of both Alex Wyllie and Laurie Mains' philosophy: if we were going to salvage anything from this scrapheap of players, then we had to start by changing perceptions.

My first target was how we trained. Like Mains had done in Otago, I built a ruck machine out of heavy timber and, at training, started players doing Laurie's 'down and ups'. We finished every session with what I called, 'honesty sprints' whereby I asked individual players a question and then, depending on their answer, give them the appropriate punishment. If the player lied to me, then everybody got the punishment.

The interrogation would vary in its subject matter. Sometimes I'd ask the group who was out drinking during the week and the guilty players, already tired from that evening's session, would refuse to own up. But I knew the most likely culprits and it wasn't difficult to bluff them. I'd say someone at Harry Byrne's pub had spotted, and named, several players who'd been up there drinking. Then I'd warn them that, if the guilty ones weren't honest with me everybody would get the punishment. It worked just about every time. After stewing for a while as they weighed up whether or not I was bluffing, they figured the smartest move was honesty. Then it'd be up and down the field, roughly two sprints for each pint.

My logic didn't always work. In fact, it failed miserably on Warren O'Kelly, a soon-to-be Munster prop who had returned to his home club, Clontarf, from Landsowne. Warro was built like a beer keg himself and, boy, could he drink. One evening, as he completed his fourteenth honesty sprint, I got fed up and shouted after him: "Just keep running Warren… We'll see you later!"

But at least Warro was very honest. I prized honesty, believing that it could galvanise team spirit. If players saw that everyone was being honest with each other, then they'd begin to realise that we really were all in this together. I imposed a drink ban in the lead-up to our AIL matches: we'd trained so hard for those two months that I wasn't going to let drink ruin the early signs that the lads were beginning to get seriously fit. I announced the ban just before our first game after Christmas – a road trip to Derry. A few of the senior players disagreed, they felt it was still okay to have a couple of quiet beers the night before a game – it was "the Clontarf way".

Adopting the stance of my old mentor, Lemons Mains, I told them the only way that counted was *my* way, and dropped them all. It was a tough thing to do, I liked the players individually and I also needed them badly. But I had to make a stand. If I'd folded on the point, then that was me gone. At the time there was war and a couple of lads left.

As things turned out, we won the game which was fortunate for me. I'm not sure I'd have kept my head above the waves if we'd lost. In the wake of the game, there was more good news – the lads who had left had a change of heart and were welcomed back with open arms.

It was taking a while but, gradually, players were beginning to buy into my methods as they realised it was my way or the highway.

The same was true of the club in general. Beyond the inner circle of coaches and management and the great gentleman of Castle Avenue, Harry Brooks, there was a lot of scepticism about my approach. After Christmas, that slowly began to change.

We began to climb the AIL, Division 3 ladder. It felt good, not just for me, but for the players. Men like Peter McQuillan and second rower, Phillip Quinn, relished the hard, physical training sessions, hitting the ruck machine like madmen, each trying to break the unbreakable machine. In the backline, the talented Fitzsimons and Smith started to run the cutter. We came together as a team and as a club and, for the next four or five years, Clontarf never looked back.

During that first season, we never lost another match and were rewarded with promotion to Division 2 of the AIL as one of the two best Division 3 teams. There was real excitement in the north Dublin club and, while there were differing views on where the success had come from, Matt Smith and I just carried on.

This was just the beginning, some of the Clontarf rugby committee men at last started to dream big.

The club was lucky enough to have some great supporters. One of those was well-known publican, Peter Hanahoe, part-owner of the Hairy Lemon in Dublin city centre. Earlier in the season, when things were going wrong, some of us were too embarrassed to be seen drinking in the club, so we'd made the Hairy Lemon our home. Peter was the brother of Dublin GAA legend, Tony, and he was a hugely generous man who, at some stage, had housed all of Clontarf's Kiwi imports. A clubman through and through, Peter never looked for anything in return.

Others were helping to shape the club's destiny. Harry Brooks, who passed away in 2012, was Mr Clontarf in his devotion and loyalty to the club and he was backed up by the committee, physios and doctors. I was lucky to have assistant coaches and managers of the calibre of Gerry Carr, Greg Howard, Dom O'Kelly and Paul (Lochs) O'Loughlan. There are too many good 'Tarf men and woman to name here, but they know who they are and they all played their part in re-establishing the club as a powerhouse in Irish club rugby.

Promotion after that first season was great, but it was clear that, to progress in Division 2, we'd have to recruit new players and raise the standards of our existing players. I spelled out the type of player I wanted – not big names, but players that needed a change from their current clubs, players who were underrated and underappreciated and hungry for success. We approached various players like Bernard Jackman. Although he later found fame as an International hooker, I'd seen Bernard play as a flanker for Lansdowne seconds. A whippet of a player with red hair, he reminded me of a former Otago teammate, Crazy Dave Latta. They were both a new breed of No. 2 – tough and fast. I knew I could make Bernard into a top-class hooker and brought him onboard, and he became a true Clontarf man along the way.

Pat Ward was another fantastic acquisition. Pat was good enough to represent Leinster, but he'd endured a terrible couple of years after a personal tragedy. Born into a staunch Lansdowne family, I could see Pat needed a distraction, something new to focus on. So I invited him across the Liffey and he went on to become one of the best players Clontarf has ever had.

Soon enough, as we continued to make progress, the players began to approach us. In my second year, my old St Mary's colleague, Nicky Barry, joined us, as did Shane Guerin from Galwegians. Despite his upbringing in the West, Shane, alongside Matt Smith and Phillip Quinn, was prepared to die on the pitch for the team and you can't really say much more about a player than that. I targeted Dave Moore from Blackrock College. A No. 8 with an Irish Schools cap, Dave was exactly the sort of player I wanted: someone who was missing out at his current club but who could become an integral part of 'Tarf's adventure. Ritchie Murphy, the current Leinster skills coach, joined us from Greystones and became one of the best kicking out-halves in the country. He was later joined by his former teammates, Alan Dignam and the Noble brothers Rob and Paul.

Clontarf and north Dublin players, exiled to the south of the Liffey, began to return, realising that they no longer had to cross O'Connell Bridge to look for higher-level rugby. Kenny Lawless, Gareth Ahern, Karl Hoffman and others came back.

Further afield, Niall Murphy travelled up from Cork and I brought in Ollie Winchester from Otago, South African Rian Vorster, and Craig Brownlie from Hawke's Bay. It was the same way St Mary's had brought me over and, in the early years, the accommodation wasn't too flash for the lads: a trailer-home on concrete slabs at the back of the club. An honest, hard-working player, Craig was a great catch for Clontarf and, later on, good enough to captain the side and play professionally for Leinster. Craig was one of the main reasons we prospered in Clontarf.But we were also all about developing our own players. We wanted to retain players that had been loyal to the club. Had our policy centred only on new blood, we would have ruined what we were trying so hard to build up. Players like Robbie Foley, Micky Fitz, Mark Woods, Rasher O'Reilly, Dermot Kyne, Tommy Hannigan, Phillip Quinn, Tony Lawless, and Colm Power remained the axis of the team.

Division 2 was tough but we learned, adapted, survived and built. Soon, with our new recruits bedded in, we started to carve a swathe through the teams above, rocketing up the Second Division as we had the Third. Future Welsh Grand Slam coach, Mike Ruddock, paid us the compliment of being one of the best rucking sides in the country. But the heart of our success was team unity. We began to claim scalps among the so-called elite clubs which featured Irish Internationals. We were a hard-nosed team that was almost impossible to beat in Castle Avenue and the club itself was beginning to roar off the field. The team relocated its HQ from the Hairy Lemon back to the club and a local bar, Harry Byrne's, and after the matches we'd spend our evenings singing songs and enjoying our camaraderie. I'd become an honorary Northsider – for a while, at least.

We snatched the Leinster Floodlit Cup against more fancied First Division teams and repeated the success a year later. As we approached the end of my third season, promotion to the glittering First Division beckoned. It was the dream that had long eluded this proud club and we were desperate to realise it.

The season came down to the second-last game: the promotion decider between Clontarf and Bective Rangers. On paper, they had a much superior team which contained Internationals like Kurt McQuilkin, Vinny Cunningham and a young Trevor Brennan.

The match was played at Lansdowne Road on a wet and windy day and I was so nervous that, in the dying minutes, I went for a walk around the block. It was a silly thing for a coach to do but the tension was simply unbearable. In the end, we won 12-3 with a brilliant ball-carrying effort into the wind in a second half, in which the likes of McQuillan, Ward and Jackman, Barry and Woods were outstanding. Moore was especially brilliant. I'd instructed him to annoy the volatile Brennan and then stay a few metres out of his reach. In those days, Trevor was a bit of a loose cannon who, if sinned against, would spend the rest of the game working out how to exact revenge. I'd once played against him in a Floodlit Cup match and, as I broke up the field, I could see this fast-moving, seething, monster steaming towards me, determined to inflict pain. Just as he reached me, I stopped dead and poor old Trev, moving too fast to halt, passed right in front of me and over the pitchside railings. A lucky escape at my advancing age.

At the end of the Bective match, we'd won the AIL Division 2 title and, with it, promotion. The celebrations back at Castle Avenue were unbelievable: Harry Brooks and other club veterans were in tears during a party that lasted several days. There was still one game left, a home game against Greystones. Tired, emotional, hung over and playing a game in which the result was inconsequential, the players switched off. By half time we were getting thrashed.

The problem was, the club had erected a marquee and thousands of Clontarf fans had come along to celebrate our great year. Yet, all they were getting to see was a bunch of no-hopers getting caned. I shouted at the players during half time: "We cannot let our season end this way. These people are here to celebrate. Where's our pride?"

The players responded with a second half that remains my proudest ever as a coach. Hung-over but with pride in their hearts, they took the visitors apart. Then they partied some more.

I stayed with Clontarf for another couple of years, but it was hard to top the emotion of that year and winning promotion to Division 1. We were recognised as the best team in Division 2 and I was nominated as one of the coaches of the season at the annual IRFU awards. Personally, even being nominated was a great honour but, at the end of the day, all I had really done was bring a simple game plan to a club that was already well motivated. With a bit of training and some self-belief, the players did the rest themselves, building themselves into a unit capable of beating any team in the land.

Our first year in the top flight was a continuation of that self-belief and we finished the season fifth in the League. If we hadn't been denied a richly-deserved penalty try in the final game against Garryowen, we'd have finished third or fourth, but that's how it goes. Notably, we finished as the top Leinster side in the country in that first year. Many of my players had been selected by Mike Ruddock for Leinster and it seemed to all that Clontarf were poised to move to the next level.

Along the way, we'd destroyed my old club, St Mary's, on their home pitch. With a team filled with Irish Internationals, they should really have beaten us, a side with no Ireland players at all. But, despite the great names in their squad, they didn't seem to play consistently as a unit. I could see it in their body language. On paper they should have won the League easily but it seemed beyond them – they'd been in a couple of semi-finals but had lost games they should have won.

After beating them that year, it occurred to me that I had unfinished business with St Mary's, that I still owed them for that Young Munster sending off. But any thought of moving there was far from my mind: I was still a relatively inexperienced coach, cutting my teeth with a Clontarf side that was only beginning to enjoy success.

Or so I thought.

Soon after, I bumped into Victor Costello and Emmet Byrne of St Mary's. They told me they had the deepest respect for their coach, Ciaran Fitzgerald, and backs coach, Steve Hennessy, but I sensed they felt they needed an extra push to get them over the line.

Personally, I was at a bit of a crossroads. I was in the middle of a great run with Clontarf but, despite just winning the Leinster Senior Cup for the first time in over 50 years, I suspected the players were beginning to grow tired of me. I've always believed that a coach's lifespan at any club is about three or four years. After that, no matter how successful you have been, how often you change your tactics or your approach, your voice just doesn't carry the same weight in the dressing room.

I made my decision to leave, though it was no easy choice. I was leaving a dressing room filled with lads who were more than just players, they were friends. My last game in charge was typical 'Tarf: we made an amazing comeback against Blackrock, scoring 10 points in injury time to send the 'Rock down to Division 2. The post-game dressing room was highly charged. There were tears on all sides and, in particular, Irish International prop, Henry Hurley, was very emotional about my leaving as we had all become so close. That meant the world to me.

It had been an incredible journey for me, both physically and emotionally. But, at the end of it all, I'd achieved much more than I ever dreamed of all those years before when I sat in that Rathmines pub with Trevor Merry. When I left, I was happy that I had left the club in much better shape that I had found it. Ironically, the man who succeeded me was ex-All Black coach, Grizz Wyllie. Grizz came to Clontarf from Argentina's national side but in his first year in the Northside of Dublin, the side struggled, only narrowly avoiding relegation.

Though I was always aware of how Clontarf was doing, I had moved on. There was little point in looking back, my future lay with the club which had brought me to Ireland, St Mary's College RFC.

*Brent Pope came to Ireland in the early 1990s and left
an imprint on Irish rugby, its players and its people. He
brought a ball-carrying style of playing that hadn't been
seen in Ireland before, but was badly needed in those early
days of transition from amateur rugby to professional sport.
I played with and against him and was one of his players
when he coached St Mary's to an AIL trophy win, in 1999.
It was Popey and Trevor Brennan who guided us home in
the final. We players knew what it meant to him after his
many, painful years of trying. He travelled the touchlines
of every game, his frustration, enthusiasm and knowledge
evident at all times. Popey is 'old school'. In today's
professional era, players gain financially from the game
and have to play full-time. By doing so, they miss out on
the purity of going into battle not for money, but for the
guy beside them, making a tackle to cover him, taking a
hit to save him knowing that your only recompense will be
personal satisfaction, closer camaraderie and a pint after
the game. Respect is everything in team sports, especially
rugby. Across the world, Popey is respected.*

Victor Costello
Blackrock. St Mary's. Leinster. Ireland.

13

Return to St Mary's

Clontarf had been great for me in many ways but my time there taught me the most important lesson I was ever to learn in coaching.

I learned to keep my long-term problems of anxiety and negativity away from my players. I tried desperately not to pass my troubled way of looking at things on to the team.

Alongside that lesson, I learned the gold rule of coaching – tell players what they can do, rather than what they can't.

In my playing days in New Zealand, I'd been a victim of the Kiwi way – if you messed up, you were dropped. It was often because there was a queue of quality players waiting to take your position but it was also a diktat that stressed the negative rather than the positive and placed the emphasis in player development on threats, rather than encouragement.

I was dubious of that attitude in New Zealand and now, in Ireland, I found it simply didn't work. The secret in Ireland was to get to know your players, find out what they responded to and communicate effectively with them. I also learned to be fair and honest with players. That might sound like so much New Age mumbo jumbo, but it was true.

And all the time, encourage, encourage, encourage. That became my new mantra for my players. It had taken me a lifetime of low self-confidence and seeing the glass as half-empty to understand how wrong my old approach was. Instead, I drilled into my players the need to believe in themselves and explained that such self-belief, allied to a strong work ethic, was the key to success.

I believed in that approach so much that I applied it to myself and began to see results. Towards the end of my time in Clontarf, Leinster coach, Mike Ruddock, approached me to oversee and coach the Leinster A side: a side crammed full of young, up and coming players who would soon become household names in Ireland. Alongside Lansdowne's Willie Dawson, I'd be responsible for bringing on a generation of Leinster players, who would help their province dominate Europe and the Heineken Cup. Among that crop of youngsters was a young centre by the name of Brian O'Driscoll who would later became the world's best player in that position, though I can't claim any credit for that. These days, there is no shortage of people who take credit for O'Driscoll's career but I am not one of them. In my book, one of the few people who can justifiably claim some role in O'Driscoll's rise to the top of rugby is his old UCD coach, Lee Smith.

By coincidence, Lee was coach at Otago University in Dunedin, but, by the time Brian was ready for UCD life, Smith had transferred to the famous Dublin college. Lee was rugby mad and could turn any conversation back to his favourite sport. Above all, Lee was a gentleman, passionate but even-tempered and I can't remember him losing his cool like many other coaches. I'm sure even Brian would still credit Lee with playing a big role in his sporting life.

Both Willie and I could see something special in young O'Driscoll and, after just three games for the As, we told Mike Ruddock as much. The then starting centre partnership for Leinster was Kiwi import and Irish centre, Kurt McQuilkin and Martin Ridge, but in our opinion the As' partnership of O'Driscoll and Dermot O'Sullivan was every bit as good, and considerably younger.

O'Sullivan was an amazing player who was the perfect foil to O'Driscoll at inside centre. Though not as quick or perhaps as confident as Brian, he was bigger and stronger in the thighs and able to create space. His only flaw, according to

232

Willie at that time, was that he did not stay in the game as long as O'Driscoll, nor did he have the same finishing prowess. But the ex-Newbridge schools player did have a rare knack of making a half-break and creating tries. My dad, who knew a thing or two about rugby, was in Ireland when the Leinster As played Morocco and he came along to watch. Despite Morocco's role as cannon fodder, Dad saw enough to convince him that our midfield pairing was sensational – the perfect mix of power and pace who, between them, cut the Moroccans open almost every time they got the ball.

I've no doubt these two would have made a phenomenal pairing for both Leinster and Ireland but life, as we know, can be cruel. Dermot suffered a serious knee injury from which he never really recovered. Brian, who at the time was planning a holiday with his friend, Leinster and Blackrock College scrum-half, Ciaran Scully (another talented player who suffered an early career-ending injury), was quickly elevated into Ruddock's squad and went on to become perhaps the greatest centre the rugby world has ever seen.

It's funny to look back on that period in charge of Leinster As, which featured other stars of the future, like Leo Cullen. But, in my own mind, it will always be the two 'Os' – O'Driscoll and O'Sullivan – who stand out for me. While neither Willie nor I would be arrogant enough to suggest we passed on any pearls of wisdom – I was just a basic Kiwi forwards coach after all – our time with the As did show that we had the ability to at least appreciate talent when we saw it.

Getting to work with both players was an honour in itself and it's amazing and, at times, difficult to look back at how fickle fate and fortunate can be.

But my time with Leinster was only a short sojourn before I headed back to my old club, St Mary's, with whom I had unfinished business. It was a big deal to me. I was finally going to have the chance to put right the wrong of getting sent off in the club's biggest ever game, and I was also about to get the chance to see if my personal philosophy on rugby would work somewhere other than Clontarf.

I was very nervous. I'd done well at Clontarf but that was with a team that had started at the bottom, and, which had been devoid of Internationals. Much of our success was built on team spirit and self-belief, not necessarily traits that St Mary's International stars, and professionals, would buy into. My old St Mary's and Clontarf colleague, Nicky Barry, came with me as backs coach. Nicky was ideal for me. He was a great player in his own right, with good ideas and confident in everything he did.

The first task was to appoint an incoming club captain. St Mary's had a tradition of bestowing that honour on a new player every year and I was keen to make sure that the captain in my first St Mary's team would be a spiritual leader as much as anything else.

A lot of players could have done the job. There were men like Victor Costello and Denis Hickie already there, but I concurred with the choice of the St Mary's rugby committee, who felt Trevor Brennan was the man for the job. Trev wasn't a St Mary's man, he hadn't even attended the local Rathmines school and, in some quarters, that didn't sit well. Worse, he was a new recruit who arrived with a bit of a wild reputation. But what was undeniable was that Trevor had, well, the X-factor we so desperately needed.

In the end, big Trev turned out to be the perfect choice, one of the best captains I'd ever coached. His work ethic was incredible and he never failed to attend training or be there for me, or Nicky. The game was now professional and, at times, Trevor dug his heels in about the players getting paid, as most club teams around the country could only afford minimal match fees. We did have some worries that he might not play certain games but, in his own way, Trevor was just looking after his fellow players. Anyway, I took the view that all of that was nothing to do with me. It was up to the club to sort it out and Trevor always took the field.

And we certainly got our money's worth from our new captain. Each Sunday, regardless of his Leinster or St Mary's training and playing duties, Trevor would attend all the mini-rugby games. Moreover, he and his wife Paula would welcome any new player to their house for Sunday lunch. In a short time, the club and its members came to love his attitude. With the Brennans it became clear that, once they made their minds up to do something, they did it wholeheartedly. Trevor's dad, Rory, became a great St Mary's man and, although we both knew that father and son's loyalties would, ultimately, end in his home club of Barnhall, it was wonderful to see how much they loved their time in Templeogue.

As things turned out, Barnhall lost out when a certain small South of France rugby outfit called Toulouse spoiled the Leixlip club's happily ever after.

That St Mary's team had talent throughout. Later I brought in an overseas player who ended up being described by George Hook as, "the worst import in Leinster history". That was a harsh judgement. Eddie Hekenui had been a New Zealand, schoolboy star, and a great player. He had never asked to play for Leinster, but was selected after new Leinster coach, Matt Williams, ran into huge injury problems at out-half. Matt parachuted Eddie in for some games and, though he was unprepared, I thought he did well under the circumstances.

The team was crammed full of talent and, during my first year, players like Mark McHugh and Peter McKenna, won richly-deserved Irish caps. We had a magnificent backrow of Victor Costello, Trevor and Leinster Rep, Ross Doyle, and suddenly we were on track.

In our first year, we had some fantastic results, beating the likes of Cork Con and Garryowen. And, in perhaps St Mary's best-ever performance in the League, thrashing a Shannon team that was playing at home and featuring all its big guns, by over 40 points. The same game was marred by a punch-up after the final whistle: Mick Galwey took exception to our hooker, Dave Lee, and a mêlée broke out in the tunnel at Thomond Park with Galwey and, of course, Trevor standing up for their respective clubs. That was his way, he played with Mick Galwey on an International level and respected him immensely, but your teammate was your teammate…

During the Cork Con game, I was right beside the action when that same man, Captain Trev, hit Munster and Ireland star, Ronan O'Gara, with a couple of, marginally-timed, big hits. On a miserable day with the rain pouring down and the pitch a sea of mud, O'Gara refused to shirk his duty. He bravely took another ball and, sure enough… WALLOP!

As poor ROG lay there, face-down in the mud and bleeding from his nose, there was a moment of quiet. Then, without looking up to see which freight train had just hit him, ROG mumbled groggily: "Is that my old friend Trevor Brennan?"

In that distinctive Dublin drawl of his, Trevor simply replied: "Yeah, it's me again, Ronan."

Trev pulled ROG to his feet, patted him on the backside and the two of them disappeared off into the rain and the mud, ready to do battle again. As rugby moments go, it was one of the best I've witnessed – hilarious, but saying so much about both men and the sport they play.

They loved and hated Trevor down in Munster and he was often singled out for special treatment in Limerick, where he was blamed for every unsavoury act, regardless of whether he was on the pitch or back in Dublin. In one very bad-tempered game against Old Crescent, Trevor was sent off and the local fans, delighted that the bad boy of Leinster rugby had been red-carded, queued up at the pitchside to abuse him as he walked off. In typical Brennan style, he marched the line in front of the irate Crescent fans with his middle finger raised. Most of the hecklers waited until his 6 foot 4 inch frame had passed before bursting into more abuse, having to fall silent every now and again as Trev backed up to challenge them. In the dressing room after the game, Trevor remained incensed at his unfair sending off and at the crowd outside baying for his blood, even trying to open the dressing room door to let them in.

To my mind, Brennan was the greatest marketing scoop ever missed by the IRFU. He was, and remains, the poster child for players from non-traditional rugby backgrounds to make it in the sport. The IRFU should have paid him to visit disadvantaged areas of Dublin and promote the game. In many Dublin schools, he could have told working-class kids, in their own language, about how, through his rugby life, he had "been there, done that".

In rugby terms, he came from the wrong side of the tracks but, despite all kinds of prejudice, he has built a life and a following in France that makes him, in many regards, the most successful of all of Ireland's rugby exports. He's rightly revered in Toulouse where they claim him as one of their own, for giving them the hard edge they needed to win Heineken Cups. His current role as a successful bar-owner in the French rugby capital just adds to his popularity.

Whichever club the ex-milkman from Leixslip went to – Barnhall, Bective, St Mary's, Leinster, Ireland and Toulouse – he always made an impression, both on and off the park.

He should have made the 2005 Lions tour to New Zealand: Clive Woodward was a fool to ignore him when he sent so many others on that tour who made little or no impression. Trevor might have struggled to make the Test XV, but he would have been ideal just to gel the mid-week side.

When the All Blacks toured, they always took an older, well-respected and liked player that would bring the mid-week team together. Given Woodward's diastrous Lions tour of New Zealand, it's hard to say if Trevor missed that much anyway, but it was an honour that should not have passed him by.

In the end, Trevor's illustrious career ended controversially when he got involved with an opposition supporter. He deserved much better but, honest and straight as ever, he was man enough to admit that the red mist had descended and he was wrong in what he did.

To many in Irish rugby, myself included, Trevor Brennan epitomises everything that's good about sport. He's walking, tackling proof that a person can emerge from outside the usual areas and bring heart and soul to the game of rugby. A New Zealander in so many ways, he remains a legend in Leinster and French rugby circles.

Led by a captain who could single-handedly change the result of a match, St Mary's ended the Munster clubs' stranglehold on the AIL that year, though their top teams stayed in the hunt for a top-four finish. The provincial team was on its famous European journey and drawing heavily on the club players. There was a lot of talk that year about how unfair it all was on the Munster clubs and, while I have no problem admitting their complaints had real foundation, that's a problem all clubs encountered at some point. In the next season, St Mary's lost an entire team to Leinster duty.

Anyway, I didn't view Munster clubs' woes as my problem: as any good coach will tell you, you play what's in front of you. In ten years of trying, no Leinster team had ever won the AIL First Division and, after we won it that year, it would take another ten for one to do it again.

I'd taken on the St Mary's challenge to win and I was going to use whatever advantage I could to gain an edge – Munster had been doing it to Leinster teams for years. The Cork Con coach summed it up after we beat them when he said in dispatches that, "Whatever about the Munster European Cup factor, we didn't lose it here against St Mary's. We lost it by only winning one of our away games when all the players were here earlier in the season."

I appreciated that. The League had started months before when all the provinces were affected. St Mary's, with its huge Leinster contingent, had been hit early on but we'd still managed to win key games.

That year was an important one for many reasons. It was my first year back with the club that had brought me to Ireland and it was my chance for redemption. But St Mary's was also coming into its centennial year and we'd managed to make the AIL semi-finals. In itself making the semis was not a big deal, Mary's had reached the last four on numerous occasions. But they'd failed to make it past that point and, this year, I was determined to win, to get the monkey off our backs.

We faced Ballymena, a tough Ulster team packed with top players like current Irish captain, and South African import, Dion O'Cuinneagain. We won handsomely with Victor Costello playing the best game I'd ever seen. Victor wanted to show the Irish selectors he had a lot to offer and he blew away his opposite No. 8, O'Cuinneagain, scoring one of his best ever tries when we needed it most.

In the final, we faced another star-studded team. Lansdowne boasted the likes of Shane Horgan and Gordon D'Arcy but we weren't to be denied. In what George Hook described on-air as one of the worst games he'd ever seen, St Mary's triumphed. George might have been right – though few finals are ever a great spectacle – but I didn't really care. The St Mary's lads, to a man, were furious with the comment: Many felt that George was trampling on the club in its finest hour but, fortunately, the rest of the media felt differently and George's comments were drowned in a sea of headlines proclaiming St Mary's as champions.

It was a magnificent result, just reward for the efforts of players like Malcolm O'Kelly, Denis Hickie, Gareth Gannon, Fergal Campion, John McWeeney and others. Trevor brought the Cup home to the club and I hoped that this victory would help him forget about his shock omission from that year's Ireland Touring party. We spent the next week celebrating a golden year for the club. It was particularly special for me. After all that had happened, I'd returned to the club where my Irish adventure began and I felt I'd repaid their faith in me. Above all, I felt I'd finally made amends for that sending-off a decade before. And that St Mary's win wasn't only about redemption for me. It was just as important for my old teammate from that Young Munster defeat in 1993, Nicky Barry, who'd coached alongside me in Clontarf and now in St Mary's. Nicky had attracted unfair criticism in the wake of that loss but, now, that was all forgotten, those old ghosts finally laid to rest.

But, if the win was extra special to Nicky and myself, I was very conscious that it was built on the shoulders of many people. I was only one cog in a greater machine which ran from the loyal groundsman to ladies who made the sandwiches. The first thing I did was present a jersey, signed and framed, to my tearful manager, Kev Conboy, in recognition of the tireless work he'd put in that year.

I hate it when coaches take all the accolades and, at St Mary's, I felt very aware that I was only part of the success story. In fact, I regarded my own role as more of a facilitator or a motivator than a coach. I stood back and let the likes of Victor, Trevor, Mal, Emmet Byrne, and especially Peter Symth, take the lead among the forwards, while Campo, Mark McHugh and Denis Hickie led in the backs.

These players didn't need coaching by me. They were Irish Internationals who needed no reminder of how to play. What they did need, at times, was to be reminded that St Mary's was their club and that winning in the blue shirt meant something very dear to the loyal supporters who turned out, week in and week out, to cheer their heroes. But, by the end of that season when they were in the hunt for the ultimate honour, they didn't need much reminding of even that – they were magnificent, to a man.

In the aftermath of the win I was also cognisant of the fact that much of the groundwork had been laid by the previous coaches, Fitzy and Steve, before I arrived. They had effectively built the winning side, all I did was add the finishing touches to a team that was three-quarters in place. I recalled that night a year previously when I'd bumped into Victor and Emmet and my feeling that all they really needed was something a little different to get them that extra inch over the fine line that divides defeat and victory. Really, I was just lucky to get them at the right time.

I was still in situ the following year, but our success was proving our downfall with many players selected for Leinster or Connacht duty. At one point, we lost an entire team to the burgeoning professional game while the academies began to pick up many of the best players at St Mary's College. The club game in Ireland was changing and, in common with other great clubs, we began to struggle.

It was disappointing. That year's president was recently retired orthopaedic surgeon, Ozzie Fogarty. Ozzie was a St Mary's man through and through, and he was one of the nicest people I've ever met. For his sake, as much as my own, I wanted to repeat our success of the previous year, but it was not to be.

We had so many defections that I barely found it possible to cobble together a team. Along with backs coaches, Conor McGuinness and then Gary Halpin, I had props trying to play on the wings, and, though we still played with an immense team spirit, I began to realise that it was time to move on. I wasn't sure that I could take St Mary's any further and RTÉ was demanding more of my time. I was also involved with Clontarf friend John Pardy in trying to establish Ireland's first ever 24-hour sports clinic and it just seemed the right time to move on.

I needed a fresh challenge. Not a fresh rugby challenge – I'd spent the past thirty years somewhere on a rugby pitch – but a total change.

The game I grew up loving was getting harder and harder to recognise. Professionalism had sunk its claws into the club game and, in many ways, brought the great club era to an end. In today's game, there are Internationals who've never experienced what it's like to play the sport at a true grassroots level. To me, that's a huge loss.

When I left, it forced St Mary's to investigate closely how they would survive and prosper in the new, professional era. In my year there, we'd been top-heavy with Internationals and professionals but that simply couldn't continue. The club had to build on its own players, lads who would be there every week for the club and who wouldn't, in the course of a last-minute phone call, be pulled away for Leinster duty. I felt that Peter Smyth, the hooker from my team, was the perfect man to replace me – he was young, hungry and a great prospect.

In a clever move, the club appointed him coach and he delivered for them, though it took them 10 years to capture a second AIL Division 1 title, in 2011. Ironically, that title came against Young Munster in St Mary's and, in another ironic twist of fate, this time it was Young Munster who had a man sent off. Swings and roundabouts…

When I left St Mary's, I was offered other coaching jobs in Ireland, the UK and even France. Though I never applied for it, I was even tipped by the press as the hot favourite for the Ulster job which was vacant. I believed I had the stuff to go and coach at a much higher level. I still believe that. I only have to look around the world at my contemporaries – the Kirwans, Coopers, Gatlands, Putts and Josephs, and others – to see how successful they have been at the highest coaching levels.

But I have no regrets about the end of that part of my life. I loved the amateur days, I wasn't cut out for the professional game, I wanted to try to do other things outside of the game. And I felt I was growing into a role with RTÉ that may give me some security compared with a past that had been anything but.

I was still successful as a coach. With Clontarf and St Mary's, I had won promotion from Divsion 3, captured Division 2 and 1 titles in the AIL, and collected a three-in-a-row of Leinster Floodlit Cups, and two Leinster Senior Cups. Not a bad return for just a few years' coaching. Granted, everything I achieved was at club level – excepting that short spell at Leinster As – but I felt I'd achieved everything I'd set out to do. And I'd collected enough memories of great times and great people to last me a lifetime.

Thus ended my on-pitch life in competitive rugby.

It had been an incredible, and emotional, journey both on the playing and coaching side. Knowing when to stop playing had been much easier than making the decision to stop coaching – my body just stopped working the way it needed to, and that was that.

Still, in my heart, I knew my coaching future lay elsewhere. I needed an entirely new challenge on all fronts of my life. On the rugby front, I decided to get back to what I loved most, grassroots coaching, and building teams from the ground up in the same way I'd done with Clontarf.

But I wanted to do it for love of the game and for love of the players. I decided to create something entirely different and the Irish Shamrocks were born. Though the name was not the most original, the concept was new to Ireland. I wanted to give young club players, who'd been overlooked in one way or another, a chance to see if professional rugby was a real choice for them in life. I intended to take them to New Zealand and expose them to the best rugby experience of their lives. Along the way, I wanted them to have fun and experience not just something new in rugby, but in life.

The Shamrock Tours were an excellent adventure for the young men Brent brought to New Zealand, which provided them with great training and a real NZ experience. While they were not all of national standard, they trained hard, played harder and partied hardest – great representatives of Ireland who left a lasting impression on those they came in contact with. It was obvious that Brent brought the Shamrocks to NZ for them to get a wonderful rugby and life experience, and not for himself. It often ended up with him paying the living costs of those with less financial means! During the 2001 tour, Brent enquired about any young boys who might be interested in coming to Ireland to play for six months. As the CBHS First XV coach, I suggested a young lad called Dan Carter, who was quite exceptional at No. 10 or 12. Also a handy goal kicker! The NZ selectors had failed to select him for the NZ Secondary Schools side so Brent contacted Dan and his family and it was all set up for Dan to go to Ireland. One of the Canterbury coaches at the time, Steve Hansen, heard that Dan was leaving and felt there was a gap in Canterbury. At the eleventh hour, Dan was convinced not to go.

Richard Taylor.
Friend. Christchurch Boys' High School Coach.

14

Shamrocks

Even allowing for the bonds that form in sport, there's something special about the link between a player and his home club. No matter what kind of success a player might enjoy, no matter how far he might travel, he can always be certain that his highs – and his lows – will be most keenly felt by the coaches, fellow players and friends who were there when it all began, watching a little boy fumbling his first ball on a cold, mucky September morning when watching Scooby-Doo must have seemed a better option.

Those bonds between a club and a player are to be celebrated and cherished, even in an era when national and provincial success sometimes seems to be prized above all else.

In August 2012 I was reminded, in the most brutal fashion, how important those links are.

A young player from Cobh Pirates, by the name of Gavin Owens, suffered a horrific accident in a parish far from home. Like many young Irishmen and women, Gavin had opted to emigrate from Ireland in 2010, judging that, at 30 years of age, he might have a more secure future in Australia.

He was working as a refrigeration mechanic for a meat plant in Scone, just north of Sydney in New South Wales, and playing rugby for the local team, the

Scone Brumbies. To mark the end of their 2012 season the team had a celebration but, later that night as he crossed the railway tracks on his way home, he was hit by an express train.

Gavin suffered horrendous injuries and, while he's expected to recover from most of those injuries, the surgeons who treated him had no option but to amputate his leg below the knee.

The locals in Scone rallied around but, understandably, his family wanted to bring him home. It was at that point that his old mates from Cobh Pirates got involved – they hadn't forgotten him. Along with other friends, the Pirates undertook fundraising to get the money to bring him back.

That's how it should be, clubs and teammates looking out for each other. After all, that's the concept that brought me into contact with Gavin Owens in the first place.

In 2004 – I started developing an idea to build an Irish Touring Rugby Team aimed at young club players.

Years ago in New Zealand, there was a concept developed called the Rugby News Youth Touring. Sponsored partly by a then-popular rugby magazine, it was a tour for young players aged about 18 to 21 years old, who were nominated from clubs across the country. The players nominated were not the top names from underage rugby – quite the opposite. Some were players who had slipped below the radar of the national selectors and whose coaches thought were capable of higher honours. Others were nominated by their clubs as a reward, a 'thank you' for sticking with the club and showing loyalty.

Whatever the reason, the Rugby News Tour was hugely successful. Ian Jones, the wiry 75-cap, All Black second row, who later played with Old Crescent in Limerick, was just one example of a number of players who were discovered on the tour and who went on to enjoy illustrious careers at provincial or national level.

I saw the same need to develop a touring team aimed at young club players in Ireland. Why should wanting to improve your game or the chance to be able to tour be the preserve of Irish Internationals or professionals?

Some clubs already had annual tours as part of their team-building plans and as a means to improving players. Old Belvedere had been developing a similar scheme for years, as had St Mary's and a few other clubs who would send players for a season in New Zealand. John Hayes was first converted to a prop whilst playing for the small Marist club in Invercargill. The Bull always credits his time in the Country 'n' Western capital of New Zealand as the best learning experience of his life and one that set him off on his road to rugby greatness. Geordan Murphy is another who spent a couple of seasons being toughened up in New Zealand rugby, locking horns with the likes of Doug Howlett – then a young All Black star in the making.

But, back in 2004, I felt we needed to be doing something more than just encouraging camaraderie, so I started working on an idea to allow clubs to reward a player with nearly two months in New Zealand, living and breathing its natural game and living like a full-time rugby professional. It would be good for the clubs, allowing them the chance to retain players instead of always losing them to the bigger, more money orientated clubs that had been pillaging players for years.

The premise was simple: junior clubs would nominate a player – not a professional – fundraise to send him and allow him to better himself. In return, that player would return to his club and impart the knowledge gleaned from some of the best rugby brains in the world.

So Brent Pope's Irish Shamrocks Touring Team was born and, luckily, it was an instant success.

I assembled a group of raw, young rugby talent from all over Ireland. Players arrived from all four provinces and from clubs as diverse as Shannon and Ballynahinch.

Some players funded themselves, while others relied on parents or clubs to help out, but all shared the same ambition – to improve their game.

Though the players were amateur, the tour was professional. The players' fitness was tested before we left, so I could track their improvements over the coming two months in New Zealand where I'd lined up some of the best coaches available in world rugby. The Shamrocks were coached by the likes of Mike Cron, the brilliant All Black scrum coach; Richard Smith, a Canterbury high-performance coach who later coached the All Black U-20s to a World Championship; and Richard Taylor, one of the coaches from Christchurch Boys' High and a well-respected national schoolboy selector.

The schedule was simple, but intense. Each morning, the players would train at the University of Canterbury gym where they were given individual training programmes and, in the afternoon, they had sessions on skill development.

Tuesdays, Thursdays and Saturdays were different. On those days we placed the players with various Christchurch clubs where they were coached by locals and got to place alongside ex-Internationals or Canterbury players.

As if that wasn't enough rugby, we tied the whole thing together with a series of games in which the Shamrocks played against the likes of Canterbury Country, Christchurch Boys' High, Christ's College and Canterbury underage selection teams.

It wasn't all about building better rugby players – I wanted to build character and the living set-up reflected that.

Accommodation was good – four players to a Riccarton motel room which were more like little apartments really. There was a room with two beds, a sitting room with a pull-out bed for the runt of the litter, and finally a double room for the quickest, or meanest.

In terms of their food, they were encouraged to fend for themselves. Breakfast was laid on, and took the form of fruit and cereal, but a strict daily budget meant the lads had enough money to eat out for lunch while being forced to cook their own evening meal. Richard Taylor had kindly fixed it for the players to walk around to Boys' High where a healthy, plentiful, three course lunch was amazing value for money.

The Irish lads got lucky with Richard. Despite losing contact with him for a long time, Richard remained – remains – one of my closest friends. A kind man with a wonderful sporting family and wife, the tours would have failed without his help in organising coaches, games and meals for the Shamrocks. The lads and I were, and are, indebted to him.

But if breakfast and lunch were healthy, the evening meals where the guys had to prepare their own culinary feasts were a disaster. Rather than a shopping list comprising the basics such as bread, pastas, milk, butter and so on, some of the rooms had a nightly diet of chocolate bars, crisps and pies from the local garage.

I knew how to cook from my university days but these guys were hopeless. Apart from a couple of players that had escaped from under their mothers' aprons, most of them couldn't cook and some couldn't boil an egg.

Things got so bad I even arranged for them to take cookery lessons with the young ladies from Christchurch Girls'. But even that turned out to be a disaster with both sides just making dates for the coming weekend and giggling.

We persevered and things did improve after a while the players started to treat their diet more seriously. The odd plate of sausage and mash started to appear in some rooms though, for some players, chocolate and crisps still formed their major part of their evening meal.

But when the oven gloves were off, the Shamrocks needed to get around Christchurch, in order to play for their 'new' clubs and reach their dates with the girls from the cookery classes.

I had three vehicles they drove and two in particular were very popular – an old ex-ambulance, nicknamed the Venga Bus, that could fit about 30 Irishmen at a squeeze and a big old Holden car.

An eight-cylinder beast that could fit four across the front seats and four in the back, the Holden was 'a fair-dinkum Australian heavies' car' – the kind of vehicle that the Irish could see themselves driving across the Aussie Outback.

My dad had bought these cars and maintained them in the off-season, but he would nearly die at the end of every tour when he saw how the lads treated them. By the time the two-month trips were up, the cars would be short on actual parts but long on dents and rubbish.

Dad always loved to bitch about it, but he couldn't wait for the Irish lads to hit Christchurch. He loved meeting the lads and they loved him – he was easy going with them and chatted away like he had known them for years.

Insuring youngsters to drive was a little more easy-going in New Zealand as well. We managed to get third-party insurance, for a few of the lads who had licenses, for a few hundred dollars each. Some of the drivers couldn't afford the huge premiums back home so they were delighted, though the joy of being one of the five nominated drivers wore thin as requests for drop-offs and pick-ups poured in – one unfortunate soul even had to drive his mate on a date like a real gooseberry.

Over the years the Venga Bus became well-known, covered in Irish Tricolours and with a serious horn, rigged up by one of the players, that made it sound like the Dukes of Hazard were hitting town. Each morning the Venga Bus – packed to the illegal rafters with mad, Irish rugby players – would make the frosty journey to the University gym and back.

Proud as they were of their flags and their horn, the lads never realised that creating a mobile landmark was a double-edged sword. An ex-ambulance covered in Tricolours and sounding – from a mile away – like the General Lee is a hard thing to hide in a place as small as New Zealand!

So, while I didn't always let on, it wasn't hard to spy a badly-disguised Venga Bus parked around the back of some of the Irish bars in Riccarton.

And if I wasn't there to spot it, I could rely on the locals to do it for me – everybody down there knew there was a serious purpose to the tour and was determined to help the Irish lads improve at rugby, even if that help had to be administered in spite of themselves.

So, I'd get regular reports on the phone about the latest sighting… "Popey, just saw the Venga Bus pulling into the pub…" or, "Popey, the Venga Bus just rolled up to the off-license… "

More often that not, I'd let it go for the evening but would make sure to always take it out on the culprits at the next training session, or two. Slowly, but surely, most of them learned.

It was a 24-hour job, looking after the guys, but I had my Clontarf teammate, Matt Smith, helping out. Matt was back living in New Zealand, so he became team manager of the Shamrocks. Problem was, Matt's one of the nicest guys you could hope to meet and was much too good a guy to be any use at being a manager – he got on far too well with the players.

The two of us shared a room opposite the main bar a well-known hostelry called Trevino's Bar and Restaurant in Riccarton. When the bar was busy people could look out its main windows directly into our lounge. On a Friday night the bar would be packed so, if I wanted a shower after rugby, I'd have to pull the blinds in the lounge before making a mad dash – wrapped in a towel – into my room, all the time paranoid someone might spy me through the gap in the blinds.

But Matt, well he was too much of an exhibitionist to worry about a detail like that. He'd leave the curtains wide open, stride buck-naked to the shower and then still naked sit in full view watching TV or toweling himself off. Ripped and with dark colouring, even from across the road he was an impressive sight.

"Matt," I told him, embarrassed for him and the people in the lounge, "people are looking at you."

He'd just look at me and smile, as if to say: "I know, Popey, I know… "

Famous for his kangaroo courts both in Clontarf and in New Zealand, Matt was also the proud owner of a notorious – not to be tried at home – trick whereby he would finish his drink, and then set about eating the glass he'd just drunk home.

As if exhibitionism and eating glass weren't skills enough, he was also an inspirational speaker – a quality he employed to great effect in the Shamrocks' drinking session in Queenstown. Waxing lyrical about how the Irish should drink, the history and the pride associated with that quality, his motivational speech reduced some players to tears and inspired others to practically attack the bar – chests swollen – with the passion of full internationals.

After three hours, the Shamrocks were kicked out.

Matt had done his job too well.

Next morning, as I sat in a Queenstown coffee shop, I overheard two Irish girls talking about the evening before.

"You should have been at the bar last night," one friend said to the other. "It was awesome. This group of Irish rugby lads, called the Shamrocks, came in and took over... dancing on the bars, singing in the band... It was brilliant – I hope they're back in again tonight."

I had to laugh. I'd been in Ireland long enough to know that getting kicked out of a pub was a mark of honour.

But I knew I had to be disciplined with the lads. Outside of a couple of beers after the odd Shamrocks game, they were not allowed to drink during the week. Mostly, it wasn't a problem. All in all, the guys were great and though we had the odd call out from the police – many of whom I knew from my old rugby days – most of the trouble was fun-based.

I didn't want to be held responsible for underage drinking so I always made sure the guys on tour were at least 18 years old and could legally have a beer, if they wanted, at weekends. I also made the player's parents always sign a waiver saying that if they were ever arrested, out of line or disrespectful then I could send them home. In all the years we did the tour and looking after almost 100 young men, I only came close to sending one player home. It wasn't for anything serious – he just seemed to want to get drunk and party instead of learning and bettering himself. But after a couple of stern warnings he knuckled down and realised that, by sneaking out at night and drinking in town, he was just spoiling it for everyone else.

•••••

I couldn't watch them 24/7 but, at times, I felt I had to. It was far more work than I ever imagined. Parents will tell you looking after teenagers is hard enough, but looking after twenty-five of them for four years in a row, all on the other side of the world and many away from home for the first time, was tough, tough work.

But I was determined to make this the experience of their lives, something that would not only shape them as rugby players but also make them better people. I like to think a lot of the players on those Shamrock Tours left Ireland as a boy and returned a man.

Certainly, a lot of parents phoned me in the wake of the tours, telling me the difference in their son was amazing. Suddenly he was cleaning up, cooking and generally being more appreciative. I've no idea how long that lasted but it was a start, at least. I noticed the difference as well. The tours brought shy players out of themselves because they were forced to mix, to communicate, to get on with their peers for nearly two months. That gave them renewed confidence in dealing with others and I am sure helped many when they returned to Ireland and college or a career.

I remember making an exception once when I agreed to take a lad at the last minute. His dad rang me, imploring me to take his son who was rugby mad. At the time, I wasn't sure I had room for the guy as I already had a lot of players signed up for the tour. It would be hard to keep an eye on all of them, especially when they went out.

The dad said he understood but told me his son never touched a drink, was a clean-living peach of a lad who would be no problem. After a series of equally glowing reports about his angelic son, I finally caved in.

On the first weekend away I heard a car screech into the car park full of laughing young girls. I heard more noise at 4am emanating from outside, and hauled myself out of bed to go and investigate what the fuss was about.

I could hear what sounded like laughter – with a distinct Irish accent – coming from the trunk of the car, so I asked the girls to pop the boot.

There, staring back at me from the dark confines of the boot, twisted drunk and with a smoke in his mouth, was the teetotalling, non-smoking, clean-living angel.

I ordered him out and we had some talk that next day. I could've sent him home or phoned his parents.

But I didn't.

He rewarded me by, not only respecting my rules, but training hard and turned out to be one of the best players on the tour. He ended up playing 1st rugby for one of the country's top clubs.

Still, I should have known better.

The players would enjoy a few beers at the clubrooms with their New Zealand mates and when it came to training on a Sunday… My God, they were in some state. But they'd be in a worse state after training. I'd make them pay for their nights out – the players who'd been out all night would spend my training sessions sweating and vomiting. Every Sunday, they had an ice-cold dip and went on mid-winter swims at Summer Beach – a bit like Dublin's Forty Foot, it's freezing cold at that time of the year.

But if the swim was a form of torture for some, it was paradise for others. The lads who came out with me were a great cross-section of life and a disappointment for people who like to paint rugby as a game for posh kids. One of the lads hailed from a less-affluent part of Dublin and had a tougher background than some of the others. He was a great young guy but had never been to the sea, and while the others just ran in and out of the freezing water at Summer Beach, he revelled in the swims. While they shivered at the water's edge, this lad refused to come out and spent ages in the water, blue cold but fascinated by the sea, much to the amusement of the Japanese tourists who were busy clicking away like crazy, taking photos of these mad Irishmen.

But it wasn't all punishment for the lads. One of the treats was a weekend away in Queenstown, the adrenaline capital of the world.

The trip was great fun but a logistical nightmare to organise – trying to mind the lads as they bungee jumped, skied and generally tried every kind of thrill on offer, was a challenge.

One member of Trevor Brennan's Barnhall club ended up in hospital after attempting to slide the length of a handrail outside a club. In the local hospital's A&E department, he insisted to the not-amused medical staff that he was a famous jockey back home in Ireland.

Thank God he was the only casualty, but I don't know how. A typical mobile phone conversation would go like this…

"Guys! Where are you?"

"Hey, Popey, look up… See that helicopter? We're just about to jump out of it!"

All weekend long, I was terrified that I'd have to call parents in Ireland and give them some awful news. Fortunately – the odd broken bone, bruised limbs and some sore heads apart – we got away Scott-free.

In fact, the Shamrocks picked up more injuries at some of Matt's kangaroo courts than from bungee jumping or whitewater rafting.

It was, in reality, a magical time for all of us. Watching these young Irishmen develop their rugby and getting the chance to face-off against a New Zealand Haka, performed on home soil, is a memory that will stay with me, and hopefully the players, forever.

In many instances these Irish youngsters lined up against young New Zealanders who have gone on to become household names – Dan Carter and George Naoupu (who ended up in Ireland) both played for Christchurch Boys' against the Shamrocks.

To be honest, a lot of players that went to New Zealand could have made it out there. Some players did stay on in New Zealand or went back to play seasons with the clubs they had been 'adopted' by.

Some were even asked to stay on and trial for various Canterbury underage Rep teams. Given that some of these Shamrocks players couldn't achieve recognition above club level back home, such an offer was a huge honour – the Canterbury Crusaders is one of the top provincial structures in the world.

All this was achieved without any help from the official Irish rugby set-up. But such offers, and honours, don't come along every day and, truth be told, I was always a bit disappointed that the IRFU failed to row in with me a little.

I know there was no onus on them to do so, but wasn't I putting something positive back into the game in Ireland?

I figured that maybe one or two of these players – properly nurtured – could have been the next great Irish player. And I wasn't alone. Some of my Kiwi experts, men who knew a thing or two about world class rugby, agreed with me. But when some of these young guys – great talents – came home, they were again ignored. Perhaps their disappearance back into the rugby mists was due to their coming from a small club which couldn't promote them properly… I don't know, but in my opinion many a talented player who toured with the Shamrocks was wasted.

In the end, the tours became too hard to manage single-handedly. My father, by that stage in his 70s, had done a huge amount of legwork back home, maintaining the cars, sorting out insurances and so on. Meanwhile I had to book flights with my own money, organise accommodation and everything else.

This was not a money making venture, I was doing it all for nothing.

At one stage, the players were getting seven weeks in New Zealand, airfares, food, accommodation, transport, coaching and a weekend in Queenstown for under €3000. It was a great deal and affordable for clubs but, obviously, as the exchange rate tightened and the recession hit, the Shamrocks Tour became too expensive for struggling clubs to consider. Suddenly, provincial rugby had taken over and clubs were struggling to find the finances to keep the club going, let alone find extra monies to send a player to New Zealand and then find, on his return, that he wasn't staying with them.

But, over the years, the Shamrocks produced some great characters. It was great to see how players from nearly every county in Ireland could get on so well. When the lads from the North marched around the parking lot, the others hurled water bombs at them, but it was all in good jest.

Frankie Feeney from Sligo was a great fella. About eight stone – dripping wet – Frankie had a great way with anyone he met, a cheeky kind of chappy. The summer Frankie was with us in New Zealand, happened to coincide with a tour by the Irish national team. There was much excitement and when the Shamrocks dressed up as leprechauns, not only did they met Peter Stringer after the game, but they managed to make the front page of the *Otago Daily Times*.

But the best was yet to come. At one point, I was in a shopping mall in Christchurch when a tall, beautiful Kiwi woman approached me.

She had spotted my Shamrocks top and asked if I was the Irish team manager. I told her I was the manager of an Irish team all right, but maybe not the one she imagined.

Then she asked me if I knew Frankie Feeney the great rugby hooker from Sligo.

Of course, I replied.

This model-like vision told me that Frankie had informed her that, if Keith Wood was unavailable for Saturday's Second Test against the All Blacks, then he was in the Irish team and would be able to get her tickets.

This beauty was all excited and wanted to know if I thought that she had a chance of availing of Frankie's VIP offer. How was Keith Wood?

I didn't want to blow Frankie's cover or potential date, so I just kind of nodded and said we had to wait on news of Keith's injury. As I tried to exit from the awkward conversation, she grabbed my arm and commented: "My God, he must be very good, then, because he's not very big, huh?"

I walked away laughing to myself, secure in the knowledge that once I told Mr Justice Extraordinaire, Matt Smith, of Frankie's bullshit then he'd be drinking all the way home to Sligo after the next court session.

Frankie's other line – common to all the Sligo lads – was that he was good mates with the Westlife lads. Who knows? It might even have been true, but regardless, it was a good opening move on the ladies. I spoke years later at the Sligo Rugby Ball and had a great night recounting some of Feeney and Co's stories.

Further down the coastline of Ireland, I remember a prop cum out-half from Kerry by the name of Humphrey Shanahan. Humps spent virtually the whole tour with hardly anyone understanding a bloody word he said because his Kerry accent was so strong. All we could ever make out was: "right good now". According to Humps everything was "right good now".

In fairness, Humphrey was an ideal tourist as he trained hard, took everything in, mixed well and always had a big smile on his face. Nothing was ever a problem for 'right good now, Shanahan', apart, of course, from every Kiwi exclaiming: "What the bloody hell's he saying now?"

In New Zealand, we don't have accents as such, apart from the odd cultural differences and young Kiwi Maoris' love of sayings things like 'sweet as bro'.

But Humps was far from being alone in his ability to stump the locals with his 'brogue' and his lingo. Across the road from the motel, the proprietors of the local garage had a real problem with one Irish saying, namely, "It's grand".

A 'grand' in New Zealand is NZ$1000 – in fact, that's a definition of 'grand' in most of the English-speaking world.

So, whenever the guys bought petrol at the garage, they usually met the attendant's version of the price with a universal, "grand".

"Sorry, mate, no, you don't understand. It's 50 dollars, not a grand."

"Thanks. That's grand".

"No, sir, it's 50 dollars."

"Ah, sure, we know. That's grand, thanks."

"No sir, you don't UNDERSTAND. It's 50 dollars, not a thousand."

"We know, we know. You're grand…"

And so it would go, on and on, like a never-ending combination of Monty Python meets Mrs Doyle from Father Ted.

One day, no doubt having filled up with a 'grand' at the garage, the lads decided to take the Holden car to the movies. The beast had one of those old-fashioned bench seats and the gear shift on the side of the steering wheel and, at a maximum, it could probably sit about six people.

But, on this particular occasion, the lads crammed eight into the car. Already stretching the law at that count, they then managed to squeeze another three hidden bodies into the huge boot, bringing the illegal body count to a grand total of 11.

But before the cops got the chance to stop them, they were intercepted at the first set of lights by an irate woman who actually got out of her own car to deliver, quite properly, a lecture about how dangerous the overcrowding was. Warning them that she was about to call the local police and tell them about the Holden with eight lads inside, the unfortunate lady's jaw dropped to the ground when a disembodied voice – seemingly originating from the departing car's boot – called out: "What about us? You might as well make it eleven!"

Off they drove down the road, laughing about the encounter and poking fun at the three in the trunk, whose heads popped out every now and again.

Luckily, the police didn't appear – something I put down to the fact that the lady in question was so shocked she never got around to dialing 999. Following the encounter, I put a strict limit on the number allowed in the Holden, but it may have come too late for the lady motorist – she may well still be there in downtown Riccarton, feet rooted to the spot at the traffic lights and jaw well and truly stuck to the tarmac.

• • • • •

As witnessed by Frankie's efforts to impress a stranger in a shopping centre, and model son's willingness to travel in the boot of a local girl's car, the Irish lads loved Kiwi women.

And vice versa. The Kiwi girls, predictably, found the accents charming and irresistible.

Often, I'd burst, unannounced, into the rooms for Sunday morning sessions, with a cry of, "RIGHT, TRAINING," only to find myself staring not at a bleary-eyed, hung-over Irishman, but straight into a pair of bright eyes, behind which was a shapely figure in bra and knickers.

One woman, with the impressive nickname of 'Tarantula Woman', took the biscuit.

To me, she was very attractive in a Goth sort of way: she had long, dark hair, piercings and wore a long black leather coat. With her striking, pale looks she could have been a model. She took a shine to one of the Shamrocks and took him home one night to her house.

On taking off her clothes, the player noticed she had a huge spider tattoo on her body – a tribute to her love of arachnids.

The Shamrock, on the other hand, was scared stiff of spiders but, in the interests of furthering Hiberno-Kiwi understanding, decided to push the thought from his mind, dismissing the tattoo as nothing more than a kinky obsession.

The evening progressed and, to the Irishman's delight, his Goth date turned out to have unusual tendencies. Leaving the Shamrock in her room for a moment, Tarantula Woman returned and promptly transformed his dream into a nightmare by producing a pair of mighty spiders which she placed on the Irishman's body. The forever-anonymous Shamrock didn't know whether to scream in terror or joy.

Traumatised – who knows, perhaps to this day – this unknown hero nonetheless picked up the Overall Tour Award after a unanimous vote among his peers.

I wonder, whatever became of Tarantula Woman?

Like any young blokes on tour, the Shamrocks were capable of making up huge stories about where they came from and what they did. We had doctors, lawyers, models, GAA stars, all sorts. But it didn't matter. They were all Irish and could tell the tallest of tales and nobody was ever the wiser. What happened on a Shamrocks Tour, stayed on a Shamrocks Tour. That's how you build team spirit.

The average age of the guys on the tour ranged from 18 to maybe 25 years old, and some were big lumps of men who had played at senior level back home in Ireland.

So when, in the first week of every tour, I suggested we play Christchurch

Boys' High as an introduction, these big men would laugh.

"But they're just school kids," every new Shamrock team would protest. "We'll bully them and put them off rugby for life!"

I smiled: "Let's see."

Without fail, the Christchurch Boys' High team thrashed us. Without fail. In the first year the Shamrocks were going to munch Boys' High, but ended up with an experience much less enjoyable than the Tarantula Woman horror tale which, at least, had a happy ending.

The Boys' High is a school that has produced forty-two All Blacks, including stars like Dan Carter, the Franks brothers, Adam Thomson, along with World Cup winning coaches, Graham Henry and Steve Hansen.

"Watch out, lads," I warned that first touring team, "for a young 15-year-old, out-half who's the stepson of an ex-Canterbury All Black, and personal friend, Vic Simpson."

I knew Vic and figured that if his stepson, Stephen Brett who later became Dan Carter's understudy at the Canterbury Crusaders, was made from the same mould then he was going to be as hard as nails.

No problem, argued the Shamrock loose forwards, we'll murder him.

In the event, Vic's 15-year-old stepson scored four tries as Boys' High trounced us by about 50 points. That game starred a future Connacht No. 8, George Naoupu, already a New Zealand schools star. That was a hard lesson to learn but, to their credit, the Shamrocks understood the gap. When the two sides met again at the end of that summer's tour, the result was a tighter affair. It was wonderful to see how far these lads had come in only seven weeks.

It was supremely satisfying then, in the last tour in 2009, to see a Shamrocks team taste victory against a Boys' High team – a huge achievement, given that Boys' High were then one of the top, if not the top, rugby school in the land.

The message for the young Irish was clear: in most instances speed, skill and teamwork will beat brute force any day, and the guys learnt that fairly quickly.

That 2009 tour was a bittersweet affair. It was wonderful to see how far we'd come in five years, but desperately sad to wave goodbye to it all.

Put simply, I didn't have the time or the finances to run the tour any longer.

It will always remain an important part of my life, and I hope that's a sentiment shared by many of the players who went Down Under with the Shamrocks.

Many of the tourists went on to play for First Division clubs. Some played provincially and, Conor McPhillips, one of our 'Kiwis' went close to playing for Ireland when he was selected to tour Japan, but was never capped.

• • • • •

It's tempting to think about the Shamrocks Tour with a sense of regret, to consider that it had a possibility of becoming something much bigger than it ultimately did.

But I like to think that the tour touched the lives of almost 100 young rugby players and exposed them to experiences they might never, otherwise, have had.

What is they say about the best-laid plans of mice and men? Things never quite work out as you think.

The tour had mixed results for both clubs and players. Some of the lads returned home heavier, faster and fitter and, as a result, left for bigger clubs. That was never my intention and I'm pleased to note that, for the best part of the four years that I ran the Shamrocks in New Zealand, the majority of 'returnees' put a lot back into their clubs.

Ultimately, the tour was about helping these young Irishmen to become better players, better clubmen and better people.

When I consider what happened to Gavin Owens, that lovely young man who was hurt in Australia, and the way that his clubs, both Down Under and in Cork, responded to his trouble, then I remain convinced that we were right to try and build stronger bonds between player, club and, ultimately, other people.

Brent and All Black, Gordy Macpherson, stopped off in San Diego around 1986 or '87 and hooked up with my club, the Old Mission Beach Athletic Club, more commonly known as OMBAC. OMBAC went on to become the most successful rugby team in the United States around that time, winning the US National Championship title in 1988, '89, '91, '93, '94 and '96, and were only a handful of games away from winning nine titles in a row. But, what I remember best about Popey was his huge influence on my play. I learned a lot from watching him train and play in matches and it inspired me to be a better player. That transformation helped me to be selected for the US National Team from 1986-1991, including the first two Rugby World Cups, and eventually captaining the team for eight of my twenty-two Test matches.

Brian Vizard
Old Mission Beach Athletic Club. USA (Eagles).

15

Tourists, Rules and Strippers

Rugby, in the old amateur days, was a different experience.

When you started out, you played simply because you loved the game. Then, as you got older, you played because you loved the teammates you played with and you loved the fun and the craic you had with them.

If you ask most retired players what they miss the most, it genuinely isn't the accolades or trophies, but the camaraderie. When you spend years playing and touring with the same group of players you become part of a big family. These players become your best friends, and in my case that feeling of belonging was probably more significant since there was only Mark and me in my own family. I envied those people who came from large families, and their ability to enjoy Sunday lunches or spend weekends laughing around a big kitchen table.

Playing rugby on any team was like that, but the most intense experiences you had were the tours, if you were lucky enough to be invited on one.

There was a number of what were known as 'composite' touring sides, like the present-day Barbarians, though maybe not quite so high profile. But the experience was always the same, you got to meet and befriend players from different backgrounds and countries. In my time, I've been lucky enough to play for a number of composite sides all over the world where, suddenly, once fierce opponents became teammates and, sometimes, friends for life.

I've travelled to exotic parts of the world like Brazil, Indonesia, South Africa, and Saudi Arabia in the company of rugby men intent on 40 per cent rugby and 60 per cent fun. One such team was the Penguins, an English-based Barbarians-type team and the brainchild of one of the nicest men in rugby, the late Tony Mason.

Tony was an absolute gentleman, a rugby ambassador of the highest magnitude and a genuine lover of the game. Alongside the regal and well-spoken Alan Wright, Tony set up the Penguins Club in an effort to bring the love and language of rugby to parts of the world that would not usually get a chance to see world stars. Penguins RFC was always about promoting the game of rugby, and so exotic trips to the likes of India, Chile, China, Russia, Mexico and other far-flung destinations were always on offer.

The Penguins had a great reputation and the number of former Internationals who have lined out for the team is almost endless, with the result that this long conveyor belt of talent has meant the Penguins have been extremely successful in winning a lot of world ranked sevens and tens Tournaments. In many regards, only the Barbarians surpassed them as the most famous composite rugby team in the world. Of course, as the years rolled on and the game became professional, it became harder for the Penguins' management to attract the elite players. The old end-of-season drinking tours had sadly passed into folklore as players opted to be fit, not hung over.

But it had been a great era. I was lucky enough to captain the Penguins on two or three overseas tours and the list of ex-Internationals under my leadership, especially from the likes of England, Scotland and Wales, is almost too long to mention, but they were very powerful sides on paper.

One player I got to know well was Stuart 'The Bear' Evans, a front-row prop, capped many times by Wales, who then successfully switched to Rugby League, an unusual move for a prop. Stu and his family owned a tough bar in Cardiff City and, according to the Welsh players, was not a man to be trifled with. But Stu and I became great friends. On one particular tour of Hungary and the Czech

Republic, hardly a region known for its rugby prowess, a contact from a club in the Czech Rugby Union invited Stu and me on a night out. It was already late and as we approached a nightclub in a seedy part of town, I looked at Stu and wondered where the hell we were going.

Another couple of turns and we ended up in front of a club that was reminiscent of a Hollywood horror movie. A dark ex-industrial warehouse, its entrance was flanked by two chimneys spitting ten-foot flames. On the door stood two giant gorillas, heavily tattooed, bare-chested and dressed in long leather coats, leather trousers and heavy boots. Each was holding back a massive Rottweiler dog on long taut chains. They were the biggest, scariest guys I had ever seen, but the liaison officer seemed to know them well, hugging them and shaking hands in some sort of gangland handshake.

He called Stu and myself over and, to our complete bewilderment, introduced us to the two thugs.

But we made nice and shook hands. Afterwards, the liaison officer explained that he just wanted us to meet his team's prop and hooker. Jesus, they were huge! And mean looking.

The following day, we discovered the team we were due to face had won the local League only because the other teams were too scared to play against them. Previous encounters had ended up in assaults, injuries and fights with the result that our opponents had claimed the League via a series of walkover wins.

Our guys were naturally terrified. The opposition were all built the same: about five foot tall and five foot wide, they looked as though they spent their days in the gym pumping iron. They were basically props who would rather fight than play, possibly inventing the modern concept of playing like there was no number on your back.

It was clear the local ref didn't have much of a clue, so we figured we were on our own. And so it proved. The very first scrum triggered a massive punch-up which involved just about everyone, including myself. At one stage, I had some massive, screaming eastern-European player on top of me, pummelling me as I tried to fight back. Suddenly Stu arrived, looked down at me, and said: "Don't worry, Popey. We can't have the captain sent off, now can we?" He proceeded to flatten my Czech oppressor, pick me up, dust me off and then trot off in the direction of the next scrum.

We were unsure what was coming next. Would it be more of the same? Suffice to say we moved the ball to the backline and I've never seen backs run so fast in my life. Not that it had anything to do with skill or fitness levels. No, the backline shifted so quickly out of sheer terror.

The combination of terror and fisticuffs worked well for us. After about twenty minutes of fighting in the forwards and running for dear life in the backs, we'd built up a fine lead.

But I was already worrying about how the locals would react, as they got closer to the final whistle and a humiliating defeat. They were liable to do anything. I had a brainwave: I called over their captain (who had presumably stuffed his long leather coat and the Rottweiler into his locker) and suggested we mix the teams up so that his players 'could learn' from their visitors. Tony Mason thought it was a 'wonderful gesture' of friendship, but I was more concerned about getting my lads out alive.

The locals agreed and the game finished largely incident-free, though there was much consternation at one point when a Czech player, now playing in a Penguins jersey, took his new-found allegiance a little too seriously and knocked out one of his former Czech teammates.

We declined to get involved in that one, Stu wisely suggesting that, "we let them sort themselves out on that score, Popey."

At the post-game function in a small room somewhere in the Czech mountains, we sat at a table directly facing the other team. At the head of the table, the other captain and I made a couple of speeches that neither of us understood, before he stood up, raised his glass, uttered a few more guttural sounds and downed a shot of what can only be described as 'poitín on steroids'. He then glared at me, before ordering, "Oh, 'im to do the same," which was the signal for about five rounds of these shots, their players following the captains and the Penguins following them. Later that evening, we made our escape, but not until we were absolutely locked.

Drink, of course, was a major part of touring in those days and on that same tour, we had an outrageous session led by a Neath and Welsh winger by the name of Alun Edmonds, who was infamous in New Zealand for once giving the great All Black, John Kirwan, the fingers during a game and on national television.

Alun had a fearsome reputation, but he was great fun and the perfect tourist.

A couple of days before a match to celebrate a significant anniversary of the Czech or Hungarian Rugby Union – I can't remember which to be honest, the game is a blur for most of us – we met to plan our strategy. Alun's contribution was the suggestion that our new caps' induction forfeit should be having to eat a loaf of bread which had been soaked in three bottles of cheap red wine. Alun's theory was that the bread would soak up most of the liquor, and the new caps would then try to eat the loaf alongside their normal drinks.

At one stage in the evening, the Welsh full-back Luke Evans (on most tours involving the Welsh there are about ten Jones' or Evans') and in a manner reminiscent of Terry 'Rat' Kennedy, the Irish winger who loved to tour, stood on a table. With eyes firmly clamped shut, and completely oblivious to the irony of the situation, he bolted out 'Bread of Heaven' with gusto. As Luke launched into it, the other Welsh lads, who had heard it all before, motioned to us to leave the bar silently. We quietly filed out the door. As we passed the window, we stole a final look at Luke, standing on the table, eyes firmly shut, completely alone save for a few puzzled, eastern European waitresses who awarded him a few mooted claps in bemused appreciation.

Luke soon rejoined us and, his anger notwithstanding, the session continued. Though, in an effort to preserve the dignity of the captaincy, I ducked out early before everybody got too twisted.

I was called in at 7am the next morning for the damage report. Tour organisers, Alan Wright and Tony Mason, delivered the verdict: Penguins were seen drunk, vomiting and singing, with one group of Penguins even 'mooning' hotel reception. Alan and Tony were disappointed with the behaviour but, as always, strove hard to only "see the best" in their players. So, when the players begged me to have the bus to the game pull over so they could hurl their toes up, Tony commented that it was, "a good sign to see the guys so nervous before the game". He was oblivious to the real reason. But that was Tony, he was just a nice man.

We played like we were hung over and, while we managed to win the game, it wasn't made any easier by the fact the locals had secretly flown in a couple of big-name players from French clubs. Their No. 8 in particular was a huge, wrecking ball of a player and not the sort of guy you'd want to square up to with a head full of red wine.

On a separate Penguins tour, I again captained the side which visited Brazil, Chile and Uruguay. Tony was getting older and doing less on the management side of things, so I took over some of his organising duties. We had a few other, old-fashioned, managers with us but many of them enjoyed the social side a bit too much (didn't we all?). One of the best of these managers was Hugh McHardy, who we promptly renamed 'Huge Bacardi'.

In Brazil, the players were given a daily payment to cover expenses. Their personal budget was to last a week so, every day, each player had to queue up outside manager Tony Jarman's room to get his money. Before too long, Tony was getting confused. He couldn't figure out why he had gone through a week's budget in a single morning. Moreover, he couldn't work out why the Penguins had brought so many players on a tour. Poor Tony. The lads had twigged that he didn't recognise any of them and so, having pocketed their allowance, they rushed back to their bedrooms, donned a few rudimentary disguises and then rejoined the back of the line at Tony's room.

One of them, Grant Ross, was a Kiwi with whom I had once played at Otago University. He was 6 foot 5 inches tall and once gave England's Martin Johnson a good grilling when Brive won the Heineken Cup. He rejoined the back of the line on about five occasions, each time wearing an ever-sillier false moustache and silly hat. I don't know how Tony never copped him.

"Who are you?" Tony would ask, as the Kiwi put on a French accent, or an Aussie accent. I think he even managed to convince Tony at one point that he was an Argentinean, even though there was only one South American on the tour and he was only 5 foot 8 inches tall! I spent the next day trying to get all the money back from the players, without much joy.

But those Penguins trips were great, great tours, full of big characters who were great craic. Some of the tourists had already established their reputations while others were only starting out. But some of them went on to great things. Among the tourists was Jason White, the 70-times capped Scottish legend. Jason was a tough nut and one of the best spot tacklers I ever saw. Barry Stewart, a prop who went on to play many times for Scotland, had to look at every tractor we passed. Barry told me once that, if he won the National Lottery, the fist thing he would buy was a tractor – he'd have been great mates with Sean O'Brien and Bull Hayes.

The Welsh were mad but brilliant tourists, backed up by a cast of Internationals from all over the world. You name the country and most likely we had them: Fijians, French, Argentineans, All Blacks, Irish, Scots, English, Aussies. I played in a back row featuring Simon Taylor, who went on to play for Scotland and the Lions. I never thought Taylor would have made it; he was a blonde, floppy-haired university kid who seemed more at home with a cravat than a rugby ball. But Simon was an intelligent footballer and, what he lacked in size, he more than made up for in his ability to read the game. A quiet, introspective player, Simon was proof again that rugby is a combination of brains and brawn.

Another Scot and former Penguin, who went on to play professionally for Edinburgh, was Iain 'Sinky' Sinclair. Sinky spent more time on top of the touring bus than in it. His party trick was to climb out of the bus window and pull himself up on to the roof, all while the bus was driving along at high speed. Then he'd just sit up there. Once, when we pulled into a late-night burger joint somewhere in Chile, we discovered that Sinky was gone. The management thought we'd left him behind at the hotel, but his teammates knew better. He'd been out on the roof during the journey and, when the bus pulled in at the fast food place, he dived down some sort of laundry shoot and ended up on the other side of the counter, wearing an apron and serving us, surrounded by a giggling chain of women.

Sinky was a tough player, too, but what I loved about him was he made every tour enjoyable. He was like a walking can of Red Bull and his rule was: if he could not sleep, then neither could you. He'd bang on the wall at all hours of the night, shouting, "Popey! Just checking if you're asleep." Then a muffled chuckle. Even as you tried to grab a few winks on the plane, Sinky would crawl marine-style under seats to grab your leg just as you were nodding off: "Popey, just checking you're not asleep." It drove me mad but made me laugh.

The great thing about the Penguins was the aim to take the game of rugby to countries that would not usually experience it. The tours travelled to almost every country in the world and spread fun and the love of the oval ball as they went. That was Tony Mason's dream, and it was extremely sad when he passed away a few years ago, many International players mourned the loss of one of rugby's true gentlemen, a man who dedicated his life to the passion of the game.

• • • • •

The Penguins wasn't the only touring side I played with. I was also part of a number of New Zealand overseas selections, including a strong New Zealand team that would play an English counties side. The selection was full of great players: All Blacks like Mike Clamp, then playing in France, and Wayne Shelford, then with Northampton, ably backed up by a host of other, former All Blacks, Aussies, South Africans and any other big-name players that were floating around Britain.

The games were always great craic, and even though the ties that bound us were the odd training session and a load of partying, we still managed to thrash most teams we met.

On one of those tours, I had the pleasure of rooming and playing with one of the legends of Welsh and world rugby, Graham Price, still part of one of the toughest, meanest Welsh cockpits ever. In the middle of the day, I arrived back at the room to find a note pinned to the door: "Pope, see you over the road at the bar, Pricey."

It was such a nice gesture. Price had no idea who I was but, since we were thrown together as roommates, he had decided to get to know me by inviting me for a few beers. We drank all that afternoon and on into the evening, me just sitting there, listening to Pricey's stories of tours gone by. We rolled into our beds at some ungodly hour, hammered and in no shape to play the following day. But we managed to switch on and thumped a team containing a good number of English Internationals and wannabes – all fresh and keen – by about 30 points.

Then we showered and hit the booze again. For us, as for a lot of foreigners, it was job done – English beaten now on the jar.

About a month later, I got an excited call from my old university mate Mark "Vogue" Hudson, better known as Huddo.

He was a great mate who, during our time in England, was a barman in a bar called Vagabonds, which attracted some of the harder drinkers in British sport. It was common knowledge that reporters and hacks left their notebooks at the door when entering this coterie of stars from the worlds of soccer, cricket, snooker and rugby. I spent some great afternoons down there, slipping in to the bar via a small door, and having Huddo point out, and sometimes introduce me to, some of these great sporting icons, all enjoying a mid-week pint and each other's company.

So, he called to let me know about this opportunity for me to play in a big game for an exclusive team called the Public School Wanderers, another International selection who were playing the circuit in the same way as the Barbarians and the Penguins. According to Huddo, it was an honour even to be considered for Public School Wanderers. Apparently, Bill Calcraft, the Aussie second row and another Penguin, who was studying at Oxford on a Rhodes Scholarship, had contacted Huddo looking for a player who could fill the shoes of a last-minute cry off. It was only a place on the bench, but according to Huddo – who was playing at the back of the scrum – I should feel honoured to be asked to be a substitute. If I was lucky, I might even get a run out.

The Wanderers were playing the English armed forces. They were obviously a collection of navy and army players, a tough bunch and a team that featured a few handy Representative players. Huddo, still excited by the prospect of the game, arranged to have me picked up. In his mind this was a big deal: it'd be a huge honour to join the list of other great players who had lined out for the Public School Wanderers. I'd never met Bill Calcraft, but Huddo introduced us at the ground. He pumped my hand warmly as Huddo looked on, and then said: "Great to see you, Popey. I've heard great things about you. I just wanted to know, can you play No. 8? What's more, I'd love you to captain the side."

Poor, old Huddo. Not only was I taking his place, but now I was going to be the bloody captain as well. I had to laugh, but I felt bad for Huddo. In the end, it worked out well. Huddo got on the pitch, we won and we had a great session drinking with Aussie Bill and the lads.

Whenever I hook up with Huddo, we still laugh about Brent Pope, the Public School Wanderers Great. Not.

● ● ● ● ●

But times have changed.

In the old days, we were all amateurs and, as such, could rightly expect that our antics off the field would remain private.

Famous Internationals, like legendary All Black winger, Bernie Fraser, were well known for their love of a few beers the night before a game. Fraser actually believed he played much better with a bit of a hangover. Who knows, maybe he did?

And Ireland's stars of yesteryear were no slouches when it came to pre-match pints. A number of them would have agreed wholeheartedly with Fraser's unusual theory. Legendary hard men, like Moss Keane and Willie Duggan, could often be spotted on the gargle somewhere in Dublin on a Friday night before a big game. In fact, Duggan was known to enjoy the odd cigarette minutes before the game, even reputedly handing a lit one to the referee seconds before running onto Lansdowne road. Duggan's mantra of, "I can train or play, but not both," was enough to secure him legendary status as being someone who played hard on and off the field.

Some of rugby's best stories have been based on exactly this kind of distinctly non-professional approach to the game.

Years ago, the Australian schoolboy rugby team was touring the UK and scheduled to meet their English counterparts on Twickenham soil. A pea-souper of a fog descended on the famous old ground, but the two teams were desperate to play despite hardly being able to see the man beside them.

One English winger spent practically the whole game freezing on the wing, unable to make out any of the players due to the dense fog. No ball had come his way and, as the clock ran down, he spied his brother and a friend passing along the sideline, making for an exit and enjoying a tin of beer and a cigarette. No doubt bored with the lack of action, and unable to see either his own team or the opposition, the youngster jogged over to say goodbye and have a quick drag on the fag.

But Murphy's Law struck and, suddenly, an Aussie burst out of mist and ran straight at the English winger, who still had the cigarette in his hand. Regardless of his numb fingers and head, the brave youngster threw himself into the tackle, hearing screams from his Aussie opponent as he did so.

But the yell of pain had little to do with the English player's bone-crunching commitment. For, as the Australian schoolboy picked himself up and limped off into the mist, the only sound that could be heard was an Aussie accent miserably shouting to his coach: "The bloody poms burnt me!"

The incident is still regarded as the only known occasion when a player burnt his opposition into submission.

In more modern times, Ireland centre, Rob Henderson, another who enjoyed the craic of touring, reputedly pulled up in a game against South Africa in the belief he had pulled a thigh muscle. There was relief all round when he discovered it was just his heavy, metal lighter that he'd forgotten to take out of his shorts, after having a pre-match puff to settle the nerves.

• • • • •

But the rules of the game have changed, and I don't just mean on the pitch.

Martin Johnson's England team discovered that during the 2011 World Cup, when some team members behaved as though the sport was still an amateur game. They and Johnson discovered, to their bitter chagrin that it's not.

The press pack's shadowing of the England team in their downtime, and the subsequent leaking of embarrassing stories about what they were getting up to in New Zealand's bars and fleshpots, left Johnson with little choice but to resign.

Stories of over-the-top drinking; minor, married-in members of the Royal Family getting offside in bars; and taking part in dwarf-throwing competitions was never going to sit well with the, expectant, English faithful back home. Especially when the team's on-field performances failed to ignite.

The England team wasn't alone, though.

When All Black winger, Cory Jane, decided to go drinking and smoking in an Auckland bar just two days before a World Cup game, he couldn't honestly have believed it would stay a secret. And, more recently, All Black winger, Zac Guildford, appearing naked in a bar and assaulting patrons on an end-of-season holiday in Fiji, was always going to make national and international news, regardless of whether he was there in a private or professional capacity.

What in God's name were they thinking?

George Hook and I will argue this point until the cows come home. Hookie will insist that the players are young and entitled to blow off some steam and, up to a point, I agree with his view. After all, as a player and a coach, I participated in and encouraged exactly that kind of thing. In fact, a good old-fashioned bonding session was, and still is, vital to fostering team spirit.

One of the main criticisms of Eddie O'Sullivan's management at the 2007 World Cup, was that the players needed to blow off some steam and allowing them to do so would have brought them together as a unit, and I agree. Over the years, some of my various teams' best performances came as a result of the players enjoying a good night together, getting all their frustrations out and starting afresh, especially after a loss.

But – and this will have former teammates and players of mine scratching their heads in disbelief – that kind of carry-on in public is no longer acceptable.

Rugby has changed.

It's a profession now and it's also become a global phenomenon – our top players are role models to millions of young kids, worldwide. They are getting paid serious coin to undertake a job that many thousands of others would give an arm to do.

Back when I played the game – and even further back, when Hookie played with T-Rexs and Pterodactyls – the sport was amateur. The biggest names in the sport worked hard during the week at their day jobs and, at the weekend, they played their hearts out for club, province or country. Aside from the odd free beer after a game, there was no remuneration. Playing or not playing was a personal choice. You played and you sacrificed because you wanted to. Like the GAA boys in Ireland, you did it for honour and for pride of club, county, province, or country.

There was a high price to be paid for participation but the players were the ones paying it, and the accepted currency was their bodies. Some of my teammates were so badly injured they struggled to keep jobs in later life, all lost money when touring and some can barely even walk today without popping pills to kill the pain. And they did it all regardless, for love of the game.

But the modern game is different. I believe that if you choose a professional lifestyle that affords you a huge paycheque and celebrity status, which in itself brings more money, then the price for that is a responsibility to represent yourself more appropriately in public.

Don't get me wrong. I know what I'm saying smacks a little of hypocrisy. I was no saint when it came to drink – I was one of the first to get twisted after a game and the last to leave many a rugby booze up. In fact, for years I acted as the judge at many kangaroo court sessions forcing players to drink heavily. But, even in the old days, I knew when enough was enough and I had a grasp of the rules of the off-field game, and I never forced a player to drink when he did not regularly drink himself. And, as I say, the rules have changed. Back then, it was a case of: "what goes on tour, stays on tour", but that's been replaced with the maxim:

"what goes on tour, goes on facebook".

Social media has been a plus for society in many ways, but it's been an unmitigated disaster for top-level sportspeople. Mobile cameras, facebook, Twitter, and a host of other technological advances, have combined to make it virtually impossible to hide. When it comes to how they live off the pitch, players know the rules of engagement have changed, and it's up to them to live by the new rules.

Funnily enough, Ireland has been fortunate that, by and large, its players have managed to avoid controversy. That's partly because, over the years, reporters have enjoyed a close working relationship with the Irish management team and players. The Irish set-up has not been hounded by red-top hacks on relentless searches for dwarf-throwing stories. On the contrary, the reporters around the Irish scene tend to be intelligent rugby men who focus on reporting the game, not what happens after it.

No doubt, the Irish team enjoyed New Zealand – especially Queenstown – just as wholeheartedly as their English counterparts. But there are a couple of key differences. The Irish are loved everywhere they go and, while, they can party and drink harder than most, they generally do so in a jovial, good-natured and respectful manner. This isn't my Irish bias here – I can honestly say that, in a couple of decades of drinking and having a bit of craic in Ireland, I've yet to meet an Irish rugby International of any generation that has been a complete ass in public. Some may have been rude to their fans or refused an autograph or a photo, but that is a personal thing, some players just want privacy. I've seen plenty of them rolling drunk all right – I was probably rolling right alongside them at some stage – but it never got too out of hand.

But there's another key factor at play, I believe. The Irish team boasts a set of leaders who can take charge of any situation, on or off the field of play. There's a good player hierarchy in the Irish set-up whereby, if a player is getting seriously out of hand, he's often taken aside and put back in line by one of the senior players. Better still, he'll be taken home by one of his teammates, knowing that bad behaviour can, and will, reflect on the team as a whole. Going back to the England example, there were many players probably just enjoying a beer and a singsong, even if a few were acting a little over the top. But the stories reflected badly not only on a handful of players who were actually culpable, but on Johnson himself. In fairness to the coach, while he may have given his permission for the bonding session, he was probably not even there. Still, he paid the price.

I've often heard that Paul O'Connell is the type of player that fulfills that big brother role for Ireland. Certainly, I can honestly say that I've never seen Paul tipsy, let alone drunk. Mind you, if he's reading this, he's probably roaring with laughter and saying, "You should have seen me when we won the Heineken Cup and Grand Slam."

But having an alert, tuned-in and responsible group of senior players is a great habit for a national team to be in and players with the attitude of Paul O'Connell and other senior members are to be treasured and admired. Successful teams and successful attitudes are built on shoulders of such men.

• • • • •

But before the Pope pontificates too much, I should pay tribute to one of New Zealand's great rugby tourists, the aforementioned Huddo.

A talented New Zealand junior decathlete and high-jump champion in his own right, Huddo was also a very good Kiwi rugby player who played flanker for Canterbury, Otago, Wellington and the New Zealand Maori.

But Huddo had other, non-sporting, skills. In fact, much of his legendary status had less to do with his on-field prowess as it did with a special talent off it.

A bit of an all-rounder, Huddo was famed, like champion British sprinter, Linford Christie, for – ahem – his lunch box. In fact, such was the size of his talent, he got a job working as a male stripper in a boat cruising up and down Wellington Harbour.

His love of 'performance art' went hand in hand with a liking for a drink and, as a result, Huddo was well practised in combining the two – a skill which came in handy when the French International team came to town to play Wellington as part of their Summer Tour.

Obliging bloke that he was, Huddo felt it was his duty to say "bonjour" and play host to our Gallic cousins. One thing led to another and, later that night – just a few hours before the game – a handful of French players and Huddo found themselves floating on a boat in the middle of Wellington Harbour. A good old-fashioned drinking session ensued before Huddo ushered the French stars up to the front row of the room and disappeared.

Within seconds, the curtain was pulled back and Huddo was revealed onstage, just inches from the French, clad in his best cape and thong. Huddo proceeded with his act, giving the French an eyeful of what the New Zealand Maori are all about.

Needless to say, by the time the next day's game rolled around there were many hung over Frenchmen in bits – the result of being stuck on the boat until the wee small hours, and forced to drink and watch a naked Huddo.

The great performer himself, on the other hand, was in tip-top shape, though he did have one minor complaint – a spot of towel rash from his act.

Against the odds, Wellington won the match and created a little bit of local history. Gallant losers that they were, the French used the occasion of the post-match dinner to award Huddo a standing ovation as the man most responsible for their historic loss and Wellington's historic win – not, obviously, for his efforts on the field, but for his antics off it.

As a ploy to put off a visiting team full of rugby geniuses, Huddo's efforts will most likely never be topped.

This age of professionalism, accompanied by the ever-present camera phone, has killed off an era of fun and craic.

I accept that times have changed but I, for one, sometimes think that we may have paid too high a price.

Once upon a Lions tour of New Zealand, Popey and I were walking around Dunedin town and chatting about Popey's TV career. "You know, Greg, back in Ireland I'm quite well known," said Popey – he may even have used the word 'famous' but I can't confirm that one! I had a little laugh to myself thinking, "He's building himself up a bit much here." Within minutes, a few Lions players walked past us, followed rapidly by a number of autograph hunters who came flying out of a bar. But, the excited fans showed no interest in the Lions players, they only wanted to get Popey's autograph – he was telling the truth! Any time I run into Irish folk over the years I always say, "I have a good mate in Ireland called Brent Pope, do you know him?" Without fail, they all know him. No doubting his celebrity status any more.

Greg Cooper
Otago. Hawke's Bay. Auckland. All Blacks.

16

RTÉ – by Hook or by Fluke

The answer machine blinked at me as I opened the front door of my home. There were more than 100 messages on it from reporters and rugby fans all over the world. Somehow, people from as far afield as South Africa, New Zealand and England had discovered my phone number and left dozens of messages for me.

Most were reporters asking for a comment and demanding a quote, but many were from irate England supporters. Some of these were abusive and, though upsetting, were harmless. But a couple were personal and quite menacing.

"You Kiwi ****! Watch your back – we know where you live…" ran the most threatening.

I was out of my depth and rattled, so I rang my then boss at RTÉ, Glen Killane, and my television colleague, George Hook. With lots of experience of dealing with controversy – courtesy of his talk radio show – George was the perfect man to give advice. On this occasion the word from George was, "Talk to no one. Let it die down." Today's newspaper is tomorrow's fish and chip wrapper, and all that.

But what had I done to deserve such attention?

My crime – as the angry England fans saw it – was to wonder aloud about the now infamous 'Water Bottle Incident' which starred England's World Cup captain, Martin Johnson and his coach, Clive Woodward.

The entire incident stemmed from the 2003 Rugby World Cup final between England and Australia or, to be precise, from a throwaway comment I'd made about England's captain, Martin Johnson.

Along with the rest of the RTÉ rugby panel, I'd been watching the final as it was beamed live into the RTÉ studio from host nation, Australia. About three quarters of the way through the match, England was awarded a penalty around the middle of the park. There was a stoppage in play and Jonny Wilkinson had stepped up to the ball to decide on taking either a kick at goal or a territorial kick down the line. It was just at the edge of Wilkinson's range, so it wasn't a foregone conclusion as to what the England kicker would do. But at the very same moment as Wilkinson was making his mind up about the crucial kick, Martin Johnson was pictured walking over to a water bottle and taking a drink.

In what seemed odd to me, as he raised the bottle to his lips, Johnson appeared to be talking to someone. But to whom? There were no visible players within earshot of him so I initially thought that, like a lot of players, he may have been just talking to himself, self-motivating which would not have been unusual. But at that very moment, the TV screen was 'split' between a shot of Johnson and a shot of the England management box in the stands where England coach, Clive Woodward, was talking into his mic. The two were suddenly onscreen at the same moment, Johnson talking strangely to himself into a bottle, while Woodward listened intently to someone on his earphones and replied into a mic. It just seemed a strange and comical coincidence and I commented on it as I saw it, pointing out that Woodward looked as though he was giving instructions to his captain via a hidden mic in the water bottle. Following Johnson's water bottle conversation, Wilkinson opted to kick for goal and duly split the posts with a great penalty which set England on their way to victory.

To me, it was no big deal and made no real difference to the game. People who understand the modern game know that, at any time during the game, the water dispensers can come on and give advice. Even Brian O'Driscoll, when out injured, has run on to the field to dispense water and instructions – either his own or his coach's.

I had never suggested that England or Johnson had cheated, nor that England had won the final because of the water bottle moment. I'd simply commented that it seemed strange and I wondered aloud had technology gone so far, that teams were able to hide some sort of walkie-talkie technology in a water bottle. I said I'd no idea how such a device might work and said that, even if there were a mic in the bottle connecting Johnson to Woodward, how could the England captain hear his coach without earphones? The whole thing was further complicated by the fact the bottle seemed to actually contain water. In any event, you had the feeling Johnson, who was clearly his own man, would not have been asking Woodward anything anyway.

So, obviously, I thought the comment would have been taken as I'd meant it – a throwaway line that was only a talking point.

I couldn't have been more wrong.

By the next day, several international newspapers were running with the headline "Cheat" and accusing England of bending the rules en route to victory. They contacted Johnson who, obviously, dismissed it all as rubbish.

But the Australian media, still seething at having lost the World Cup to England on home turf, refused to let it go and were making the most of it. One media outlet even employed a lip-reading expert to try and figure out what Johnson was saying in the TV footage.

On this side of the world the English press was going crazy as well, and I got an up-close lesson in how the English tabloids work.

I was contacted by one very well-spoken English gent from a popular red-top paper who wanted to know about my side of the story. I told him, honestly, that my comment had just been a small observation and, in my opinion, there was no way that the incident influenced Wilkinson's penalty, let alone the final World Cup result. I said it was comical, given Clive Woodward's imposition of near martial law during the Tournament in a bid to keep prying eyes and hidden cameras away from his team, that there was now speculation that someone in the England camp had come up with a two-way device disguised as a water bottle.

The reporter said he understood that the whole thing had been blown out of all proportion. As a matter of interest, he asked, what did I think of Johnson as a captain? Again, I answered honestly that I felt Johnson was a great captain and player.

The next day a two-page, centre spread in the tabloid screamed how, "Pope Grovels to English Captain". It was hardly a grovel: I'd purely said the whole thing had been blown out of proportion and that it did not cloud my feelings on the type of player Johnson was.

The funny thing about it all was that I've always thought the world of Johnson, both as a player and as a captain. As an out and out player, Johnson was a big, hard bloke – a modest man and a great leader in the mould of Paul O'Connell, Lawrence Dallaglio, and Anthony Foley. As far as I was concerned, Johnson was the guiding force behind England winning the 2003 Rugby World Cup and, following that, the winning British and Irish Lions Tour in South Africa. While he has been less successful as a coach, I'd still put Johnson down as one of the most influential captains and players ever, with regards to the Northern Hemisphere game.

But following my water bottle comments, the merry-go-round kept on spinning and, despite following George's advice to lie low, the story refused to go away. I was asked to appear on a number of English TV talk shows, including the popular Frank Skinner show, who wanted me to appear on the show along with Johnson. I declined but the show went ahead anyway and, in my absence, Skinner made great sport of it all, jokingly throwing the question – and the water bottle – to Johnson. So, for a couple more weeks, I continued to be a media star. Later that year, I even made the Conspiracy Theory of the Year Award in a major Sydney paper.

Then my fifteen minutes of world fame came to an end. The media circus left town and everyone focused on rugby again.

It had all been a storm in a water bottle.

• • • • •

The water bottle controversy is a pretty good microcosm of what it's like to live life in the full glare of the public spotlight. Everything you say is picked up on and, if it suits someone else's agenda, blown up out of all proportion.

Still, despite the obvious pitfalls, working with RTÉ has been an incredibly wonderful part of my life. It's allowed me to stay in Ireland, build a life here and, along the way, meet some of the best people I've ever had the pleasure of encountering.

My introduction to television came in 1994 when the then Head of RTÉ Sport, Niall Cogley, asked me if I would be interested in sitting on a rugby panel show at the time, called Rugby After Dark. It was the only rugby show that went out in those days, being broadcast late on a Sunday night and with a small, but enthusiastic, following.

I didn't really know much about the game of television rugby. Like everyone else, I'd grown up in an age when rugby coverage was fairly basic, especially when compared with its soccer equivalent, where programmes like Grandstand and, later, Match of the Day featured panels discussing the finer elements of the game.

With rugby it was just usually one main match commentator, like the great Bill McLaren, who covered the entire game from start to finish. Viewers never got to see his face, and instead made do with his dulcet tones. In Ireland there was Fred Cogley and, just across the water, the famous Welshman, Cliff Morgan.

That all changed when the game turned professional. Suddenly, rugby folk became more interested in the game and audience numbers grew. TV rights for rugby began to run into the millions as the threat of Sky TV loomed large on the horizon, and television channels had to start thinking about entertainment as well as the rudiments of the game.

So, when Niall rang me I wasn't sure what to make of his call. Still a relatively young St Mary's rugby man, Niall had a strong sports pedigree handed down from his commentator dad, Fred. Even then, Niall was obviously being groomed for higher things with the national broadcaster and was very highly regarded, not just in sport but in all things RTÉ. Niall had a vision of creating an RTÉ rugby panel that could compare with the soccer line-up of Johnny Giles, Eamon Dunphy and Bill O'Herlihy.

Already on the panel was one of the first pin-up boys of Irish and European rugby, and a player I'd admired from faraway New Zealand, Tony Ward. Ciaran Fitzgerald, another good St Mary's man and a former captain and coach of Ireland was there and, alongside those two, was another former Irish coach and player, the late, great Kerryman, Mick Doyle. Rounding out the panel was Alan Lewis, Lewy, a trend-setting referee who, I suspect, started the fashion of tanned legs and high-cut shorts.

The whole thing was headed up by the soccer anchor and affable Corkonian, Bill O'Herlihy. More comfortable with the round ball than the oval one, Bill was nonetheless a true professional who knew enough to allow his panel or guests to talk about what they know best.

Though I didn't think much about TV as a career – I was a rugby player first and foremost – I didn't hesitate too long before saying yes to Niall. Anyway, he'd advised me that this would be a once-off appearance and I had no reason to think otherwise. I was told to be in RTÉ the following Sunday for about 9pm. My Irish television debut would follow a Five Nations, Ireland v Wales match. Not knowing much about TV, I presumed that the show would comprise of a pre-recorded analytical piece, lasting only a few minutes.

So, undaunted by a few minutes' TV work, I ended up on the Saturday night, like clockwork, in my favourite haunt of the '90s, Leggs. Hours later, I stumbled out, just as the birds were getting up and by Sunday afternoon my hangover was killing me. In tatters, I headed in to RTÉ for my debut and found myself being led wearily into makeup

As I sat there with my fellow guests, my caked makeup combined with the hot studio lights, my hangover and my nerves, led me to believe I was about to be the first – and last – person to throw up on live TV. I couldn't stop thinking about being sick and the more I thought about it, the worse I felt. I was deathly white under my makeup and sweating profusely. Worse, instead of the few minutes I thought it would take, the programme lasted an astonishing couple of hours. Somehow, I made it through with the others who were probably feeling a bit like me, such was the nature of after-match celebrations in those days. But Bill O'Herlihy just threw his arm around me and told me how great I was. Thankfully, Bill didn't know how close I came to being sick and scuppering his show and my future TV career.

But I hadn't hidden my hangover from everyone. Straight after the show Mick Doyle asked me back to the RTÉ Sports and Social Club for 'a straightener', as he called it. For Mick, a straightener meant a few straight whiskeys. I went along and so began a great friendship with a remarkable man. I loved Mick's company. He was the ultimate raconteur: Mick the talker, Mick the supreme storyteller and me, the patient listener. But I loved it and I spent hours listening to Mick's flamboyant and wonderful stories of Irish rugby characters and tours.

The rule used to be, "What goes on tour, stays on tour," – but not with Mick. He could turn someone tying their bootlaces into a hilarious story that might have taken three whiskies and three hours to tell. He was a highly intelligent and well-read man, a natural storyteller of pure wit and humour and I relished the hours we would spend in the RTÉ Sports Club, him always calling his wife and blaming me for leading him astray. Sadly, Mick passed away far too early after a shocking car accident near Quinn's Corner, outside Ballygawley, County Tyrone, in May 2004. I am honoured to have known Mick 'Give It a Lash' Doyle, and I am delighted I remain good friends with his son, Andy.

After that first night's TV appearance, and fuelled with Mick's whiskey and Bill's confidence, I headed up to Faces nightclub, another popular watering hole. It was a Sunday night haunt just up the road from St Mary's RFC where I was due to meet the St Mary's gang. As I waited at the bar for a drink, I spotted a rather attractive woman and her friends looking over, pointing and smiling at me.

I was delighted. Maybe they had seen my rugged movie star features during my TV debut. Maybe they knew me as a rugby player. Had I met them before? So, buoyed up by their obvious attentions, I gingerly said hello.

That's when I overheard one of them turn to her friend and exclaim, "I told you that big eejit was wearing makeup".

I tried to explain that I'd just been on TV, but they shook their heads and replied, "Yeah, right," before walking off, laughing.

A quick trip to the toilet revealed a face like Marilyn Monroe – well maybe more Barry Humphries, aka Dame Edna Everage. In my haste to get off air and have a chat in the RTÉ Sports Club with Mick, I'd forgotten to take my makeup off. Mick must have known but, ever the prankster, he never let on. The stuff was caked on me, but he was happy to let me go to a nightclub with a face made up with creamy powder and mascara.

Mortified, I made a quick exit past the bouncers who must have wondered what sort of club they were running.

● ● ● ● ●

For a while, that eventful Sunday seemed as though it really would be my only foray into Irish television. The Rugby after Dark show continued without me but Clontarf was doing well and the club was pleased with me. So, in 1995 I decided I'd go home, via South Africa, for a holiday. It was the Rugby World Cup year and a few mates – Ginge, Mike Brewer and Jamie Joseph – were in the All Black team so I figured it'd be fun to stop off in South Africa and see how they got on.

But, at the last minute, I got a call at my girlfriend's house. It was Niall Cogley. Ireland were playing the All Blacks in the opening game of the World Cup and, given my knowledge of the All Black and Irish players, would I appear on the panel for that first game?

I turned Niall down. I had my own World Cup plans and also wanted to go home to see my parents – the tickets were bought. But Niall persisted and persuaded me to stay and do the show. I rearranged my travel plans to fly out the day after the RTÉ appearance.

So, once again, I joined the panel which still featured Wardy, Mick Doyle, Bill O'Herlihy, Fitzy and Lewy. Some guy I didn't know at that stage – by the name of George Hook – was in South Africa reporting on the game for someone or other.

There was no repeat of my Leggs hangover this time and I turned up for work in what I thought was a fashionable waistcoat. I perched my little furry kiwi mascot up on the desk in front of me. The game started well for the Irish with big London Irish prop, Gary Halpin, going over for a great opening try.

The try went on to become an iconic moment of the tour, not least because of what happened next. Halpin, high on scoring and brimming with confidence, obviously thought to himself: "This is easy, these All Blacks aren't that great – we can win this." So, he ran backwards giving the All Blacks the one-fingered salute.

Good move, Gary!

It got the Irish fans fired up but, unfortunately, it did the same for the Kiwis. Incensed by the gesture, the All Blacks proceeded to smash the Irish from then until the end of the game, with Halpin's try being Ireland's only visit across the opposition try line. In that same game, popular Irish winger, Simon Geoghegan, was the first player to get one arm around Jonah Lomu's gigantic thighs, hanging on for dear life, like a tick on a buffalo's bum.

At least Geoghegan showed prowess in slowing the human bulldozer down. Later in the competition, in the semi-final, the English were convinced they'd come up with the perfect plan to neutralise Lomu. But the undoubted star of the

1995 World Cup neutralised the English instead, scoring four tries and flattening England full-back, Mike Catt, en route to one of them.

In the wake of that Irish defeat, it was difficult for me as I knew a lot of players from both sides. I was not, nor will I ever be, anything other than adopted Irish and, as any patriotic Irish fan will appreciate I was honour-bound to support my homeland. But I didn't want to be hyper-critical or condescending to the Irish, something that I still try to avoid being today. I appreciated that the Ireland and New Zealand sides were operating in two different hemispheres of the game against very different competitors. The All Blacks were professional in all but name and money – though that was about to change, too – whilst Ireland was still bravely clinging to the amateur game and ethos, one of the few bigger rugby nations to do so.

After the match, Bill O'Herlihy pulled me aside and confided that the RTÉ switchboard had lit up during the show. It seemed that people liked what they had heard from me. I reckoned I'd been okay on the panel. I was honest and I knew a lot about the All Black Camp – I had a lot of friends on the team and the All Black coach, Laurie Mains, had been my Otago coach for almost a decade. The accent helped as well and, looking back on it now, I think the Irish viewers liked hearing someone who knew about the Southern Hemisphere teams. Bill bluntly told me I'd be an idiot to go home, that I had a future in this TV game.

I was still unsure: staying on would mean cancelling my chance to go to the World Cup and also to see my parents. But when Niall Cogley rang me that night to ask me to work with RTÉ for the duration of the World Cup, he quickly dealt with my worries by saying RTÉ would pay for a new ticket home. My decision was made. I said yes and RTÉ got a month's television work out of me for the price of an airline ticket to New Zealand. But I didn't mind. I'd enjoyed the match between Ireland and New Zealand and my parents, and girlfriend at the time, had impressed upon me that this was the opportunity of a lifetime. They were right, of course.

As the tournament progressed I grew in confidence. Bill O'Herlihy was an amazing mentor, so professional in everything he did. He helped me immensely, as did Tony Ward and, especially, Mick Doyle. After every game Mick and I would again sit up in the RTÉ Social Club, he on his whiskey, me with my pint and he'd help me gain confidence. At the end of the tournament we had a dinner out in town somewhere, and Bill stood up and made a toast to me as the star of RTÉ's World Cup rugby team. He didn't have to and it was gracious and thoughtful of him to single me out. I think he also knew the other panellists had worked a lot on television, but this was my first foray. Everyone drunkenly cheered and clinked glasses: the coverage in general had been a success with good viewership figures and, according to Bill and the tabloids, so had I. That was that, I was hooked – literally.

The nice thing about that original panel was that there was no animosity within the group, no egos. They were all good, knowledgeable rugby men that I still respect today. But it was Niall Cogley who I had to thank for changing the direction of my life. In time, Niall moved on to Setanta and, more recently, has relocated to TV3. I've no doubt that he will do well in whichever station he's with.

When Niall left RTÉ, he was replaced by the young and upwardly-mobile Glen Killane, who went on to join the RTÉ Executive Board as Managing Director of Television, in May 2010. It was Glen who put together the current panel of Tom McGurk, George Hook, Conor O'Shea and myself and I regard both Niall and Glen as consummate professionals. They have been a pleasure to work with and people I like to consider friends.

When Glen moved up, the baton of RTÉ sport was taken up by Ryle Nugent who's busy building his own team and implementing his own vision. These three men have each introduced their own approach to dealing with sport. All three are smart, innovative thinkers who, between them, have produced some of the best sporting television anywhere in the world. Other stations, especially international rivals, have often enjoyed far bigger budgets than RTÉ, but, in fairness, RTÉ sport has worked remarkably well with what it's been given.

Critics will say they'd expect me to say that, given the fact that I'm fortunate enough to work in a job I love, dealing with a subject that is very dear to my heart. But even as far afield as New Zealand, unbiased people have called my parents to say they've seen me on RTÉ and they think the show is great. RTÉ's had its well-documented woes over the past few years and I can only really speak about my own dealings with the broadcaster. But, hats off to those involved in sport: they are passionate about what they do and I honestly think that, in 90 per cent of cases, they do a great job.

•••••

By the late 1990s, I was appearing on TV regularly, covering the annual Five Nations.

Back then, I hadn't heard much of a gentleman named George Hook – apart from the odd broadcast from South Africa during the Rugby World Cup of 1995. But, by coincidence, he'd helped coach the USA team which appeared in the 1987 World Cup in New Zealand. I'd spent a season with Old Mission Beach Athletic Club (OMBAC) in San Diego and had actually played a lot of rugby with that 1987 Eagles team. OMBAC had won the US title during my year with them and, as a result, many of their players were key Eagles men: like Brian Vizard, now a rugby commentator, Mike Saunders and centre, Kevin Higgins, one of two of my teammates who would sadly take their own lives a few years later.

But I didn't know George back then and, truth be told, I can't actually remember the first time 'Hookie' came on the RTÉ scene. He seemed to just arrive! One day he wasn't there but, suddenly, he was a permanent fixture. According to George's own, possibly embellished, account he was asked by Niall Cogley to come in one day and cover a single rugby match. It was apparently on the same day that a lot of sports fixtures were being systematically cancelled due to a horrible snow storm and RTÉ's sports coverage was in crisis. According to George, an emergency call went out for someone to fill in for a couple of hours by talking about anything and everything. George replied to the RTÉ's distress beacon saying, "There's no better man… " and, boy, was he right.

After that, George and I just kind of evolved. Despite having a few years of experience under my belt, I suddenly began to feel I was a step behind George in the talking and opinion pecking order. It was Hook and Popey, not Popey and Hook and that's pretty much where I've found my role ever since. That's because things work that way: George is a wordsmith and his comments can often go off on a humorous tangent of biblical or historical quotes, many of which are lost on me.

So, by the time we get past The Battle of Little Big Horn or Moses parting the sea and back to the game at hand, George has used up a good percentage of on-air time. But, to be honest, it works. Over the years, I've come to see that, if it's not broke why fix it?

Still, it requires a certain degree of patience on my part, at times. Everywhere I go people ask me how George and I get on. Or ask, would I ever just lean over and whack him? Of course, they don't really mean it and their comments are mostly in jest but, over the years, George has certainly teed some people off, and mightn't be the first on a lot of former, or current, players' Christmas card lists. One former International even called George and told him, in no uncertain terms, that he'd take him down a dark alley and show him just what he thought of him. The player was incensed at George's criticism of him, and knowing the player in question, if George had gone anywhere near a dark alley it could have happened. But that has always been George's style and it has brought him recognition – positive and negative – all over Ireland. It's worked to the point that George, now also a radio man, is one of the most recognisable faces in this country.

Many people wonder if any of our spats are premeditated, that the arguments are scripted to boost viewer enjoyment and ratings. Hand on my heart, absolutely not. That's never happened. It doesn't need to – George is an opinionated, strong-willed man. And he's entitled to his views. Sometimes, when I've found him to be overly negative or critical of players, I've said it. It's the same with coaches: if I think he's not giving someone a fair go, I've become annoyed with him onscreen. We've had genuine rows both on and off-air and, on a couple of occasions, I've actually found myself becoming incredibly incensed with him – red-faced, seething angry. After one heated argument in an RTÉ meeting, George turned his chair around and just looked out the window, leaving me absolutely enraged.

Over the years, he's been a difficult man to work with at times. Not so much for me as I've come to recognise what kind of mood he might be in on any particular day, but certainly for some other staff. Some of them have experienced his wrath, especially if he considers them incapable of doing their job to his standards or in the way he'd prefer things done. At times, I've had a lot of empathy for our hard-working production staff who may not always have known a lot about the game of rugby – but why should they? They may have been trying to juggle five different sports at the time and not everybody understands where the prop should have his arm in a scrum.

But in fairness to him, and unlike some others, George has always been man enough to apologise if he thinks he was over the top and it takes a big man to admit when he's wrong.

We're very different in how we prepare for matches. For me, it's all about watching the game as it unfolds, I was always the type of coach that would stand away from the players and other coaches so I could get an overview of where the game was going. I'm more off the cuff than George because I believe games, results and tactics can and do change in a heartbeat. On the other hand, George seems to devote more time to pre-game research or to what information he wants to convey. His trademark is the effective use of vocabulary while my own philosophy is more along the lines of, "Why use a long word when a short one will do?"

But that mix of styles, accents and opinions has built a rugby brand as strong as the one I wanted to be a part of so many years ago.

Are George and I considered the Giles and Dunphy of rugby? I'd be honoured to think so, though, if you want to light George's fuse, just compare him to Eamon Dunphy and then stand well back and watch the firecracker explode. George dislikes the comparison, possibly because they are both radio men who have had their own spats over the years.

As far as I am concerned, if people think I'm the Giles side of that equation, then that's just fine with me.

At some of his after-dinner talks, one of George's jokes is that Tom McGurk, our panel chairman, is like a corpse at a funeral – "he doesn't do much but you can't start the bloody gig without him."

George is joking, of course – I think. Tom is an essential part of the programme and a quick-thinking and extremely intelligent man. You have to be on guard with Tom as you never know just what question he will throw at you or in what order, which can be a terrifying experience on live TV. In the early days we never, unlike viewers at home, got a chance to see the replay of tries or significant plays at half time so Tom would tell us what to concentrate on when we came back live.

"George," Tom would say in his broad Northern brogue, "I will come to you first and you can explain O'Driscoll's try. Popey, you take O'Gara's try... " Finally, in the days before Conor O'Shea came onboard, a third guest panellist would usually be given something simple, or more insignificant, like the Italian dropkick. So George and I would be busy working out our pieces, with Hookie frantically writing down what happened in the lead-up to O'Driscoll's try so that, when live, he would flow. But when we came back, Tom would turn to George and ask: "George, what about that Italian dropkick?"

Cue panic. Eyes would go everywhere. George would be caught and none of us would know what to do.

Tom has never learnt the error of his ways. He still does that kind of thing to this day, only now we are ready for it and cover all our bases. If he gets the order wrong, I'll just bat it over to Conor with a quick, "I think Conor is covering that, Tom." He still gets some people – this year Donal Lenihan got caught rotten. I was meant to discuss the Scottish backs while Donal was set to analyse the forwards. Tom duly reversed the roles with a blunt, "Donal, the Scottish backs please."

Donal, caught in the headlights, simply didn't speak. It was hilarious for a couple of seconds but I eventually stepped in and pointed out that Donal was looking at the forwards. Suffice to say that Donal now knows to anticipate sudden change.

Tom, despite sometimes wearing two different coloured socks, is easy enough to work with though he'll often come out with some howler that has us all looking heavenwards and wondering, "Holy Moses, where are you going with this?" He's also extremely passionate when we're watching the matches live from the studio, often screaming, beating his chest and firing off opinions about the opposition or referee.

Usually that's fine, though, on occasion, it has resulted in a heated panel, especially if he's watching a game involving the All Blacks where he wants to see them beaten. I can understand that opinion when Ireland plays New Zealand but, at times, I think that the lads forget, or are not sensitive to the fact, that I am still a New Zealander. That's hurtful at times, especially during the last World Cup when I knew what it meant to the people of my country, with all they had endured through the earthquake, to do well in the competition. Yet, it's hard not to feel that sometimes people just want the All Blacks to lose simply because they are the All Blacks.

I understand that too, but I'm still a New Zealander and proud of my heritage. I always want Ireland to win, except maybe when they are playing the All Blacks.

Still, sometimes with George and Tom it's smarter to keep my head down. They've had some humdingers over the years. At times, it's seemed as though their rows have been about to pass the point of no return but, somehow, we've managed to pull it back together and be man enough to shake hands and get on with things. One thing I will say about Tom is that he is the man for a crisis: he never gets flustered, well almost never. If things go down, or he loses his feed, he doesn't panic, he calmly tells us to get ready to go live. Like Bill O'Herlihy, Tom's an asset to RTÉ rugby and a consummate professional in what he does. He calls us the oldest boy band in the country.

I've worked with different panellists over the years and, while some have worked out and some have not, I'd have to say that Conor O'Shea is one of the nicest people you could ever meet. The definition of a true Irish gentleman, Conor adores his wife and children and is always talking about them – it's refreshing. He's a pleasure to work with and, from a rugby point of view, astute and very successful. He makes his points succinctly and calmly and demonstrates an articulate intelligence. Unlike George, Tom, or myself, he's never been really flustered, other than the very odd time he's been frustrated and angry at something he has seen on screen or in the studio. Even then, he generally calms down within a heartbeat. I know Conor's very well respected both at London Irish and now at Harlequins, where he's currently doing an amazing job. He came into a club that, only a few years ago, was in turmoil both on and off the field and has worked hard to steady the ship and start turning the famous club around. RTÉ's very fortunate to have someone on the panel of his calibre. He's a talented coach and a potential club CEO, and I hope he will continue to be able to commit to television. If he is to return to these shores as an Irish coach – which is a real option for the future – he will be a major asset to Irish rugby. I hope by the time this book goes to print that, alongside Joe Schmidt, he's included somewhere in Warren Gatland's plan for the Lions' Tour to Australia and New Zealand. Conor's ability to manage and get on with people from all the nations involved marks him out as a great potential cog in Gatland's management team. He's the kind of bloke you feel will be a success in anything he does in life, be it coaching, administration or television punditry and I can't say more about the man than that.

• • • • •

At the other end of the diplomatic scale, George has courted controversy with players and coaches for years, calling for their heads on many occasions.

I don't always see it as black and white as that. I always believe that a player, if he's wearing the colours of his country, is trying his best to honour that jersey. All players make mistakes and have off days, especially if they are carrying some fall-out from injury. So, in general, I try to give constructive criticism and never attack a player on a personal level. I may have said that a particular player wouldn't be happy with his game or that he made a serious error of judgement but that's fair comment and, in any event, the player will know that better than anyone. In my own playing days, I always respected fair and constructive commentary. In fact, I always felt like an imposter if the media said I had played well when, in my heart of hearts, I knew I had not.

On occasion while out and about, I've met players or coaches who, especially if they have drink on board, have had a swipe at me or have just blanked me. That, of course, is their prerogative: they do their job and I do mine.

But I believe I have a right and, after a life of rugby involvement, the experience to comment on rugby at national and international level. I do warrant an opinion.

Coming from my Kiwi background, rugby is in my blood and my soul.

I played more than 100 first class games for Otago, in an era when you didn't get a provincial cap for coming on as a sub and when you only played about ten games a year. As documented elsewhere, I was unfortunate to miss out on consideration for the 1987 Rugby World Cup but I have lined out for Canterbury, South Island, Mid Canterbury and Otago provincial teams and represented my country as well. I formed loose forward trios with some of the greatest players in the world, and helped Otago to its first ever First Division title in 1991. I've captained international touring sides and played provincial rugby in England and USA, with only illness preventing me from taking up an offer to play in South Africa. Since coming to Ireland, I've played and coached at both St Mary's and Clontarf RFC and won numerous trophies with them.

That national and international experience of playing across four continents and in both the Southern and Northern Hemispheres has given me an overview of rugby on a worldwide stage.

I feel I've earned the right to have an opinion on rugby.

I understand where some players and coaches are coming from when they complain about TV pundits' critical opinions. You can see how sensitive the situation is when recently retired players come into the studio in an attempt to break into media work. When it comes to the crunch, even they will admit it's difficult to critically analyse former teammates or coaches who are still involved in the game. But it goes with the territory and, at times, it can't be avoided. The public demands that you don't sit on the fence and you have to call the matches as you see them.

Anyway, I think much of the criticism of TV sports panellists is missing the point. In New Zealand, even the top players are not immune to criticism and that's got to be good for the game: no one takes their place for granted. Moreover, the role of the media has been very positive in many instances. No coach will ever admit to listening to, or reading, our opinions. Why should he? But at times I believe that we've played a major role in helping players gain recognition and selection, especially players who play abroad. A few years ago, Mike Ross, the Irish tighthead prop, seemed to have been left out in the wilderness. But, after being propelled into the limelight via TV commentary and newspaper coverage, he suddenly became a crucial part of the team.

The same could be said about Sean O'Brien and – hard to believe now that he has gained international recognition – Stephen Ferris. How long was Ferris left knocking on the door, a player of his calibre? I'd like to think that the RTÉ panel generates discussion about players and, in an advocacy role, has challenged coaches who favoured maintaining the status quo over picking based on current form.

• • • • •

I guess in a lot of ways George and I are like an old married couple by this stage. We've spent so much time in each other's company over the years and we've travelled to far-flung places, both for rugby games and, at one point, for the RTÉ tourism programme, No Frontiers.

People seem to continue to be fascinated about our dynamic, and for the past ten years George and I have become, in many ways, the brand for rugby in Ireland. But we don't share much time in each other's company outside of rugby.

I'm not particularly sure if we're friends. It's hard to say. I'd like to think there's a mutual respect between us and I have a lot of time for his wife – the lovely Ingrid – and his family. George Hook Junior was of great help to me when I was organising my tours to New Zealand and I very much appreciated being invited to his wedding a few years back. I've also come to know George's lovely daughter Michelle and her husband, Mick, and I have helped on occasion with Michelle's worthy charity, Comer. His daughters have played a big part in his life: when Hookie first came into RTÉ, his daughters would label his clothes. George is colourblind, so the girls would pin notes in big, bold letters – shirt 'A' with tie 'B', and so on – pinned to each garment. These days, George would describe his wardrobe as akin to an explosion in a pizza parlour, although he does have the appreciation of a good tie.

I respect George greatly. By his early 60s he was depressed, bankrupt, and away from his wife and family. But he changed all that, resurrecting his life and career and becoming a high-profile, national figure along the way. He forged a successful and lucrative career in radio, writing, rugby and he's a wonderful after-dinner speaker – an ex-debating champion who's still a first-class wordsmith.

Hookie also shares a common interest with me in helping countries whose people are lacking basic living conditions. For George that's meant working with his daughter, Michelle, in the cause of Haiti and Romania while, for me, it's meant helping in Zambia via the charity, Habitat for Humanity Ireland. George's RTÉ documentary on Haiti showed Irish audiences a very different, empathetic side of the man.

It might not appear so but, like me, George suffers hugely from nerves when he has to do something live. He will pace up and down, reviewing his notes and getting into a highly agitated state. But he works hard at overcoming those nerves and making a success of whatever he's doing. His dominant personality means he needs to be the central person in most conversations and, at times, he can find it hard when people, including me, begin to question his views.

But he's also first-class company when he is in good form and we've had some laughs along the way.

During one panel show, there were shots of Brian O'Driscoll clearly endorsing some sports drink in the pre- and post-game interviews. He had not only one drinks bottle, but two, and was alternating the bottles between each hand and between each question. His sponsors must have been delighted but, to George and me, it was great fun. We grabbed an old water bottle in the studio and stuck a label on it saying, 'Hookie's Hooch'. When the action came back to the panel, Tom questioned George and Hookie swigged his Hooch in a perfect take-off of Brian. I'm not sure how it went down with viewers, but it was hilarious in the studio.

During the No Frontiers trip to San Francisco, we spent the day filming around the beautiful wine country of the Sonoma Valley. At one point, we both had to strip naked and sit in a spa made of heated sawdust from redwood trees. George was hilarious as the humourless woman in charge tried to convince us of the benefits of emerging hot and flustered from the spa, with chips of bark in places that took them a month to be removed from…

We filmed in various vineyards, sampling different wines, and gaining a new level of expertise in the swirl and spit technique so beloved of the wine-tasting community. Now, George will admit that he's not a big drinker, in fact, he tends to get a little inebriated on the tonic in his gin and tonic. But as we were making our way through our Sonoma Valley tastings, he made the mistake of swallowing more wine than he spat out. After a long day's filming our last stop was a trendy, new age wine shop. George, by this stage, was a little tipsy and when a bus load of college students, mostly attractive sophomores, pulled up, Hookie was suddenly in his element. The more he talked to them the more they were enthralled by his Cork accent and, in turn, the more he played up to the ever-increasing crowd.

The owners of the shop had hung a huge Chinese gong on the wall of their store. For anyone who can remember, the wall decoration resembled the gong that an-oiled up beefcake, by the name of Ken Richmond, used to strike before the start of Rank Organisation movies. Thinking of the similarity in age, I suggested that George was a dead ringer for Richmond – a former British Olympian who passed away not long ago at the age of 80. But George, overjoyed at my comparison of him to the rippling athlete, sank his choppers into the bait. Stripping off his shirt to reveal a rather less tanned, less smooth and less muscular physique than Richmond's, George grabbed hold of the gong's gavel.

Bong!

Or, maybe … boink!

George's first strike was a little meek so, à la Mick Doyle, I suggested he give it a decent lash.

Buoyed up by the crowd's adoration, George puffed up, wound up, and bashed the gong.

BOOOOONNGG!

He caught the gong with a fearsome blow and impressed everybody with the sound he produced.

Well, nearly everyone. The owners looked on in horror as the gong came crashing down on top of poor old George's head, whacking him on his noggin and shoulder and knocking him to the floor. The gong landed beside, rattling and reverberating like a discarded hubcap which had spun off a car at high-speed.

It was perhaps the funniest thing I've ever seen in my life and, even better, it was all caught on camera. George demanded that the episode be kept out of the show, but I'm sure it's there, buried somewhere in the RTÉ archive, waiting to be aired on another day.

The trip was memorable for a lot of reasons. Before we'd left Ireland, I'd worried that two weeks in each other's company would result in open warfare but, actually, it was great fun. George is in his element on trips like that, a well-read guy who will pull facts out about anything, and have a good laugh along the way.

We visited where Alfred Hitchcock filmed 'The Birds' – the famous horror movie from 1963 which starred Rod Taylor and Tippi Hedren. Then we headed for San Francisco where we'd hoped to rent an old Mustang and restage a scene or two from Steve McQueen's classic 1968 movie, 'Bullitt'. Sadly, we wound up with a silly-looking, three-wheel trike which, after two 17-stone men had been levered into it, looked more like an over-populated sardine tin than anything. Still, at least my driving up and down the famous San Fran 'humps' managed to terrify George.

In turn, George, ever the professional in these matters, managed to terrify the crew, keeping them to the minute – and not a minute after – of scheduling.

When we booked into the five-star Fairmont Hotel in San Francisco for the last night, I was told by reception that, due to an overbooking, I'd been upgraded. We were staying in the hotel courtesy of the American Tourist Board and changing rooms didn't really impress me. I wasn't intending to spend much time in there anyway, I just wanted to head out into the city, grab a burger and a beer and relax. But when George got to the desk and heard I'd been upgraded, he demanded the same treatment on the basis of, "If Pope got one, then I'll get one!"

The chap on reception apologised and explained my upgrade was the result of a mistake on their part. That didn't impress George who glared at the young man.

"But, I'm George Hook!"

The chap was unsure if he'd failed to recognise a leading actor or famous politician. In fairness to George, there's probably a bit of both in his make-up. The clerk apologised again, but once more pointed out that he could do nothing.

"But, I'm George Hook!" exclaimed a now clearly frustrated and impatient George.

I don't know if George ever got his upgrade but the young guy on reception certainly knew who he was by the time we checked out. Happy to have claimed one rare victory over him, I headed up to my new room to enjoy a few hours comfort, unsure if poor old George was slumming it or not.

● ● ● ● ●

In terms of punditry, George has engaged in many media wars with players and coaches during an often turbulent relationship.

For the first few weeks of Joe Schmidt's Leinster tenure, George said that the, "Kiwi had lost the dressing room and really should go".

He was wrong – incredibly wrong – on that occasion and, in my opinion, he has also been overly harsh in his assessment of some players while, simultaneously, overrating others. One memorable occasion led to George unfortunately feeling the wrath of John Hayes' wife, Fiona, herself an Irish International. Fiona, rightly, tackled George head-on about what she saw as his unfair criticism of her husband's ability to scrum.

But, at the end of the day, George will call it as he sees it. It's his opinion and he's entitled to it. When questioned about his opinions or, at times his credentials, George's normal retort is that the best rugby coaches were not always the best players, so why should a pundit, as some players demand, have been a great International?

His statement is borne out in fact: World Cup winning coaches like Graham Henry, Steve Hansen, Bob Dwyer, Kitch Christie, Rod Macqueen, and Jake White, failed to be capped as players. Nearly three-quarters of the men put in charge to lead their respective nations to victory have not actually pulled on the nation's jersey. In fact, a couple never even played at First XV schools level. It's the same story with Ireland's successful coaches, Eddie O'Sullivan and Declan Kidney, or Leinster's former Heineken Cup winning coach, Michael Cheika. Though it might be ironic to use Joe Schmidt to defend George, the fact is that

Schmidt was not an All Black, but look at what a marvellous coach and reader of the game he has shown himself to be.

The point is, whether people like it or not, George is still entitled to what he thinks. He is controversial, he is biased, he can be unfair and harsh and it wouldn't be far off the mark to describe him as an old grouch at times – but that's why he makes good television. As a spectator watching rugby coverage, I've found much of it quite sterile. Most people don't actually want to know the intricate details of every scrum and lineout. In fact, if you looked at the hundreds of thousands of people who tune in to rugby coverage, only a small percentage want all the bits and bobs. They tune in for the extra factor of hearing George talk about Rommel in the desert or the Battle of Britain and think, "What the feck does this have to do with anything?" The answer is zero, and the viewers know it but that is exactly what they love and hate about him. They want to enjoy the coverage and they want entertainment. A bit like a Bond villain, George gives them that and, as biased as I am, that's why I think RTÉ makes some of the best sports programmes anywhere in the world, and on a smaller budget than many of the world's bigger stations. The various sports chiefs at RTÉ, Niall, Glen and now Ryle, are astute enough to know the programmes must entertain as well as give informed opinions.

I hate to say it – in fact it riles me – but that's why the rugby panel will be a sadder place when the Hookie Monster decides to hang up his boots.

I'll miss when he does.

I just won't tell him to his face.

Hookie Bites Back

Here are some of the best, or worst depending on your point of view, of what I like to call 'Georgisms' – lines that could only ever be uttered on national television by George Hook!

"Back up the truck. If you just listen for a minute, Tom, I will tell you why Munster will never beat Biarritz." *Munster wins.*

"Joe Schmidt has clearly lost the changing room, who brought that guy over anyway?" *Schmidt delivers two European Cups.*

"Leinster will not beat Harlequins, nor will they win the European Cup." *Leinster win both.*

"I have a large ass and a big backside and when they give you these sport seats, they're not meant for fellas with big backsides. It was tight when I sat into it." *On looking uncomfortable in studio.*

"Kevin Maggs running is like Popey's face – it's not pretty but it gets the job done."

"That player [Gordon D'Arcy] is so unlucky that he actually gets a letter every week from Reader's Digest saying he hasn't won a prize."

"Tommy Bowe does not have the speed to make an International winger, over half the length of the field I could give him a go."

"I admit it. Ronan O'Gara is the illegitimate son I always wanted."

"Eddie O'Sullivan telling it is like Custer telling them at The Battle of Little Big Horn that they ran them close..."

"They're using statistics in the same way that a drunk uses a lamp-post ... to prop himself up."

"That team is like a eunuch in a brothel. They see what's to be done, they know how to do it, but when the time comes they just can't do it."

"I am the face of erectile dysfunction, but I suggest the problem is elsewhere."

"The problem with Brent Pope is that he thinks he's Brent Pope."

Popey's intellectual ability dwarfed many a rugger bugger around him. In 1988, he mentioned, to much laughter in the Otago shed, that he was going to write and publish a children's book. Yeah right! But, of course, the big guy did exactly that. A good read, too, but what inspired most was that he was giving himself to the children. His skillset in life was all over the place. When the Otago touring team needed a pick-up, Popey would bring out the RABBIT. Yes, he transformed himself into a human version of the pest by twitching his nose and ears at the same time. It was a sight to behold and one that cracked up everyone who saw it. Ask him to show you and prepare to be amazed. Of course, the lookout for the PERFECT woman at the time was all-consuming for Brent. Many were interviewed over the years in our university town of Dunedin, but none could muster up the perfect ten. Time after time, I warned him to lower the bar, son, and get on with it! Brent was the rugby rockstar who didn't get to the big stage. That was a shame as he would of made a great, explosive All Black. He was a great, great teammate, outstanding player and ahead of his time with his vision and abilities. Guys like Popey make the game of rugby, and life, even more rewarding to all around him. Weren't we the lucky ones?

Paul Henderson.
Otago. All Black (1989-95). All Black Captain.

17

Outsider Art and a 'Good Book'

Charity begins at home.

That's certainly where it began for me. I've been involved with community work or charities for much of my life and, alongside rugby, I've found it the most rewarding part of my life.

My parents have always been particularly empathetic people who taught Mark and I to be kind to others and treat them as we'd like to be treated ourselves. I don't always get it right – who does? – But I do try and live my life with that constant mantra in mind. I certainly don't believe that where you grew up, your accent or your wealth in any way defines you. To me, it's about how big your heart is, how wide your smile is.

Many people see wealth or power as the best, or only, indicators of success but, to me, it's more like when Jack Nicholson and Morgan Freeman sit atop a mountain in the Hollywood movie 'The Bucket List'.

As they contemplate their mortality and survey their lifetimes' accomplishments,

Freeman asks Nicholson: "But have you made a difference in someone else's life?"

It might sound corny, but that's a consideration that's driven me for much of my life. There are more important things than rugby, my own life's experiences taught me that a long time ago. I doubt I'll be long remembered for my rugby legacy – though my ability to fail university-level maths might go down in history – but I'd like to think that, through my charity work, I've made a difference in other people's lives.

It's in the genes. Dad was actually awarded a Queen's Medal in the 2007 Queen's New Years Honours list for his own community work. He's worked for years, beneath the radar, for the community in Ashburton and, while it's a small rural community, both Mum and Dad are well-respected for what they've given back. At one stage, Dad was Captain of the Ashburton Golf Club, at the same time as Mum was President of the Ashburton Racing Club. As a friend comically put it, they were a bit like the Kennedys of Ashburton.

On top of that, my parents have always been quite religious. Dad especially, was heavily involved for years at the local Catholic Church and Mark and I were press-ganged into helping, especially at a younger age. I guess the clue is in the name. So, my upbringing helped shape my views on working voluntarily and, added to my natural empathy for people, doing charity work came pretty naturally to me. That empathy for people is particularly important to me and is why I first began writing children's books, about twenty-five years ago.

I'd always been interested in storytelling and how words can be combined with drawings. Early in my career, I'd worked with a talented, self-taught artist called Gillian Brocke and, every week after I'd played a weekend game for Otago, I'd arrive at my desk to find a cartoon caricature of me in some rugby pose. Working with Gillian was great that way, we were always mucking around with stories and pictures, developing new characters.

Years later, when I was running a successful commercial and residential valuation practice in Dunedin, as part of the Robertson Real Estate group, one of my colleagues told me about a relative who was suffering from leukaemia. The patient in Dunedin Hospital loved anything to do with the ocean or dolphins and whales. The topic helped her relax as she fought the terrible and painful disease that eventually took her life.

The sad story really touched me and I started to write little short stories to try and brighten up her day, give her some respite. The stories were about the things she loved. My first attempt was about a big, blue whale named Wally who had his infected teeth removed by a tugboat. I drew the pictures myself, printed up the story at work and sent them to this brave little girl. After a while I started to get more and more requests, not only from my new friend, but also from the nurses and doctors at the hospital who wrote or called to say all the kids on the ward loved my little photocopied books.

Things just spiralled from there. I was contacted by a Dunedin publisher who said that the feedback from the kids at the hospital, combined with my high-profile status as an Otago rugby player, had convinced them to offer me a book deal. I agreed, but only on the proviso that every cent raised went to a charity of my choice.

And so, my career as a children's author was launched. I didn't have too many ambitions for the project. I thought we'd shift a few copies and that would be that.

Wally the Whale was the star of my first published book, a poor unfortunate whale who thought he was too cool to use sun lotion but, as a result, got badly sunburnt and was in great pain until all the other sea creatures licked runny ice-cream off his big, tickly belly. It sounds silly, and it was, but silly is great for children who love to have their imaginations fired. My writings weren't immune to criticism. A dentist who read the earlier Wally adventure in which he'd had his sore tooth pulled out took me to task. He informed me that blue whales do not, in point of fact, have teeth and asked me if that was the message I wanted to convey to children. I thought, Who cares? Kids just want to have fun. I'm not sure that fire-breathing dragons ever ruled the earth either, but that never stopped children from believing in them, or loving them. Make-believe, imagination, fantasy – those are the things that make children, well, children.

In the wake of publishing 'Wally the Whale' – the dental profession notwithstanding – I didn't expect much of a reaction. At that time the publisher reckoned I was possibly the only rugby player in the world to have ever published a non-sporting book for children. I don't know if he was right, though I haven't heard of any others. But, truth be told, though I got a bundle of nice thank you cards, drawings and letters from youngsters, I was just delighted to see Wally's book selling in the shops, raising much needed money for the treatment of children's leukaemia.

Then, I came home early one day to the digs I shared with Gordy, Cumby and Mike Brewer and Mike's girlfriend, Nicky Walker, up in the Dunedin Hills. The flat was often called the 'Half-way House', as we had a spare room out the back that became the place of choice for any friend who was undergoing some relationship trauma: if someone broke up with their partner, then they moved in until they made up their mind about the next step. That year we nearly had to have a revolving door fitted, there were so many requests for the relationship trauma room. It was after work and I was rushing to get ready for rugby training but, when I pulled up outside, I could see a couple of television Outside Broadcast units parked outside. I went white with worry – there must have been a murder or something sinister must have happened. Was everybody okay?

A reporter spotted me and walked straight over and stuck a big mic in my face: "Brent, will you tell the nation why a top rugby player is writing a children's book?"

I was mortified. What could I say?

I'd never wanted any media attention for writing the books. It had never occurred to me that the press might show an interest. Worse, I was an aspiring young All Black – what kind of message was I sending out to the tough rugby scene by writing silly books for sick children?

But there was no hiding from the press. The story hit the newspapers, TV and radio and I was asked to do talkback interviews wherever Otago was playing. And always the same angle: Why would a rugged No. 8 who spent a fair bit of his time as a rugby 'enforcer' even contemplate writing a children's book?" I read the book at various libraries around Otago and featured on a number of national radio shows, including an Australian talk radio show. A full-page feature entitled, Pope's Passions, appeared in the *Otago Daily Times* and won its author, Brent Edwards, the New Zealand Sports Feature of the Year Award. But, as shocked as I was, the publicity was good for sales as the money rolled in. My mother weighed in and did a great job of promoting the book, forcing it upon anyone she knew. She even arranged for a full window display, complete with rugby jerseys and soft toys in the biggest bookstore on the main street of Ashburton.

Fortunately, it didn't dent my rugby career too much. Though I received a lot of support from some of New Zealand's top sporting icons, there was probably a mixed reaction to it from the Otago and All Black players and coaches: New

Zealand rugby was not a place for burly forwards to be showing a soft underbelly. But I'd written the book and that was that. I later learned, to my embarrassment, that some of the All Blacks had seen copies of it while they were playing a Test in Carisbrook. As the story goes, rugged All Black assistant coach and ex-player, Grizz Wyllie, leafed through a copy before declaring, to no one in particular, "F**kin' good book."

Once the initial furore – and ribbing – died down, I suddenly started getting 'quiet chats' from most of the Otago team, asking if they could be in the next book.

"Popey, I want to be the shark?"

"Popey, can I be the rabbit?"

A year after 'Wally', I wrote a second book called 'The Adventures of Herbie Hotton'. Herbie was based on Hotty, a legendary member of the Otago team. Also known to his mates as 'Slack', Hotty had a big, bushy moustache and was known across New Zealand for his rugby talent. The story was about Hotty, a local policeman with a splendid handlebar moustache, who eventually foils the robbery of a rare aniseed ball collection from a small sweet store. Once again, the children loved it and it sold well but that was that – end of story, so to speak.

My life took a different turn and my personal ups and downs put an end to my creative writing career.

Then, years later, while strolling down Grafton Street, a woman approached me, two young children in tow. She'd been on holiday in New Zealand a year previously, and by chance had visited Dunedin Library. As she thumbed through some books for her children she spotted 'Wally the Whale' by Brent Pope. Pope was an unusual name and, realising I hailed from New Zealand, she asked the librarian about the author. The librarian confirmed Brent Pope the rugby player was the author and said the book was a hit with the local kids. Then and there this Irish woman read 'Wally' to her children and they loved the story. In fact, they'd liked it so much that she'd photocopied the book and brought it home, on the off-chance that she might, one day, get me to sign it.

Why didn't I write some more? she asked, dismissing my explanations that the uniqueness of the book had more to do with my status as an Otago ruby player than with the story itself. Her kids, she said, had no idea who the author was but 'Wally' had become one of their favourite books.

When I went home that night, I thought about what this stranger had said and I decided to give my children's author career another go. I'd use the story of Wally again but, this time, I'd adapt the it to my new surroundings. Wally became Woody, whose smooth, bald head and trendy sunglasses were based on Irish hooker, Keith Wood. There was Mr O'Driscoll, the Mayor of Ballybahoo; the Italian ice-cream vendor, Mick Galwey; Mr Hickie the local policeman and Malcolm the mud-crab, named for Irish second row Malcolm O'Kelly. I knew how I wanted the characters to look but, in the years since 'Wally' was published, the world had moved on. I needed someone in the animation world to bring my creations to life. Fortunately, I had the perfect person right under my nose. Parry Jones was one of my best friends from school in Ashburton: in fact, he had once painted a wonderful mural on the boot of one of my old VW 'bugs'. Parry hailed from an artistically talented family and many of his cartoons had been published back home in newspapers and magazines. An amazing animator, and award-winning film-maker, he'd also worked for Disney Studios. He agreed to come on board and, after securing a publisher in Belfast, 'Woody' was launched into the Irish market. Shops like Hughes & Hughes and Easons, along with many others around the country, waived their cut of the cover price and all proceeds went to aid the Irish Hospice Homecare, which was and is doing such incredible work looking after terminally ill children, giving them the dignity of being treated at home surrounded by love.

As in New Zealand, the books sold well, in part because they broke down the stereotype of how a macho rugby player should act. I didn't really have any great strategy for writing. I didn't have any children nor did I gear the book towards a particular age. I just liked writing them, and loved the fact that the kids liked reading them.

Most importantly, they raised much-needed money and awareness for vital charities.

'Woody' led to more books which have raised money or awareness for a lot of worthy charities including Cancer treatment, The Irish Asthma Society and the Irish Osteoporosis Society. My next book, entitled 'Hip-Hop Opotomus', generously illustrated by Ben Hennessy, is going to help The Make a Wish Foundation and Pieta House. The books feature characters like Arnold the Noseless Anteater, a poor, unfortunate anteater who is born without a snout;

The Wheezing Wolf, an asthmatic wolf who's having problems blowing down the Three Little Pigs' house; Bones, a troubled teenager who looks a lot like Ryan Tubridy and ends up changing his lazy, unhealthy lifestyle; and now Hip-Hop Opotamus, a shy Hippo who transforms from a boring poet into a gangster-style rapper to win the first ever Jungle X-Factor.

I'm as proud of the books as I am of covering rugby on television and I like the fact that I'm different from a lot of what people think, that I'm my own person. A woman who grew up in New Zealand recently contacted me from London to say that 'Wally the Whale' remained her favorite book from childhood. Reactions like that are what drive me. I have never written these books because I thought I was particularly talented, rather I did them because I felt they could help either by way of raising money or by way of making children feel better about their lives. In 'Bones' and now 'Hip-Hop Opotomus', children always win out in the end. I need that message to be positive and that, somehow, 'everything will be okay'. The shy, bullied Hippo will show them all that he has talent; Bones will grow up healthy and Woody will have his painful sunburn relieved.

I'm not a parent – to my huge regret – nor a teacher and I don't reckon I'm even a great author, but I do believe that the books must try and teach and inspire children. I want to make the kids smile and show them that it's okay to be a little different. Whatever happens, I hope I can look back and think that one of my books or characters touched the life of one child somewhere, sometime and made them smile and enjoy the moment.

• • • • •

In the days of the Celtic Tiger I was marketing manager for an overseas property company. I was working maybe fourteen to fifteen hours a day, travelling around Ireland during the week and spending weekends overseas in far-flung places. At the same time I had my rugby column with the *Evening Echo* and my usual media work with RTÉ. I wasn't driven by money, that's never really been my motivation with anything I have done. Rather, it was about always keeping busy. I get very bored and distracted if I'm not constantly on the go, constantly looking for new challenges in life.

But something had to give, I was burning out. So, I left the property company in 2008. I felt I wanted to dedicate at least three years to charity work – not because I felt a need for halo-polishing, but because it gives me a huge sense of satisfaction. I love TV shows like Secret Millionaire or Undercover Boss – programmes that pull at my heart strings, that make me feel that I should be at least trying to make a difference.

One of the charitable projects I embarked on in my three-year project was the Brent Pope Rugby Build in Zambia for well-known charity, Habitat for Humanity.

My interest began when I was asked by Karen Kennedy to put my name forward as an ambassador for the organisation that was beginning to build its reputation in Ireland. I wasn't sold on the idea of just being an ambassador, of just lending my name to something without putting in any effort. To me, that's always seemed like a bit of a cop-out. I prefer to be hands-on, working in the trenches with the other charity workers who get no recognition but deserve it all. After talking to Karen, I liked the idea of helping a charity whose focus was not just in places like Africa and Haiti, but also at home in Ireland. Most importantly, I loved the concept of giving people a hand-up and not just a handout. Allying charity with dignity is something I've always valued.

In my first year with Habitat for Humanity, we travelled to Lusaka in Zambia and Malcolm O'Kelly, the International second row, came with me to film a documentary for RTÉ television. The trip was nothing short of life-affirming and the people, especially the Zambian women, were nothing short of amazing. We roughed it, living and staying with the locals in their own environment. I didn't want to go all the way to Africa to help the locals and not even make the effort to understand their way of life. I didn't want to work alongside them and share their hardships during the day, only to wave goodbye to them and check into some plush hotel by night. For, sharing everything – and that includes sleeping accommodation – comes down to respecting a different culture.

As a consequence, sleeping was almost impossible; there was no running water, no power and an old-fashioned, long drop toilet that serviced many houses. I don't think I've ever wanted so badly to be constipated than during that trip, and the morning toilet ritual was probably the worst part of the day. Firstly, you had to be quick off the mark: if you didn't get to it before the rest of the village, the stench later in the morning or when the sun came out was stifling. The problem was that, to beat the rest of them to it, you had to go in the dark.

There are more graceful ways to spend a morning than balancing precariously, like a ballet dancer, over a small hole, grasping a torch and aiming carefully. Men aren't good at multitasking at the best of times…

But the Zambian culture is amazing. There are no beggars in this society, just proud, good people forced to live in deplorable conditions with maybe three generations of families squeezed into the small space. Living in a plastic sheet covered shack, and ravaged by AIDS, even getting water means a daily hike that can take hours. The education and health system for these people is almost non-existent and the average life span in the village where Malcolm and I were building homes was about 35 years of age. Yet they seem to smile and love life more than people who, on the outside at least, seem to have a lot more. When Malcolm and myself helped coach a local rugby team – in exchange for some manual labour on our next trip – the players were so keen to learn, that many of them turned up in bare feet just to train. One player, who only possessed one pair of trousers, was so keen to play that he ran around the park in just his underwear. Now that's dedication!

● ● ● ● ●

One of the best ideas I've come across was a suggestion that all Irish gap year students should be made to work for charity – like an alternative to military national service in other countries. The government could pay them the equivalent of the dole in a system in which everybody wins. It'd be a great way to teach our young people to appreciate what's important in life as well as giving them time to consider what they want to do with their futures.

I'd have liked such an opportunity but, in the end, I kind of fell into charity work via my creative writing. Combining the two worked perfectly for me, so it wasn't really a new departure to use my love of art to try and raise awareness of mental health issues in Ireland. During a trip back home, Mark took me to a small art gallery in Wellington which featured work from self-taught artists who had faced adversity in their lives. Among the obstacles these artists faced were problems like homelessness, incarceration, addiction, Down Syndrome, or mental health issues. I was amazed at the skill, passion and talent of these artists.

In reality, I know very little about art. I know nothing about brush strokes or other technical aspects, but I do know that, in the past, artists like Picasso, Andy Warhol, Jackson Pollock or even Damien Hirst would have been referred to as 'eccentric' which is shorthand for 'different'. And though I can't define exactly what the Outsider, Raw or Brute movements in art were, I do know they originated many years ago in France with art by the criminally insane or institutionalised patients. Today, this kind of art is growing rapidly with mainstream collectors prizing such Outsider Art.

Art galleries, specifically dedicated to this genre, have sprung up everywhere, especially in the US. Suddenly, the art world has discovered that art does not have to originate from some well-heeled artist behind an easel on the sidewalks of Paris, but from anybody from any walk of life that has the talent.

But, standing in that Wellington art gallery, I knew none of that. I only saw art which was full of emotion. Each painting or sculpture had a story. Many were raw but, to me, that's real art. These pieces were not just about a canvas or a piece of clay, they were about a journey and I was inspired and moved by them.

It got me thinking about Ireland. Surely there had to be artists like this back there, people willing to showcase how art can be used as therapy? Back in Dublin, the city was full of empty buildings, deserted during the recession. I contacted Johnny Ronan, the property tycoon. Johnny's son, Johnny Junior, had been to New Zealand with me as part of a Shamrocks Tour. Johnny Snr has had his ups and downs in business and media but I've always found him to be a very kind man. He loves art and, often under the radar, has done a lot to promote and sponsor art in Ireland. He generously allowed me to move into a vacant space in one of Treasury Holdings' Spencer Dock properties and the Outsider Art Gallery was born.

I sourced the art from charities and individuals throughout Ireland, approaching organisations like Art Link Rehabilitation, the Simon Community, Shine, Down Syndrome Ireland and the prison system. I received a piece of work from an amazing cartoonist from Drogheda, by the name of Jock McHale. Like many of the artists featured in the Outsider Art Gallery Jock, who tragically took his own life, had spent his life battling mental illness and addiction. But in the midst of the chaos and mayhem of his life, he had a dream to be an artist and he certainly achieved that: his work was, is, inspirational. With the help of his family, I set up a small memorial to him at the gallery and RTÉ covered his story.

Listening to his family speak so bravely and eloquently about this vastly talented man, I was given a glimpse of how vitally important it is to let other people see the incredible vision many of these unique artists have.

Another one of the artists I met was Taz, from the Simon Community. Covered in tattoos and with a tough personal history that included drug addiction, homelessness and running with the wrong crowd, Taz was a scary-looking man. He'd grown up alongside Aboriginals in the Outback of Australia and had even married an Aboriginal woman and had a family there – possibly the only modern-day Irishman to be so intimately accepted by Australia's founding people. Taz had learned the Aboriginal art form of dot painting and created amazing work for someone who had great problems keeping a steady hand. I was at a complete loss when Taz missed the opening night of his exhibition in the gallery but, when he turned up a couple of days later, I understood. He'd been beaten black and blue as he'd tried to defend a homeless friend who'd been attacked on the street. Art meant the world to Taz and, beneath the tattooed exterior, this hard man had a heart of gold. He eventually sold all his works of art and, as a result, had the money and the confidence to return to Australia and reunite with his family. Last I heard, he was doing well.

Taz's story is the reason I set up the Outsider Art Gallery. I wanted to showcase some of these amazing people's art, not just for their good but for the wider good of society. Taz was the walking definition of why we shouldn't judge a book by its cover. But he isn't alone. Many of the people whose work I display are exceptional, skillful artists who, for a myriad reasons, fell through society's ever-widening cracks. Art is their voice and a way back from the edge.

Some of their stories were shocking. Some had faced discrimination all their lives, were misunderstood or struggling with depression or mental health issues like schizophrenia, or disorders like autism. Some of these artists had been raped, attacked, bullied or forced to grow up on the streets, ostracised from society and drugged until they could no longer feel … anything.

On our original opening night, we had an incredible array of artists, their proud families and visitors. Taz's biker mates rubbed shoulders with corporate suits and, on a great night, we sold nearly 50 per cent of the work on display.

I felt that I had achieved something. I felt we – the artists, the buyers, the families, me – had achieved something together.

For the next six months I tried to juggle the gallery with my other charity work and my rugby career. It was tough. Ireland was in a recession and footfall in the Spencer Dock area was low. At times, sitting in the middle of a large concrete floor without heating, especially with snow piled up outside, was disheartening. I felt a bit like a busy fool. But just when I thought I would give up, an artist would visit and I could see what just showing their work meant to them. I learned by email that one artist had sadly passed away, but that the last six months of her life had been her happiest seeing her work on show, and selling, for the first time. That's what inspired and motivated me.

I wasn't always alone. In fact, on many occasions, I was joined by Conor, a young guy with a tough history whose surface I couldn't even begin to scratch. He would come in and work on his art, and it gave me a great kick to see someone with real talent who, at last, had a chance to work in a positive way. Like many young artists, he had his dark days, but for the months he visited me in the gallery he had a purpose to get up of a morning, and it gave him hope that his talent was at last getting a chance to breathe.

And surely that's what art is. Talent.

The fact that a Picasso painting can hang upside down in a gallery for six months without anybody realising just goes to show that art appreciation, like beauty, really is in the eye of the beholder. Different strokes for different folks. Not everyone wants a shark or a cow suspended in formaldehyde in their living room, not everybody gets Banksy – but that's what it's all about.

Last year, I visited the Outside Art Fair in New York. It was an amazing experience seeing some of the best work that the alternative art world can offer. Celebrities like David Bowie and numerous actors and band members are now big collectors of this kind of work, and it's easy to see why: it's colourful, passionate and is often the artist's biography on canvas. I spent a weekend meeting the artists and they, in turn, were fascinated about what the Irish were doing. Inspired by their example, I am currently trying to organise a stand to feature Irish Outsider Art and represent Irish Outsider Art at the New York Fair. Raising sponsorship is hard in recession-hit Ireland but the world needs to see that Ireland, like many nations, is prepared to promote these incredible talents and, more to the point, understands the importance of using art as a therapeutic form of rehabilitation.

I'm not sure how, but it's my burning ambition to make sure we're there at the 2013 New York fair – a Tricolour-draped stand, the first ever, proudly putting Ireland's Outsider Art on an equal footing with the rest of the world.

● ● ● ● ●

There's not much I haven't done for charity over the years. I jumped off the roof of The Aviva Stadium last year for Concern, and sang – badly – for the IRFU Charitable Trust during RTÉ's Charity Eurostar programme a couple of years ago. To me, it's always been an honour to get involved in that kind of thing. I don't take my lucky position in life for granted. I want to give something back. I don't know how long my media persona will last but, for as long as it does, I intend to milk every moment of it in a positive way.

I love the fact that I meet a wide range of people doing extraordinary things. These are brave, sensitive human beings doing so much more than I can ever do and who often work tirelessly without thought of praise or recognition. They are the real heroes in my life and are the inspiration behind my efforts to do what 'The Bucket List' boys said, and make a difference to someone's else's life.

Back in 2008, I'd decided to spend three years of my life working for charity. That's long since come and gone, and I'm still involved, purely because I'm enjoying it so much. The Outsider Gallery has been closed for a while since I had to move from the premises which had been so generously given to me, rent-free, but I hope to re-open soon. In the meantime, I've 'Hip-Hop Opotomus' coming out early in the new year, and I'm still hoping to get my inspirational artists to New York.

I'm also currently convincing some broken-down, old Irish rugby players to grab a hammer and join me in Argentina on the next Rugby Legends build for Habitat.

Plenty done, but plenty more left to do.

Otago had a plethora of loose forwards in our era. At one stage, the starting trio was Brent at No. 8, Paul Henderson (All Black) at 7, and myself at 6. The back-up loose forwards were Arran Pene at No. 8 (All Black), Josh Kronfeld at 7 (All Black), Jamie Joseph at 6 (All Black) and a young 17-year-old was introduced into the squad, called Taine Randell, who also went on to captain the All Blacks. Competition for a starting place was pretty hot. That meant that, if you so happened to have the jersey and the team was winning you were very reluctant to miss a match through injury. If you did, you were leaving the door open for one of the 'new brigade'. So, we played with injuries, getting injections to play, and playing on in matches where the modern player would immediately come off, as it's now their profession. During one game towards the end of the season, we were playing at our beloved Carisbrook and most of the loose forwards were heavily strapped. Popey was having issues with his shoulder, elbow (previous dislocation), wrist and fingers, hamstring and probably both knees. The commentator was Steve Davie, a radio veteran and a die-hard Otago supporter. In his pre-match run-down of the two teams, Steve came to the forwards: "... and now the Otago loose forward trio, who all look heavily strapped for today's game. Mike Brewer will captain Otago from the blindside flank position wearing the No 6 jersey. The incumbent All Black openside, Paul Henderson, will wear the No. 7 jersey and ... when the bandages burst, we'll know who's wearing the No. 8 jersey."

Mike Brewer
Otago. Canterbury. All Blacks.

18

The Future

It's raining here. Again.

The wind is driving torrents of water against the glass doors that separate my kitchen from the garden.

It's beautiful; my favourite spot. As the storm outside whips the fierce winds in from the Irish Sea I sink back even deeper into the sofa and feel the heat from the roaring fire wash over me.

I'm so happy here – in Blackrock, in Dublin, in Ireland.

Like everyone else, I overspent in the good times, buying an old house and pouring all my savings and heart into it. I spent every weekend for three years demolishing much of this house, designing the interior, making pilgrimages to bathroom centres, kitting it out. The house bears not only my imprint but my father's, also. Every couple of years he travelled halfway around the world to help me: father and son working side by side, building something together. This house means a lot to me.

In retrospect I spent foolishly, like a lot of Irish people. I was advised that waiting a year would push the house beyond my financial reach. So I bought. It wasn't a gamble, more a calculated risk in which I believed the equity in my house would keep me dry through any future rainy days. Now, my house is worth less than half of what I paid for it, and every drop in house prices pushes me further towards negative equity.

It wasn't the only poor decision I've made. I invested in other property that I can neither rent nor sell, and my pension plans have been washed away.

So, I understand what it's like to not know what's coming around the corner. Being on TV doesn't inoculate you against this recession.

But here I am and, for as long as I can, here I stay.

Twenty-one years after I swapped Dunedin for a three-month jaunt to Dublin, and spent those first few years going home and then being drawn back again, I'm still cluttering the place up. It's hard to believe how quickly time has come and gone. I've lived most of my adult life in Ireland, on and off.

Nowadays, New Zealand seems … so far away.

Though few people believe it, I've almost five years more 'television caps' than my current, veteran panel colleagues, George and Tom. My life changed that first day of the 1995 Rugby World Cup when I perched my little kiwi furball on the panel desk in front of me and, while I didn't have a vision for the future of broadcasting, I'll be forever grateful that Niall Cogley – and subsequently, Glen and Ryle – did.

Thanks to their vision, I'm recognised in the street and people come up to me to talk rugby. It's been – it is – a wonderful experience and a privilege.

I've always wondered what life might have been like if I'd made that All Black team back in 1987. Would I have become as famous as Zinny or the other lads?

Maybe.

Maybe not.

But at least, in Ireland, there are compensations. When one of the most revered All Black ever, Sean Fitzpatrick, came here a few years back he flew into Dublin airport. Fitzy was in town for an event hosted by myself and Hookie and featuring some of rugby's greatest stars. Along with David Campese and Will Carling, Fitzy hopped into a taxi and, being the bulkiest of the three, he sat in the front seat.

"Jayzus," said the taxi driver, "you're all big fellas. Do you play rugby by any chance?"

Despite knowing there was a combined total of around 250 International caps and a couple of World Cup winners in the taxi, Fitzy modestly replied, "Yeah, we play a bit."

"Sure, that's great," came the reply, "you must know Popey from the TV?"

When Fitzy recounted the story to me, all I could do was roar with laughter and tell him, "The worm has finally turned Fitzy, you're on my patch now."

Arran Pene tells a similar story. When the All Blacks toured Britain around 1993, Arran and Stu Forster came to Dublin to visit me. The lads stayed with Henno and me in Kimmage, but when Arran announced there were more All Blacks on the way we had to find extra crash space for some of them at my then-girlfriend's house. On a wet and windy Friday night I happened to be at my girl's house when the doorbell rang. I opened it to find a bedraggled Zinzan Brooke standing on the doorstep, bag in hand. No one had given him an address and I was stumped as to how he'd found us – even I had problems finding my girlfriend's house.

"Gee, Popey, this place is unreal," said Zinny. "I got into a taxi at the airport and asked the driver if he'd heard of a guy called Brent Pope. The taxi driver said he thought you played with a team called St Mary's in South Dublin so he dropped me in Sundrive Shopping Centre. I asked the local butcher and he told me you sometimes go in there. Then he said he thought the local grocer knew your girlfriend, and told me to wait. Five minutes later, the butcher came back with the grocer – he brought me outside, told me to get in the back of his grocer's van and he brought me here."

I looked at Zinny, stunned.

"Don't worry, Popey… It's easy when you have connections," said perhaps the world's greatest-ever No. 8 as he shuffled past me through the doorway.

When I go home to Queenstown to see my old friend Ged, he often takes me with him on his whitewater rafting trips for tourists. If there're Irish onboard, Ged shouts out: "Who here knows Popey?" and the Irish tourists would all yet out. He thought that was great, that the small, chubby-faced kid from Ashburton had made something of his life in another country.

I've always believed you make your own luck in life and I think I've made a good fist of my professional, academic and sporting life, achieving more than I had ever dreamt of.

But I know that fame, like jobs in TV, can be fleeting and in constant flux. I never forget that we're operating in recessionary times and that, amid such uncertainty, no one's future is secure – not even the rugby panel in RTÉ. My contract with the broadcaster is up for renewal soon and, while I hope and pray I have done enough for the station and the public to want me to stay on, I know, like anything in life, there are no guarantees. For someone like me, it's a daunting prospect to think about the future, about where I would be without my television work. The answer may involve leaving the home I've made in Ireland and the wonderful friends I've come to know and love. That's a sad prospect to even contemplate but until that day comes, I fully intend, along with Tom and Conor, and the Hookie Monster, to keep on trying to deliver. I will call games as I see them, listen to Conor's sporting wisdom, dodge Tom's live TV ambushes, and wonder at George's ability to invoke Churchill or insert George Custer's 7th Cavalry into a Six Nations game. Priceless.

• • • • •

I love the Irish people. Straight up.

I know that, though I hold an Irish passport, I'm not Irish and never will be. There have been many moments when I've viewed it as an honour to even be allowed to share the Irish experience – none more so than when the Irish and English anthems were played before that spectacular game in Croke Park. For a Kiwi who marched during the anti-Apartheid era against Springbok tours and who believes that rugby is more than just a sport, it was a life-affirming moment which brought tears to my eyes. I was bursting with pride to be connected to this country.

The best I can hope is that I continue to be 'adopted Irish' and, in truth, that suits me fine – I'm still proud to be a Kiwi and have no intention of abandoning my NZ birthright. Whenever Ireland plays I'll always cheer for the green… Unless the green are playing the All Blacks. I think that people in Ireland understand that. They respect patriotism and I don't think they really expect me to shed my Kiwi heritage and become more Irish than the Irish themselves. Besides, I think they like the accent.

When my dad came over, people treated him with great respect when they discovered he was my father. They chatted to him in the streets and shops and their courtesy made me feel very proud that I'd become someone – however insignificant – in Irish society.

But their hospitality to my dad was not unexpected. After all, people here have been extending their hospitality to me for decades.

In 1991, I really had no intention of staying in Ireland and my choice to come here instead of Italy was based purely on a single weekend I'd spent in the West during my season playing rugby in England. Back then all I knew was how much I wanted to get out of New Zealand. My leaving home was for negative reasons.

But it's funny how things work out.

●●●●●

Despite the huge leaps I've made in my personal life and the resilience I've shown in dealing with my mental health issues, I still over-worry about a lot of things. I worry about my family back in New Zealand and my parents' health, about whether I've told them enough how much I love them. I worry that I'm going into my 50s and I'm still alone without a family here, or one of my own.

And despite working so hard on being able to just seize the day, I worry I won't completely get a handle on my anxiety or dysthymia. I wonder if the years of stress to my mind and body are already taking their toll and if my health will continue to hold out.

But I can't, and won't, worry forever.

My charity work has taught me that. I can't simply curl up into a ball and shake with fear: in the face of my anxieties, I will show resilience. I get up, dust myself off, get on with the business of life and count myself luckier than most.

That's not difficult. In my mind I'm only young, and there's still so much I want to pack into my life. I harbour a secret desire to design a range of 'Popey's Clothes for Men' and I'd love to see my movie script up on the big screen, maybe get involved in directing or making movies myself. I'm trying to figure out how to move my children's book to animation and I have an innovative mental health programme for teenagers which I'm trying to develop with professionals and roll out through the schools system in Ireland. Separately, I'd love to make a documentary about the young Irish who have emigrated in the current recession to Australia and New Zealand.

And I feel lucky about life.

In Ireland and New Zealand, and, for that matter, in England and the United

States, I've been lucky to play top-flight rugby with and against some of the greatest players in the sport's history but also with the greatest characters. Not everybody has a World Cup winner's medal or an All Black test jersey. In fact, most of the greatest people to play rugby remain anonymous to all but their own families and friends. Injury, mental health, politics, loves, kids, bad timing – all have played their part in denying countless players their chance to fulfill their potential on their chosen field of dreams.

I should know, it happened with me. The sport I love has bequeathed me an injury list that reads like a medical dictionary: dislocated and broken elbow; numerous concussions; cauliflower ears; various nose breaks; fractured cheekbone; cracked teeth; cuts to eyebrows and face; neck and disc problems in my back; dislocated shoulders; AC joint fracture; broken wrist, hands and fingers; popped rib cartilages; broken ribs; hip problems; severely bruised kidneys; torn hamstrings (chronic); cruciate and medial ligament tears to both knees; torn calf muscles; stress fractures to my shins; and broken feet and toes.

On occasion in games, I've worn so many bandages and so much strapping that I looked like a deep-sea diver. One New Zealand TV commentator once said during a broadcast: "We'll know who's playing No. 8 when the bandages burst."

The most painful injuries were the infections, caused by dirty studs, that would swell up and collect puss. In my playing days, forwards wore 22mm long studs that some of the dirtier players would sharpen by scraping them on the concrete so they'd cut like razor blades. Refs checked for that kind of thing but the offending players simply stayed in the toilets during the pre-match checks, or showed the ref another pair of boots. The refs must have known – big burly props wouldn't have had much call for low-cut, flashy boots and plastic studs better suited to running than rucking – but few ever said anything. So, the forwards would spend their games rucking, raking, stamping and slicing and spend their post-game time trying to repair the damage done to themselves. My ritual after every game was to scrub my wounds as hard as I could. I'd grit my teeth, look the other way and just do it till they bled profusely and then I'd douse them with peroxide or iodine and they would be right until the next week.

In every way, the physical pain has been the easiest to bear. I still wince on a cold morning, but it is the emotional pain that often hurts the most. In the past, the game of rugby has broken my heart and I've wondered if it would have been easier if I hadn't come so close to achieving my dream of World Cup glory and immortality with the All Blacks, if I hadn't thought I was good enough?

But still…

Things keep getting better and better. I drown out the negatives with the faces, names and voices of the men I've played with, for and against. Rugby hasn't given me everything, I've learned that I've got to do that for myself.

But it has given me a lot; friends, a career, memories. My love of rugby has allowed me to lead an extraordinary life in which legends of the sport have played a variety of roles. People like Greg Cooper, Arran, Mike, Ginge, Gordy, Laurie, Zinny, Brian O'Driscoll, Paul O'Connell, Paddy Johns, Conor O'Shea, Victor Costello, Trevor Brennan, Hookie and too many others to mention here, have all walked across the stage of my life. And that's only in the sporting arena – there are many others from the worlds of art, charity, TV and business who have inspired me and offered me their friendship.

How privileged am I?

•••••

I hope my future lies in Ireland and that I continue to work in TV. Who knows, maybe I have another shot at rugby coaching in me? Personally, I hope my family continues in good health and that we stay in contact more often in the years ahead. Despite the distance between us, the Sundays without them and the lonely Christmas Days, I concentrate on the positive and am grateful for the qualities they have instilled in me. I hope to see them soon.

Sentimentalist that I am, I love old tunes and when Old Blue Eyes sings 'My Way' I can see the words in my mind. Regrets? Yes, I've had a few but, really, too few to mention. More importantly, I've learned to live life my own way and accept who I am, flaws and all.

Over the years I've made friends and I've lost friends. I've surrounded myself and still felt alone. I've loved and lost. But I'm still here and I'm still driving for that try line. And that's, perhaps, the greatest lesson rugby has taught me about life. Never give up, never give in. Be resilient and, no matter what problem faces you, stand up and fight and never be afraid to look for help. Good, loyal, strong teammates are everywhere – in life as in sport. Just ask.

I was never meant to go to university, never meant to make it as a rugby player. I abandoned a good career and fled to the other side of the world to try and reinvent my life. More than twenty years later, I work on TV in the sport I adore, I've become an author, learned to play a musical instrument, I work with talented artists, and help fund-raise for charity. If I can do it, so can anyone.

I don't mind if this autobiography fails to top the best-sellers' chart. I didn't write it for that reason. Neither did I write it because I see myself as a victim, or as some kind of poster-child for mental health issues. I'm not and I don't ever want to be.

I've put my life down on paper as honestly and emotionally as possible so that, if there's anyone out there who thinks they are in this battle alone, they will know there are others like them. None of us is alone – we all have our own story, we all have our own issues. I hope my story might strike a chord with someone in a similar position. I struggled because I was too afraid and too ashamed to ask for help when I needed it most. I was so wrong and, if writing my story down helps one other person to reach out for help then, to me, it will have been worth it.

Though, at times, I didn't realise what I was fighting, my struggle with anxiety issues has affected me my whole life.

But it does not define me.

It's one thread of a wonderful, positive, full life that I've been lucky to live. It's part of the story, but it's not the ending. That has yet to be written.

In the meantime, I will continue to embrace my life and try to seize the moment. If the Munster men will permit me to borrow their rallying cry, I will continue to, 'stand up and fight'. I will continue to think about Morgan Freeman and 'The Bucket List' and I will always ask myself: "Did I make a difference to someone else's life?"

I hope, when all is said and done, that the answer is unequivocal. Yes!

Epilogue

Otago 1990

Come on. Let's go!

    The thunder of our tags echoes in the tunnel of Eden Park Stadium.

    Everyone is waiting for us. Auckland, the fans ... history.

    I'm in pain. I can hardly walk. The pain-killing injections are useless and the pad is strapped so tight, I can hardly breathe.

    But Laurie can't know or he will, rightly, replace me here and now and I've worked too hard, survived too many disappointments and heartbreaks to sit this game out.

    It's only pain.

    I've played with pain all my life.

    Mike knows the score. Arran knows the score. They have faith in me and the team needs me almost as much as I need them.

    Though none of us yet know it, we will lose today.

    Despite our anger, our talent, our sacrifices, our camaraderie, our desire, our pride – we will lose to Auckland, once again.

323

Greatness, immortality – whatever name it goes by – won't be denied us forever. A year from now, we will win Otago's first ever Division 1 title and fulfill our potential. We will lay to rest, forever, the ghosts of all past defeats, including this defeat.

On the back of that future win, great careers will be founded. Laurie Mains will coach the All Blacks in front of Nelson Mandela at the famous 1995 World Cup in South Africa. Many of the players sweating, heaving and steaming beside me today will become All Black legends in their own right.

I will not be among them. I will never join the ranks of the All Black elite, never be part of that great legacy. Instead I will wrestle, for decades, with my disappointment and my belief that only injury and fate denied me.

Eventually, I will be okay.

My broken, half-empty heart will mend.

But today – right now, right here – we will lose.

It will be a bitter pill, washed down with more heartbreak.

But even defeat will be only one more step.

It's not about losing.

It's never been about losing.

It's never really been about rugby.

It's about life.

It's about fighting.

It's about playing.

I want to play.